The Capitalist University

The Capitalist University
The Transformations of Higher Education in the United States, 1945–2016

Henry Heller

PlutoPress
www.plutobooks.com

First published 2016 by Pluto Press
345 Archway Road, London N6 5AA

www.plutobooks.com

British Library Cataloguing in Publication Data
A catalogue record for this book is available from the British Library

ISBN   978 0 7453 3658 9   Hardback
ISBN   978 1 7837 1975 4   PDF ebook
ISBN   978 1 7837 1977 8   Kindle ebook
ISBN   978 1 7837 1976 1   EPUB ebook

This book is printed on paper suitable for recycling and made from fully managed
and sustained forest sources. Logging, pulping and manufacturing processes are
expected to conform to the environmental standards of the country of origin.

Typeset by Stanford DTP Services, Northampton, England

Simultaneously printed in the European Union and United States of America

To Ethan Heller

Contents

Preface

Following World War II colleges and universities became key institutions of American society, second only in importance to private corporations and the military. Indeed, universities became closely tied to big business especially through the research sponsored by private foundations. At the same time, their ties to the military and to the CIA made them into virtual instruments of the U.S. state. In the Gramscian sense, they became a part of the non-coercive state apparatus. One of the aims of this book is to critically investigate their connection with the evolving capitalist political economy of the United States after 1945. A second core objective, however, is to acknowledge and celebrate the accomplishments of American scholarship and higher education, particularly in the humanities and social sciences.

The wealth generated by American capitalism provided the material foundation for the achievements of American higher learning during this period, but it was also responsible for its limitations. These limits took the form of a consistent bias in research and teaching against Marxism—and, indeed, against a historically based understanding of culture and society—in favor of defending liberalism, capitalism, and American imperialism. It was this ideological program which unified the humanities and social sciences. The student and civil rights revolts of the 1960s briefly helped to expose the ideological functions of higher education but did not fundamentally transform them.

Charting the development of academe will illuminate the economic, social, and ideological functions of the universities during the last part of the twentieth century and the beginning of the twenty-first, and will help in sketching out their likely future. Doing so is important because the universities have reached a major crossroads and their future prospects are in serious doubt. Under the influence of neoliberalism the operation and purposes of universities are being transformed from serving the public good into approximating as closely as possible those of private corporations, thereby imperiling the possibilities for independent and critical teaching and research. In reaction students and faculty are growing increasingly conscious of this neoliberal attack and attempting to organize resistance in defense of intellectual and academic freedom. This work is meant to help to further that resistance by giving it a historical and theoretical context.

The early part of the book focuses on the period when American power was at its zenith. Higher education in the post-war years based itself on mass education and scholarly research which reflected U.S. global ascendancy. American universities became the standard bearer of higher education throughout the world. The narrative centers on the evolution of the humanities and social sciences with some side-glances at other disciplines like environmental studies. The humanities and social science disciplines proved highly prolific, accumulating vast amounts of positive knowledge which helped to reinforce the economic and political power of the United States. As such this text aspires to be a contemporary intellectual history of America, something curiously both grand and insular. Grand because the vast resources available to American universities made possible an unprecedented outpouring of new knowledge in fields like psychology, economics, literary criticism, anthropology, and history. Insular because the ideological biases that were institutionalized in American higher learning inhibited (though did not completely suppress) Marxism, which, globally, was entering a period of great creativity from which America cut itself off. As we shall see, hostility to Marxism is accordingly an important part of the history of teaching and scholarship in America.

This study, on the contrary, analyzes this increase in positive knowledge on the basis of a Marxist or critical perspective. The distinction between positive and critical knowledge needs to be underlined. Positive knowledge aims at so-called objective, disinterested, or value-free learning, while critical understanding sees this approach as necessary and valid but inherently incomplete and, at times, even illusory. It is not fully true because it assumes that the knowledge generated within the present capitalist mode of production can be objectively true in some ahistorical sense, whereas critical understanding views such knowledge as historically contingent or part of an ongoing and unfinished process. Critical analysis makes use of positive knowledge but sees it as constrained by the consciousness generated by the capitalist mode of production; it views existing knowledge from an open-ended and evolving perspective hopefully moving toward a future socialism. Positive knowledge tends to cloister knowledge into reified categories and specialized departments based on subject matter. Critical analysis takes into account disciplinary differences but analyzes their institutionalized boundaries from the perspective of their ideological contradictions and connects them to the greater totality of a materialist understanding and sense of historical progression. Positive knowledge assumes that the concrete and the particular are the starting point of knowledge of first principles. Critical understanding views the concrete and particular as the focal point of previous determinations by means of which these principles are verified.

It is our premise that the enormous scholarly achievements of American universities, the inter-relationship between the disciplines and their ties with American economic and political life, are historically noteworthy and especially worth understanding through a critical analysis. The more so as these university disciplines play an increasing role in what is called knowledge capitalism and are developing within institutions which are increasingly the site of important ideological and social struggles.

I wrote this account as a reflection of the fact that I was a product of American higher education's glory years during the 1950s, got caught up in the unrest of the 1960s and 1970s, and have lived through the epoch of postmodernism and neoliberalism. Throughout this entire period I have studied and worked in academe, and for most of it I have been mainly concerned with my own field—history—especially early modern religion and society, the beginnings of capitalism, the French Revolution, and contemporary history. While I kept an eye on other academic fields—it is incumbent on a historian to do so—I tried as much as possible to ignore the management of universities, mine included. In retrospect management reciprocated, seeming to prefer my indifference and that of most of the rest of faculty toward it, which allowed it more or less a free hand. In any case one could afford to adopt a blasé attitude as the bureaucratic regime which controlled the university was a relatively benign affair for most of my career. As a faculty member I made my living teaching at the University of Manitoba in Canada, a perch which allowed me to observe the United States and its academic life from both inside and outside. Universities, like other institutions in Canada, are different from those in the United States. For one thing the prevalence of unions is much greater. Likewise, universities as public institutions are more important. On the other hand, the development of Canadian universities, including the University of Manitoba, has in other respects been modelled on that of the United States. Despite a veneer of faculty and student participation, the administration of universities in both countries, however paternalistic and enlightened, was essentially despotic.

But if one did not rock the boat, or rocked it only occasionally, it seemed that one was largely left alone to work as part of a community of scholars. This is what constituted academic freedom. Behind this screen of apparent openness, however, was the haunting memory of the purges of the McCarthy period. During the 1950s, the anti-communist purges had established the boundaries of academic freedom, with the near elimination of Marxists and

Marxism from university campuses. Distinguished scholars like W.E.B. Du Bois, Philip Foner, Paul Sweezy, F.O. Mathiessen, Owen Lattimore, Chandler Davis, and Moses Finley proved beyond the pale of American academe. In the sciences there was room for the pursuit of a significant amount of pure inquiry, i.e., independent theoretical and empirical investigation, despite overall dependence on financing by government and business. But in the humanities and social sciences the parameters were more closely drawn and were backed up by fear of further repression setting definite limits on freedom of expression. Ideological considerations played a decisive role in the patronage of research by private foundations and government, and freedom of thought was clearly restricted. On the face of it this was simply a matter of banning Marxism, as the official ideology of America's arch-enemy the Soviet Union. Given the dogmatic quality of Marxist doctrines under Stalin and his successors this could be rationalized as more gain than loss. On the other hand, the fact that such teachings were suppressed raises suspicions about the limits of free thought in America— suspicions which turn out to be entirely justified. The more so as Marxism freed from the constraints of Soviet orthodoxy is key to understanding both the meaning of knowledge and the nature of the capitalist system on which American society bases itself. In our view then, the rejection of Marxism in American universities at the height of the Cold War and indeed afterwards was blatantly ideological. Indeed, as we see it, hostility to historical materialism is central to understanding the entire history of American higher education post-1945. Granted the importance of higher education, understanding this ideological antagonism is key to comprehending the counter-revolutionary role of the United States in the twentieth century—a role which, all things considered, is comparable to that of the Roman Catholic monarchies of Spain and Austria in the early modern centuries and of royalist, Anglican and liberal Great Britain following the French Revolution. Anti-Marxism was not merely an ideological matter. It was rooted in the bureaucratic and hierarchical structure of universities and their close ties to government and business. Accordingly, institutionalized anti-Marxism is an important theme of this work.

In the wake of what became the established political orthodoxy, the community of American scholars in each discipline had its own hierarchy and intellectual paradigms which it enforced on its members. These paradigms were internalized by researchers and teachers constituting an ideological consensus imposed by the ruling class institutions including the administrators and trustees of American universities. It entailed a rejection of the Marxist point of view and the defense of liberalism, capitalism, and

American imperialism in the Cold War. Theorizing was allowed but more often than not turned out to be a rationalization or reinforcement of the existing economic and political order rather than a critique of it. However distinguished some of this work proved to be, the normative nature of the scholarship and teaching in the humanities and social sciences will be a principal focus of this narrative.

On the other hand, we should not press this perspective too far. Within the overall context of enforced conformity certain distinguished Marxist scholars like Meyer Schapiro, Leslie White, Paul Baran, Herbert Marcuse, C. Wright Mills, and Walter Lafeber were able to survive the repression of the McCarthy epoch. Beleaguered as they were, they deserve honorable mention in their own right, but especially as they prepared the ground for the student revolts of the 1960s and the spate of Marxist-inspired scholarship which followed. Their continued presence in academe also justifies the view that, despite themselves, some American universities did serve as refuges for critical thought even in the worst of times. Moreover, we will argue that the influx of Marxist professors into the universities since the 1960s has strengthened rather than weakened this stream of intellectual dissent. It is the threat that this influence poses which is in part responsible for the postmodern, poststructural and neoliberal offensive that has characterized academic life since the 1970s.

However, since the 1980s, this relatively liberal environment has become increasingly embattled through the tightening of the role of university management. Within universities—mine not excepted—administrative management has intensified at the expense of professional autonomy as part of a drive to make academics more productive or to proletarianize them, erasing the difference between more or less self-ruling tenured faculty and contractual labor. Universities increasingly began to operate according to the rules of private business and in some cases actually to become profit-based corporations. This trend also brought with it the narrowing and channeling of curriculums and the privatization of knowledge, which by definition involves limiting the growth of positive knowledge, to say nothing of critical thought. In this light the future of the humanities, the social and indeed the natural sciences—the core subjects of the university—are threatened.

As we have noted, despite their limitations universities are key institutions within which critical thought has found a place and has extended into society at large. It is our belief that the ability of university academics to produce and freely disseminate knowledge—especially in the natural sciences, engineering, and agriculture but also in the humanities and social sciences—was central to the success of post-war American capitalism. Moreover, as the upheavals of the 1960s demonstrated, universities proved to be important sites of struggle whose impact made itself felt throughout society. In the neoliberal period they are moving toward so-called knowledge capitalism, the goal of which is to turn the campus into a locus of productive, i.e. profitable, activity and privatized knowledge and which is transforming it into an important site of class conflict. Finally, we will argue that universities are crucial to the possibility of creating a future socialist society in which what Marx called the general intellect will be allowed to reorganize society on the basis of freely available knowledge, democracy, and a concern for the natural environment. In contrast, an imperiled and crisis-ridden capitalism desperate to survive is trying to make the university an adjunct of private enterprise and in the course of doing so to undermine its positive and critical functions. I believe that this movement will be self-defeating, not only damaging the university, but crippling capitalism's capacity to innovate scientifically while also undermining its legitimating ideological functions. This contradiction between the university as a site of critical knowledge and as an adjunct to capitalism surfaced, we will argue, during the Free Speech Movement at Berkeley in the 1960s, and it has increasingly come to the fore since the 1980s.

In the face of this threat, remaining indifferent to the fate of the universities would be irresponsible and, indeed, is impossible. The crisis of the universities is part of the crisis of a global capitalism of which the United States is still the center, although for how much longer is open to question. Accordingly, we have undertaken to write a critical history of the American university from the time of its emergence as a key institution centered on mass education and research. Our narrative is focused on the major humanities and social science disciplines whose principal purpose was to forge and disseminate ideological tools that helped support the liberal and capitalist pillars of the American state during the period of U.S. global ascendancy. We are interested in understanding the knowledge that was generated, for example in sociology or anthropology or English, what contribution it represented to positive knowledge, and what ideological function it served, in order to understand better its connection with the overall needs of American state power and capitalism. Instead of merely studying the generation of positive knowledge on its own terms we aim to understand its social, political, and psychological roots and common ideological purpose, as well as its contradictions, its relationship to the Marxist viewpoint and its historical significance.

In the United States most academics, while pursuing their academic specialties, in one way or another defended liberal and capitalist institutions as well as American foreign policy during the Cold War. But we will also pay close attention to those few who dissented during the 1950s and whose critical perspective prepared the way for the revolts of the 1960s. The achievements of the scholars of the 1960s and 1970s—including Eugene Genovese, Immanuel Wallerstein, Fredric Jameson, and Eric Wolf—will be celebrated. Moreover, despite the ascendancy of postmodernism and neoliberalism, the voices of critical intellectuals like Jameson, Robert Brenner, Perry Anderson, Bertell Ollman, Marshall Berman, Michael Hardt, and a host of others have become institutionalized and will not be silenced without struggle.

The precedent for this work was a long article by Perry Anderson called "Components of the National Culture" which appeared in the *New Left Review* in 1968. In it Anderson attempted a survey of the key disciplines of British academic life from a Marxist perspective. His critique was designed to lay the intellectual foundations of an alternative revolutionary culture. According to Anderson, the key feature of the dominant culture in Britain at the time was the absence of sociology, which, he argued, was the central discipline developed by the European bourgeoisie at the end of the nineteenth century in reaction to the rise of the proletariat and revolutionary Marxism. This absence was a consequence of the lack of a serious revolutionary danger in Britain, as compared to the situation in Germany, France, and Italy, which saw the theorizing of Max Weber, Emile Durkheim, and Vilfred Pareto in the face of precisely such a threat. Furthermore, Anderson pointed out that the later structural-functional synthesis offered by Parsons—in a United States now at the center of the post-1945 Free World—was meant to provide a model discipline and ideological justification for capitalism and liberalism, not only in American society but for the rest of the world. What Anderson seems to have missed at the time was the strength of Marxist history in England, which was coming into its own and whose intellectual triumph reflected the economic and political crises affecting British society.

In contrast, our own history of American academic culture takes as its premise not the absence of sociology but *the refusal of history*. The striking feature of American academic culture—in economics, political science, psychology, English, sociology, anthropology—is its repression of history, especially a history based on conflict. Indeed, it is our contention that from an intellectual point of view the upheavals of the 1960s were based on a return of history—the suppressed past of American racism and class conflict, and the United States understood not as an exception but as an integral part of the world history of capitalism and imperialism. Likewise, the more recent period dominated by postmodernism, cultural studies, and neoliberal economics saw an attempt once again to suppress the contradictions of capitalist history, only for those contradictions to resurface following the crisis of 2008. Indeed, it is Jameson—not a historian, but a towering Marxist literary critic and Hegelian philosopher—who above all has kept the light of critical dialectical method and historical materialism burning in these politically sterile and culturally fragmented times. It is Jameson's conception of Marxism as the master narrative or "untranscendable horizon" against which all other narratives must be judged that has inspired this work. The fact that Jameson is a pure product of American academe is important in celebrating the American system's achievements. We should also acknowledge the significance of the dialectical analysis of social thought undertaken by the British-Hungarian scholar István Mészáros, especially in his two-volume work *Social Structures and Forms of Consciousness* (2010–11).

The core disciplines in the humanities and social sciences are thus the focal point of our study. Probing their ideological assumptions and uncovering their ideological interconnections is a distinctive feature of this analysis. We have also tried to integrate this approach with an institutional history of the universities, including their relationship to the evolution of American political and economic life. In Chapter 3 especially—focused on students as the central agents of the 1960s revolt—the connection between the universities and the history of American society becomes manifest and their political centrality becomes incontestable. Indeed, we argue that the political importance of the university campus has once again risen to the surface following the crisis that began in 2008.

Writing this history has been facilitated by the fact that an enormous amount of critical scholarship on the universities has accumulated in recent years, although it has not been brought together in a connected narrative until now. I hope that approaching this history through the analysis of its core disciplines gives this work a perspective which readers will find instructive.

Introduction

The fact that today there are over 4,000 colleges and universities in the United States represents an unparalleled educational, scientific, and cultural endowment. These institutions occupy a central place in American economic and cultural life. Certification from one of them is critical to the career hopes of most young people in the United States. The research produced in these establishments is likewise crucial to the economic and political future of the American state. Institutions of higher learning are of course of varying quality, with only 600 offering master's degrees and only 260 classified as research institutions. Of these only 87 account for the majority of the 56,000 doctoral degrees granted annually. Moreover, the number of really top-notch institutions based on the quality of their faculty and the size of their endowments is no more than 20 or 30. But still, the existence of thousands of universities and colleges offering humanistic, scientific, and vocational education, to say nothing of religious training, represents a considerable achievement. Moreover, the breakthroughs in research that have taken place during the last two generations in the humanities and social sciences, not to speak of the natural sciences, have been spectacular.

But the future of these institutions is today imperiled. Except for a relatively few well-endowed universities, most are in serious financial difficulty. A notable reason for this has been the decline in public financial support for higher education since the 1980s, a decline due to a crisis in federal and state finances but also to the triumph of right-wing politics based on continuing austerity toward public institutions. The response of most colleges and universities has been to dramatically increase tuition fees forcing students to take on heavy debt and putting into question access to higher education for young people from low- and middle-income families. This situation casts a shadow on the implicit post-war contract between families and the state which promised upward mobility for their children based on higher education. This impasse is but part of the general predicament of the majority of the American population, which has seen its income fall and its employment opportunities shrink since the Reagan era. These problems have intensified since the financial collapse of 2008 and the onset of depression or the start of a generalized capitalist crisis.

Mounting student debt and fading job prospects are reflected in stagnating enrollments in higher education, intensifying the financial difficulties of universities and indeed exacerbating the overall economic malaise.[1] The growing cost of universities has led recently to the emergence of Massive Online Open Courses whose upfront costs to students are nil, which further puts into doubt the future of traditional colleges and universities. These so-called MOOCs, delivered via the internet, hold out the possibility, or embody the threat, of doing away with much of the expensive labor and fixed capital costs embodied in existing university campuses. Clearly the future of higher education hangs in the balance with important implications for both American politics and economic life.

The deteriorating situation of the universities has its own internal logic as well. In response to the decline in funding, but also to the prevalence of neoliberal ideology, universities—or rather the presidents, administrators, and boards of trustees who control them—are increasingly moving away from their ostensible mission of serving the public good to that of becoming as far as possible like private enterprises. In doing so, most of the teachers in these universities are being reduced to the status of wage labor, and indeed precarious wage labor. The wages of the non-tenured faculty who now constitute the majority of teachers in higher education are low, they have no job security and receive few benefits. Although salaried and historically enjoying a certain autonomy, tenured faculty are losing the vestiges of their independence as well. Similarly, the influence of students in university affairs—a result of concessions made by administrators during the upheavals of the 1960s and 1970s—has effectively been neutered. These changes reflect a decisive shift of power toward university managers whose numbers and remuneration have expanded prodigiously. The objective of these bureaucrats is to transform universities as much as possible to approximate private and profit-making corporations, regarded as models of efficient organization based on the discipline of the market. Indeed, scores of universities, Phoenix University for example, have been created explicitly as for-profit businesses and currently enroll millions of students.

Modern universities have always had a close relationship with private business, but whereas in the past faculty labor served capital by producing educated managers, highly skilled workers, and new knowledge as a largely free good, strenuous efforts are now underway to transform academic employment into directly productive, i.e., profitable, labor. The knowledge engendered by academic work is accordingly being privatized as a commodity through patenting, licensing, and copyrighting to the immediate benefit of universities and the private businesses to which universities are increasingly linked. Meanwhile, through the imposition of administrative standards laid down in accord with neoliberal principles, faculty are being subjected to unprecedented scrutiny through continuous quantified evaluation of teaching and research in which the ability to generate outside funding has become the ultimate measure of scholarly worth. At the same time, universities have become part of global ranking systems like the Shanghai Index or the Times Higher Education World University Rankings in which their standing in the hierarchy has become all important to their prestige and funding.

Several intertwined questions emerge from this state of affairs. In the first place, given the rising expense and debt that attendance at university imposes and declining employment prospects especially for young people, will there continue to be a mass market for higher education? Is the model of the university or college traditionally centered on the humanities and the sciences with a commitment to the pursuit of truth compatible with the movement toward converting the universities into quasi- or fully private business corporations? Finally, what are the implications of changes in the neoliberal direction for the future production of objective knowledge, not to speak of critical understanding?

Universities during the Cold War produced an impressive amount of new positive knowledge, not only in the sciences, engineering, and agriculture but also in the social sciences and humanities. In the case of the humanities and social sciences such knowledge, however real, was largely instrumental or tainted by ideological rationalizations. It was not sufficiently critical in the sense of getting to the root of the matter, especially on questions of social class or on the motives of American foreign policy. Too much of it was used to control and manipulate ordinary people within and without the United States in behalf of the American state and the maintenance of the capitalist order. There were scholars who continued to search for critical understanding even at the height of the Cold War, but they largely labored in obscurity. This state of affairs was disrupted in the 1960s with the sudden burgeoning of Marxist scholarship made possible by the upsurge of campus radicalism attendant on the anti-war, civil rights, and black liberation struggles. But the decline of radicalism in the 1970s saw the onset of postmodernism, neoliberalism, and the cultural turn. As we will argue, postmodernism represented an unwarranted and untenable skepticism, while neoliberal economics was a crude and overstated scientism. The cultural turn deserves more respect, but whatever intellectual interest there may be in it there is little doubt that the net effect of all three was to delink the humanities and social sciences from the revolutionary politics that marked the 1960s. The ongoing presence in many universities of radicals who took refuge in academe under Nixon and Reagan ensured the survival of Marxist ideas if only in an academic guise. Be that as it may, the crisis in American society and the concomitant crisis of the universities has become extremely grave over the last decade. It is a central contention of this work that, as a result of the crisis, universities will likely prove to be a key location for ideological and class struggle, signaled already by the growing interest in unionization of faculty both tenured and non-tenured, the revival of Marxist scholarship, the Occupy Movement, the growing importance of the Boycott, Divestment, and Sanctions movement, and heightening conflicts over academic freedom and the corporatization of university governance.

The approach of this work is to examine the recent history of American universities from the perspective of Marxism, a method which can be used to study these institutions critically as part of the capitalist economic and political system. Despite ongoing apologetics that view universities as sites for the pursuit of disinterested truth, we contend that a critical perspective involving an understanding of universities as institutions based on the contradictions of class inequality, the ultimate unity of the disciplines rooted in the master narrative of historical materialism, and a consciousness of history makes more sense as a method of analysis. All the more so, this mode of investigation is justified by the increasing and explicit promotion of academic capitalism by university managers trying to turn universities into for-profit corporations. In response to these policies scholars have in fact begun to move toward the reintegration of political economy with the study of higher education. This represents a turn away from the previous dominance in this field of postmodernism and cultural studies and, indeed, represents a break from the hegemonic outlook of neoliberalism.[2] On the other hand, most of this new scholarship is orientated toward studying the effects of neoliberalism on the contemporary university, whereas the present work takes a longer view. Marxist political economy demands a historical perspective in which the present condition of universities emerged from the crystallization of certain previous trends. It therefore looks at the evolution of the university from the beginning of the twentieth century, sketching its evolution from a preserve of the upper-middle class in which research played almost no role into a site of mass education and burgeoning research, and, by the 1960s, a vital element in the political economy of the United States.

In contrast to their original commitment to independence with respect to the state up to World War II, most if by no means all universities and colleges defined their post-war goals in terms of the pursuit of the public good and were partially absorbed into the state apparatus by becoming financially dependent on government. But from start to finish twentieth-century higher education also had an intimate and ongoing relationship with private business. In the neoliberal period universities are taking this a step further, aspiring to turn themselves into quasi- or actual business corporations. But this represents the conclusion of a long-evolving process. The encroachment of private business into the university is in fact but part of the penetration of the state by private enterprise and the partial privatization of the state. On the surface this invasion of the public sphere by the market may appear beneficial to private business. We regard it, on the contrary, as a symptom of economic weakness and a weakening of civil society.

The American system of higher education, with its prestigious private institutions, great public universities, private colleges and junior colleges, was a major achievement of a triumphant American republic. It provided the U.S. state with the intellectual, scientific, and technical means to strengthen significantly its post-1945 power. The current neoliberal phase reflects an America struggling economically and politically to adapt to the growing challenges to its global dominance and to the crisis of capitalism itself. The shift of universities toward the private corporate model is part of this struggle. Capitalism in its strongest periods not only separated the state from the private sector, it kept the private sector at arm's length from the state. The role of the state in ensuring a level playing field and providing support for the market was clearly understood. The current attempt by universities to mimic the private sector is a form of economic and ideological desperation on the part of short-sighted and opportunistic university administrators as well as politicians and businessmen. In our view, this aping of the private sector is misguided, full of contradictions, and ultimately vain if not disastrous. Indeed, it is a symptom of crisis and decline.

The current overwhelming influence of private business on universities grew out of pre-existing tendencies. In Chapter 1 we note the already corporate nature of university governance both private and public, and the influence of business on universities in the first part of the twentieth century. In reaction there developed the concept of academic freedom as well as the establishment of the system of tenure and the development of a rather timid faculty trade unionism. We will stress the importance of private foundations in controlling the development of the curriculum and research in both the sciences and humanities. In their teaching, universities were mainly purveyors of the dominant capitalist ideology. Humanities and social science professors imparted mainly liberal ideology and taught laissez-faire economics which justified the political and economic status quo. The development of specialized departments reinforced the fragmentation of knowledge and discouraged the emergence of a systemic overview and critique of American culture and society. There were, as noted earlier, a few Marxist scholars, some of considerable distinction, who became prominent particularly in the wake of the Depression, the development of the influence of the Communist Party, and the brief period of Soviet-American cooperation during World War II. But the teaching of Marxism was frowned upon and attacked even prior to the Cold War.

The post-1945 university was a creation of the Cold War. Its expansion, which sprang directly out of war, was based on the idea of education as a vehicle of social mobility, which was seen as an alternative to the equality and democracy promoted by the populism of the New Deal. Its elitist and technocratic style of governance was patterned after that of the large private corporation and the American federal state during the 1950s. Its enormously successful research programs were mainly underwritten by appropriations from the military and the CIA. The CIA itself was largely created by recruiting patriotic faculty from the universities. Much of the research in the social sciences was directed at fighting Soviet and revolutionary influence and advancing American imperialism abroad. Marxist professors and teaching programs were purged from the campuses.

Dating from medieval times, the curriculum of the universities was based on a common set of subjects including language, philosophy, and natural science premised on the idea of a unitary truth. Although the subject matter changed over the centuries higher education continued to impart the hegemonic ideology of the times. Of course the notion of unitary truth was fraying at the seams by the beginning of the twentieth century with the development of departmental specialization and the increasingly contested nature of truth, especially in the social sciences in the face of growing class struggle in America. However, the notion of the idea of the unity of knowledge as purveyed by the university was still ideologically important as a rationale for the existence of universities. Moreover, as we shall demonstrate, it was remarkable how similarly, despite differences in subject matter and method, the main disciplines in the humanities and social sciences responded to the challenge of Marxism during the Cold War. They all developed paradigms which opposed or offered alternatives to Marxism while rationalizing continued loyalty to liberalism and capitalism. As if on cue, sociology, psychology, literature, political science, and anthropology all took sides by explicitly rejecting Marxism and putting forward viewpoints opposed to it. History itself stressed American exceptionalism, justified U.S. expansionism, minimized class conflict, and warned against revolution. Indeed, this work will focus on these disciplines because they defended the capitalist status quo at a deeper cultural and intellectual level than the ubiquitous mass media. As Louis Althusser pointed out, the teaching received by students from professors at universities was the strategic focal point for the ideological defense of the dominant class system. That was as true of the United States as it was of France, where institutions of higher learning trained those who would later train or manage labor. Criticizing the recent history of these disciplines is thus an indispensable step to developing an alternative knowledge and indeed culture that will help to undermine liberal capitalist hegemony.[3]

The approach of this work is to critically analyze these core academic subjects from a perspective informed by Pierre Bourdieu and Karl Marx. Bourdieu points out that the deep involvement of the social sciences (and the humanities) with powerful social interests makes it difficult to free their study from ideological presuppositions and thereby achieve a truly socially and psychologically reflexive understanding.[4] But such reflexive knowledge was precisely what Marx had in mind more than a century earlier. Leaving a Germany still under the thrall of feudalism and absolutism for Paris in 1843, the young Marx wrote to his friend Arnold Ruge that

reason has always existed, but not always in a reasonable form ... but, if constructing the future and settling everything for all times are not our affair, it is all the more clear what we have to accomplish at present: I am referring to *ruthless criticism* of all that exists, ruthless both in the sense of not being afraid of the results it arrives at and in the sense of being just as little afraid of conflict with the powers that be.[5]

His task as he saw it was to criticize the existing body of knowledge so as to make it as reasonable as possible, i.e., to undermine its illusory and ideological character and substitute knowledge which was both true and helped advance communism. Such a project entailed deconstructing the existing body of knowledge through rational criticism, exposing its ideological foundations and advancing an alternative based on a sense of contradiction, social totality, and a historical and materialist understanding. It is our ambition in surveying and studying the humanities and social sciences in the period after 1945 to pursue our investigation in the same spirit. Indeed, it is our view that a self-reflexive approach to contemporary knowledge, while woefully lacking, is an indispensable complement to the development of a serious ideological critique of the crisis-ridden capitalist society of today.

Marxism is still regarded with suspicion in the United States. As a matter of fact, anti-Marxism in American universities was not merely a defensive response to McCarthyism as some allege. Anti-communism was bred in the bone of many Americans and was one of the strongest forces that affected U.S. society in the twentieth century, including the faculty members of its universities. An *idée fixe* rather than an articulated ideology, it was compounded out of deeply embedded albeit parochial notions of Americanism, American exceptionalism and anti-radicalism.[6] The latter was rooted in the bitter resistance of the still large American middle or capitalist class to the industrial unrest which marked the late nineteenth and early twentieth centuries and which had a strong bed of support among the immigrant working class. Nativism then was an important tool in the hands of this class in fighting a militant if ethnically divided working class. Moreover, the anti-intellectual prejudices of American society in general and the provincialism of its universities were ideal terrain for fending off subversive ideas from abroad like Marxism. Later, this anti-communism and hostility to Marxism became the rationale for the extension of American imperialism overseas particularly after 1945. The social origins of the professoriate among the lower middle class, furthermore, and its role as indentured if indirect servants of capital, strengthened its position as inimical to Marxism. Just as careers could be lost for favoring Marxism, smart and adroit academics could make careers by advancing some new intellectual angle in the fight against Marxism. And this was not merely a passing feature of the height of the Cold War: from the 1980s onward, postmodernism, identity politics, and the cultural turn were invoked to disarm the revolutionary Marxist politics that had developed in the 1960s. Whatever possible role identity politics and culture might have in deepening an understanding of class their immediate effect was to undermine a sense of class and strengthen a sense of liberal social inclusiveness while stressing the cultural obstacles to the development of revolutionary class consciousness.

This overall picture of conformity and repression was, however, offset by the remarkable upsurge of student radicalism that marked the 1960s, challenging the intellectual and social orthodoxies of the Cold War. In reaction to racism and political and social repression at home and the Vietnam War abroad, students rebelled against the oppressive character of university governance and by extension the power structure of American society. Overwhelmingly the ideology through which this revolt was refracted was the foreign and until then largely un-American doctrine of Marxism. Imported into the universities largely by students, Marxism then inspired a new generation of radical and groundbreaking scholarship. Meanwhile it is important to note that the student revolt itself was largely initiated by the southern civil rights movement, an important bastion of which were the historically black colleges of the South. It was from the struggle of racially oppressed black students in the American South as well as the growing understanding of the anti-colonial revolutionaries of Vietnam that the protest movement in American colleges and universities was born. Equally important was the Free Speech Movement at Berkeley. Indeed, it is the contention of this work that the issues raised at Berkeley over democracy in the universities and the free expression of ideas not only shaped the student movement of that time but are still with us, and indeed are central to the future of universities and intellectual life today.

At the heart of the Berkeley protest lay a rejection of the idea of a university as a hierarchical corporation producing exchange values including the production of trained workers and ideas convertible into commodities. Instead the students asserted the vision of a democratic university which produced knowledge as a use value serving the common good. It is our view that this issue raised at Berkeley in the 1960s anticipated the class conflict that is increasingly coming to the fore over so-called knowledge capitalism. Both within the increasingly corporate neoliberal university and in business at large, the role of knowledge and knowledge workers is becoming a key point of class struggle. This is especially true on university campuses where the proletarianization of both teaching and research staff is in process and where the imposition of neoliberal work rules is increasingly experienced as tyrannical. The skilled work of these knowledge producers, the necessarily interconnected nature of their work, and the fundamentally contradictory notion of trying to privatize and commodify knowledge, have the potential to develop into a fundamental challenge to capitalism.

Structure of the Book

Chapter 1 traces the evolution of the universities and colleges from being finishing schools for the middle classes at the beginning of the twentieth century to their transformation post-1945 into institutions orientated toward mass higher education and research. Big business and the foundations had an overriding interest in these changes but the influence of the U.S. military and state also played a major role, especially during World War II and the onset of the Cold War. As such the universities in this period must be seen in the Gramscian sense as an integral part of the non-coercive element of the capitalist state. The major universities where the bulk of research and the main articulation of social science and humanities ideas took place are the focal point of investigation. University faculties in the first part of the twentieth century became indirect servants of capital and the capitalist class. On the other hand, professors tried to retain as much autonomy as they could by fighting for academic freedom and tenure, and in the case of the American Federation of Teachers for the thorough unionization of faculty. Marxism established a limited presence on campuses as a result of the Depression and Soviet-American cooperation during World War II. But even in the inter-war period the weeding out of left-wing radicals was an ongoing process. The onset of the Cold War set off a widespread purge of Marxist professors as part of the McCarthyite attack on the American left. Meanwhile the intellectual and scientific resources of the universities were mobilized to fight communism and revolutionary change worldwide through the CIA and other covert activities headquartered in the elite universities. Administrators and many members of faculty enthusiastically joined this struggle to their own and their institutions' benefit. Higher salaries, the spread of tenure, increased professionalization, the comparmentalization and fragmentation of knowledge based on departments further served to depoliticize faculty.

The second chapter demonstrates how quickly and almost in lock step the humanities and social sciences fell into line with the opinions and demands of the U.S. state in the Cold War. Indeed, top academics more often than not had close ties to the U.S. government. It furthermore shows how the content of the academic disciplines was harnessed to defending capitalism, liberalism, and American imperialism while attacking left-wing ideas. The respective disciplines rapidly redefined the norms and substance of their teaching in accord with the assumptions of the Cold War. Reviewing academic research in the United States during the 1950s we take note of its commitment to methodological individualism, scientific positivism, and social engineering, especially in the social sciences, thereby fending off Marxism and helping to put weapons in the hands of those who wielded economic and political power at home and abroad. A bias toward social equilibrium and instrumentalism as against a sense of historical change and class conflict, and a preference for specialist and cumulative knowledge rather than theorizing and a sense of the whole, marked most scholarship in the 1950s. Those academics in the humanities and social sciences who served as apologists for American capitalism in the Cold War rose to the forefront, fitting the Gramscian category of traditional or, better, establishment intellectuals. Through the influence of the highly influential Talcott Parsons, sociology did take a systemic view but one which tended to be static and scholastic, denying the reality of history, imperialism, and class conflict. The influential historians of this period likewise tended to minimize the importance of class conflict in America, emphasizing an underlying capitalist and liberal consensus. The phenomenon of revolution could not be ignored but was viewed not as a feature of the global historical process but as an affliction whose symptoms were foreign to the American experience and were in need of treatment. Literature meanwhile was essentially aestheticized and insofar as possible divorced from social relations.

In Chapter 3 we turn our focus to the protests of the 1960s. Students, who had mainly stayed mute during the McCarthy period, suddenly abandoned their passivity and rebelled in large numbers against the corporate university while attempting to change society at large. Their uprisings were inspired in the first place by the civil rights struggle and were then reinforced by the anti-imperialist revolution in Vietnam. Student protest, which started with the Free Speech Movement at Berkeley, broadened as a result of the emergence of the Black Power and women's movements. Having been sites of corporate and intellectual power, the universities proved surprisingly effective launching platforms for ideological and social movements that resonated broadly in American society, challenging the existing political and social order. Black, women's, Chicano, Asian and gay and lesbian study programs were introduced into the curriculums as a result of student demands. In a case of the return of the repressed, Marxism flourished both inside and outside the classrooms. The writings of third world Marxist revolutionaries like Mao, Ho Chi Minh, Fidel Castro, and Franz Fanon, as well as British Marxist historians and the theorists of the Frankfurt School, were incorporated into the social sciences and humanities curriculums. Marxist scholarship bloomed in both the humanities and social sciences as never before. Meanwhile, a tide of demands for the liberalization and democratization of governance was contained by university authorities through a combination of concessions and repression. The students' struggle did not lead to the development of a broad-based revolutionary politics in America, but it did help to advance the civil rights struggle and frustrate the immediate imperialist ambitions of the United States in Vietnam. It also forced universities to liberalize their rules, broaden their curriculums, and to become more inclusive with respect to women, blacks, and other identity groups. Contrary to a common conservative opinion, universities in the United States at the end of the 1960s were far more cosmopolitan and stronger institutions than they were at the beginning of that decade, and students were treated with more respect.

In hindsight we take the view that the movement initiated by the events at Berkeley constituted a struggle over nothing less than the purposes of creating knowledge. In that sense the protests at Berkeley that spread to other campuses during the 1960s were of enduring importance. They prefigured the emergence of so-called cognitive capitalism toward the close of the twentieth century, in which the accumulation of an ever-increasing abundance of knowledge is at one at the same time vital to capital and constrained by it, i.e., forced to remain within the boundaries of commodification and profitability. Insofar as knowledge continues to be limited by the requirements of capitalism it is narrowed, distorted, and debased. At the same time, in cognitive capitalism knowledge workers occupy a strategic economic and political position while their social and economic condition is rendered more insecure as a result of their increasingly precarious employment situation. By the same token, their skills and strategic location within the capitalist accumulation process give knowledge producers a significant and perhaps decisive political and economic leverage.[7] It is our contention that the struggle at Berkeley in the 1960s foreshadowed this situation.

Chapter 4 deals with developments in the following period, covering trends in the humanities and social sciences, most notably the emergence and significance of postmodernism and neoliberal economics. Both had in common the goal of revoking history by insisting that it was possible to return to the past willy-nilly. Both celebrated the benefits of market capitalism. Both were made more plausible by the flight of much productive capital from the capitalist heartlands and the consequent disappearance from consciousness of collective productive activity in favor of individualized consumerism and a largely intangible finance capital. The student protest movement inspired by Marxism withered as students retreated from politics in favor of networking, careerism, and consumerism. While capitalist growth continued it became more unstable as speculative activity increased. Meanwhile the incomes and prospects of the working class declined. Under the presidencies of Reagan and Bush the Vietnam syndrome faded and U.S. imperialism and militarism raised their heads in a new phase of the Cold War against both the Soviet Union and revolutionary developments in Central America and Southern Africa. Business and government responded to radicalism and the profit squeeze with economic austerity, the disciplining of the poor, and the so-called culture wars.

With the waning of protest on campuses, university administrators gradually gained the upper hand once more, whittling away concessions made to students and faculty during the 1960s and 1970s. Still, the upheavals of that period had made universities more open than ever before. American universities took the lead in the trend toward globalized higher education, paralleling the extension of U.S. overseas investment and imperialism from the 1980s onward. Increasing numbers of foreign students, especially from Asia, entered university campuses. At the same time a greater diversity among American students was also evident. A growing cosmopolitanism also reflected itself in the increasing interest in postmodern theorists like Jean-François Lyotard and Michel Foucault, the sociology of Pierre Bourdieu, and postcolonial scholarship. Marxism survived as an academic approach shorn of politics.

Postmodernism was a product of French theory, late capitalist consumerism, and anti-Marxism. Its skepticism attacked objectivity, abstraction, and foundationalism rooted in the Enlightenment and Eurocentric thought. But as it turned out the most important theorist of the postmodern was the Marxist-Hegelian Fredric Jameson, who actually named it as a zeitgeist or historical condition and understood it as rooted in universal commodification, the fetishism of commodities, and the denial of history. Jameson's ideas, French theory, and British cultural studies boosted the development of cultural studies in the U.S. and the tendency toward interdisciplinarity rather than fragmentation. Feminism saw the progress of socialist-feminism, anti-racist feminism, so-called intersectional thought, and the post-feminist theories of Donna Haraway and Judith Butler. A politically neutered Marxism persisted in the higher criticism of Jameson and Eric Olin Wright's sociology, the latter based on an analytical Marxism with its misunderstanding of dialectical thought. Bourdieu's influence was widely felt in sociology and other academic disciplines. Clifford Geertz's idealist symbolical anthropology made itself felt in anthropology but also in cultural studies. Edward Said's work spurred the emergence of postcolonial theorists marked by hostility to Eurocentrism, which at least in their eyes included Marxism. In history Hayden White tried unsuccessfully to promote postmodern irrationalism, while epigones of E.P. Thompson attempted to undermine the objective foundations of the concepts of class and class struggle. Revisionist schools of history tried to overthrow the Marxist view of the English and French Revolutions, which had viewed them as bourgeois and capitalist revolutions.

In the field of economics neoliberalism was propagated by Frederik Hayek, who promoted it both in Europe and the United States and found a headquarters for it in the economics department of the University of Chicago. Neoliberalism became the dominant paradigm in economics, driving before it Neo-Keynesian, Marxist, and other economic ideas. Despite its anti-state rhetoric, neoliberalism does not in practice believe that the implementation of its program requires the lifting of government constraints. Rather it is a question of active political and ideological intervention in which the state plays a key role in freeing markets. The goal of neoliberals is not to destroy the state but to control and redefine it in the service of the market. The market is nonetheless represented as an autonomous machine or device that is the most powerful imaginable processer of information. Government attempts to guarantee social entitlements like health care, education, and pensions are regarded as limitations on individuals' freedom of choice. The question of popular legitimacy is addressed by viewing the state as much as possible as itself part of the market, assimilating political institutions to the model of private institutions, and regarding citizens as consumers. Freedom is not the positing of a political or social ideal but conceived rather in terms of the protection of private property, unconstrained markets, and the production of autonomous individuals equipped with a neoclassical sense of rationality and a deep self-interest in striving to improve their lot by engaging in market exchange. Freedom without capitalism is unthinkable. Those who cannot cope under such conditions should be given charity or put into prisons or other institutions. For neoliberalism, free markets are essential for capital both nationally and internationally; corporations can do no wrong and are the bedrock of wealth creation. If there are anomalies the market can correct itself. Inequality is essential and promotes progress. Gary Becker and Richard Posner of the University of Chicago were instrumental in the development of what came to be called "economics imperialism." Economics imperialism refers to the economic analysis of seemingly non-economic aspects of life. In this way neoliberal economics attempted to turn itself into a hegemonic culture by analyzing anthropological, legal, sociological, and political phenomena in terms of liberal economics.

The influence of neoliberal economics at Chicago was reinforced by the tough-minded revival of classical philosophy, with its notions of inherent inequality, by Leo Strauss, the most influential neoconservative philosopher. Meanwhile Richard Rorty tried unsuccessfully to restore a pallid liberalism but was more successful at using pragmatism and postmodernism to knock down the epistemological claims of traditional philosophy. At the turn of the millennium Alan Sokal exploded the dubious skepticism of the postmodern enterprise and exposed the sterility of American humanities and social science in the absence of a Marxist analysis of the crisis of U.S. capitalism and a program of socialism and democracy.

The last chapter returns to the institutional analysis of the university, examining the neoliberal university. Underfunded and driven by neoliberal ideas, universities have increasingly striven to become as much like private corporations as possible. Indeed, some are already private enterprises. As such they operate according to the principles of total quality management, which entails continuous scrutiny of all aspects of university operations and especially of the teaching and research activities of the academic staff. Already most teaching is done by non-tenured employees who have few if any benefits and no job security. The objective it seems is to reduce the tenured faculty to the same level, i.e., fully dependent wage workers. Indeed, tenured faculty could be largely eliminated by Massive Open Online Courses. In the interim, university managers are obsessed with their endowments, real estate development, research parks, patents and licenses, as well as student tuition fee increases and debt financing. Still in large part publicly funded, the adoption of this business approach if allowed to go unchecked is likely to undermine objective research and teaching in the natural sciences, social sciences, and humanities and kill off the traditional college and university. Doing so will undermine one of the most important ideological pillars of capitalism as well as jeopardize the production of technological and scientific innovation. Despite its difficulties, the unionization of tenured and non-tenured faculty is the best means of fighting these trends.

I

The Birth of the Corporate University

In the first part of the twentieth century the influence of big business and private foundations over American universities steadily increased. These trends were already strong following World War I but became overwhelming during World War II and the Cold War. Businessmen and corporate lawyers came to dominate university governing bodies while private foundations acquired extraordinary influence over university-based research and the organization of the disciplines. In a more belated fashion the influence of government over universities expanded during World War II and the Cold War. Much university research was harnessed to winning the hot and cold wars while contacts between top academics and administrators and the state deepened. Following the end of World War II the government at both the federal and state level financed a massive expansion of university enrollments, infrastructure, and research.

Universities became an element in what has been called the ideological or non-coercive apparatus of the state. They came more closely under state control and their teachings helped to tie students more closely to the existing political and social order. At the same time the growth in the size and functions of universities made them more and more resemble private corporations even though many were public institutions. With their president and trustees at the top, provosts and deans, chairs of departments, ordinary faculty, graduate and undergraduate students, and non-academic staff, universities had a corporate chain-of-command and division of labor.[1] The façade of the ivory tower, the disinterested pursuit of learning and the public good were nonetheless insisted upon even as the outside influence increased enormously. The fig leaf of university autonomy was maintained because it kept the government at a certain distance while serving the interests of private business overall, and fed the illusions of faculty about their intellectual independence. As the number of administrators grew the internal operations of universities multiplied and assumed a hierarchical character that reduced what there was of faculty internal self-government. The specialization of learning into departments largely separated from one another rewarded research and publication at the expense of teaching and the acquisition of a global view of knowledge. Marxism, which had acquired a certain limited influence during the Depression and World War II, was more or less proscribed during the Cold War. Communists or their sympathizers were silenced or dismissed.

Prior to World War II the middle class sent their children to colleges and universities in growing numbers. Between 1919 and 1941 enrollment quintupled from 250,000 to 1.3 million. Part of a process of class reproduction, the offspring of the middle class went to college to find prospective mates and make social contacts. In the course of acquiring higher learning students received a discipline which enabled them to manage and control those socially beneath them. As such they acquired the education necessary to become entrepreneurs, engineers, physicians, lawyers, managers, administrators, and educators. The number of institutions of higher learning in the United States was vast, numbering around 2,000 in the first part of the twentieth century, of which some were private and others controlled by state governments. Of the private colleges there were some of high quality like Williams, Wesleyan, Carleton, Oberlin, and Pomona, and a great number which were ordinary or mediocre. A few private schools with large endowments were among the elite, like Ivy League Harvard, Yale, and Princeton, which devoted themselves to educating the upper reaches of a ruling class that was increasingly recruited nationally. Indeed, attendance at these schools became a marker of upper class status—and still is. It was widely understood that upward mobility went with acquisition of a university degree and attendance at a prestigious school was particularly desirable.

Other colleges and universities that were mainly public institutions had clienteles composed of the sons and daughters of the regional business and professional elites. A few public institutions like Berkeley and Michigan were distinguished. Most of the top private and public schools at the beginning of the century have retained their dominant role to this day, having the largest endowments and attracting the most distinguished faculty and researchers. The upper tier of colleges and universities set the tone of learning and scholarship for less distinguished establishments. Universities benefited from their *alma mater* role, attracting the largesse of local and national elites based on loyalties formed through their networks of fraternities, team sports, and alumni organizations. The structure of the emerging American system of colleges and universities essentially mirrored that of the American ruling class. It constituted a mechanism for reproducing that class across the country.

Once upon a time the clergy and local politicians had had an important say in how institutions of higher learning, both private and public, were governed. But by the 1930s religious and local political influence was waning if not completely gone, and governing bodies, especially in elite institutions, were increasingly dominated by the business class and corporate lawyers who loomed over what was by now the phase of monopoly capitalism.[2] Through their control of governance and the flow of philanthropic cash, from 1880 to 1940 large corporations assumed indirect control over the major research and educational institutions and harnessed them to meet their needs. This was simply a reflection of the overwhelmingly dominant position that business and private corporations had assumed in American life. The universities' connection with business needs to be underlined as it was extremely close and ongoing. The muckraking author and socialist Upton Sinclair, for example, described Columbia University, which he had attended, as "the political university of the House of Morgan, which sets the standard for the higher education in America."[3] Stanford and the University of Chicago, two of the top 20 American universities, were created directly out of the fortunes of the Stanford and Rockefeller families. Universities nonetheless continued to enjoy a certain internal autonomy and there was lip service given to the pursuit of the public good and academic freedom. Such freedom was sharply qualified with respect to cases of sexual or political deviance.

Aside from training the managerial and professional class, a growing body of research activity in the social sciences, sciences, engineering, and agriculture was carried on based on grants from private businesses, foundations, and government.[4] Research and graduate training at this point were confined to no more than 20 institutions in the Ivy League and major state universities like Illinois, Michigan, and Berkeley. The role of big business over the organization and research activities of American universities was extraordinary. Research in the humanities and social sciences was largely made possible as a result of the funding of private foundations. As a result, the influence of business over universities loomed even larger. Somewhat overshadowed by the greater role of government from World War II onward, the neoliberal period has seen a revival and even deepening of that influence.

The Role of the Foundations

Concerned by industrial and racial unrest at home and by the repercussions of the Russian Revolution abroad, foundations controlled by big business took the lead during the 1920s in creating an academic infrastructure to study what were considered obstacles in the way of the unimpeded global expansion of American capitalism. The Rockefeller, Ford, and Carnegie philanthropies proved most important, but they were seconded by the Brookings Institution, the John Simon Guggenheim Memorial Foundation, the Phelps-Stokes Fund, the Julius Rosenwald Fund, the Russell Sage Foundation, and others. These foundations had been created out of the fortunes accumulated by some of the great American capitalists in the late nineteenth and early twentieth centuries. They helped shape the curriculums of undergraduate and graduate education, insisting on efficiency and the avoidance of duplication in programs.[5] Part of the capital of these foundations was invested in the development of a new infrastructure based in the universities for the production and dissemination of social science knowledge.[6] The funds made available were not aimed at making the social sciences more scientific for their own sake but rather at promoting social stability and developing more effective means of social control. In other words, the foundations were used by big business to finance the production of the social and technical knowledge necessary to their operations at home and abroad. As the skilled expertise needed to produce such knowledge was located in the universities the foundations funneled this money to a select number of universities designated as centers of excellence—Chicago, Columbia, Yale, Harvard, Chapel Hill, Stanford, Berkeley, and Pennsylvania. In this way they underwrote the vast majority of all social science research in the inter-war period.[7]

The Rockefeller Foundation, to take a key example, was created in 1913 to counter the hue and cry against the Rockefeller family's monopoly control of the oil industry and its brutal policies toward labor. In its initial manifesto the Foundation claimed to be interested in nothing less than the promotion of the welfare of the whole of humanity. Its stated mission was to develop solutions to the problems of sickness, poverty, underdevelopment, and ignorance in America and in the rest of the world.[8] The Rockefeller philanthropies alone poured some 50 million dollars into the advancement of the social sciences during the 1920s and '30s. Indeed, reflecting their worldwide interests, the Rockefeller Foundation and the other foundations were notably internationalist in a period when U.S. public opinion had generally retreated into isolationism following World War I. More significant than the funds allocated to specific projects was the new institutional framework created to support future research. Most important to the humanities and social sciences were the American Council of Learned Societies, founded in 1919 and heavily subsidized by the

Rockefeller Foundation and other great foundations, and the Social Science Research Council (created in 1923), likewise a largely Rockefeller-inspired body.[9] Through these institutions business was in a position to shape the kinds of knowledge produced by research in American institutions of higher learning. That these research bodies, which in other countries were state-sponsored, were the creation of private enterprise underlines the extraordinary influence of business over American society. The scholars appointed to the boards of these foundations and its funding committees were those who comfortably fit into the parameters of the existing political and ideological system. It was they who were in a position to determine which kinds of knowledge were acceptable and which were not. Academic careers at the highest level were made or unmade by these determinations. Setting up these foundations through which control could be exercised over research was a remarkably cheap way of buying the vast brain power of the United States.[10]

The Professors

In elite private institutions like Harvard and Princeton faculty enjoyed limited autonomy based on tenure. Paid employees, academics were nevertheless able to appoint their own colleagues and had extensive say in establishing their conditions of work. In early twentieth-century America a professor occupied a middle position between a small businessman and a wholly dependent proletarian. This afforded professors some independence from the president and managers of the university. But autonomy was not extended, or not for very long, to free thinkers, socialists, communists, or those whose sexual behavior was morally questionable. Autonomy was yet more restricted in public institutions as their budgets came from state legislatures, and such universities remained under close scrutiny often from narrow-minded politicians. During the nineteenth century there had already been bitter conflicts over academic freedom. Prior to the Civil War, for instance, the question of slavery was a central political issue leading to the dismissal of faculty at various colleges and universities for taking one side or the other. The matter of religion proved especially controversial as skepticism toward religious teaching aroused the ire of clergy and local public opinion. The teaching of Darwinism in the latter half of the century was especially fraught.

The term academic freedom or teaching freedom (*Lehrfreiheit*) came into use toward the end of the century as part of the growing influence of German higher educational practices. Academic freedom was both a genuine demand for the right to pursue critical inquiry free of external pressure and a self-serving attempt to gain leverage over those who controlled academic employment. Freedom to teach had become an increasingly serious issue in the face of growing pressure to control the teaching of professors stemming from churches and local bigwigs but especially from big business.[11] The teaching of economics proved notably controversial, especially the professing or espousal of socialism, which a few brave academics ventured. But the issue of racism also could arouse passion and led to the dismissal of faculty who challenged discrimination in the southern states. American higher education overall was plagued with insularity, a sense of American exceptionalism, and a general suspicion of foreign ideas. These were abiding problems that would not really be overcome until the 1960s.

Such conflicts as well as a growing sense of professionalism played a part in the creation of the American Association of University Professors (AAUP) and its issuance in 1915 of a Declaration of Principles of Academic Freedom and Academic Tenure. In its founding statement the AAUP defended academic freedom, especially underlining the threat from the tyranny of public opinion. It justified freedom of research and teaching as necessary to society as a whole rather than as the pursuit of an individual or institutional good. On the other hand, it cautioned against individual faculty speaking out, especially in public on issues beyond their competence.[12] Moreover, in response to concerns expressed by prospective members worried about their middle-class status, it repeatedly affirmed that it was a professional organization and not a labor union.[13] It is a commonplace that such anti-union feelings were prevalent among much of the American lower middle class including professors. The latter were fearful of proletarianization as well as committed to preserving their tenure, and such sentiments constituted a persistent barrier to unionization.

Such attitudes inevitably shaped the intellectual presuppositions among many if not all American academics interested in the humanities and social sciences who adopted an apolitical, neutral, objective stance in the pursuit of knowledge. A position of value-free neutrality or objectivity is useful as a method but philosophically can never be thought of as entirely pure nor considered the motive or goal of research. Such an approach did help to produce positive knowledge but was often defended with tell-tale vehemence. This reflected the denial of the fact that the academics' middle posture or position of objectivity in a class-divided society was itself an ideological position and, therefore, intellectually untenable. More often than not, what was being denied was the fact that the roots of this stance of intellectual objectivity lay in attempts to retain a middle-class status. Semi-autonomous employees like professors had little or no control over either investment or resource allocation, or over the physical means of production. However, even though such employees worked indirectly for the self-expansion of capital and even though they had lost the legal status of being self-employed, they can still be viewed as having occupied residual islands of petty-bourgeois relations of production within the capitalist mode of production. They ardently defended this vestigial autonomy by claiming an intellectually independent position. In their immediate work environment, they maintained the work process of the independent artisan while still being employed by capital as wage laborers.[14] They controlled how they accomplished their work and had at least some control over what they produced. They enjoyed relatively high status in the eyes of the public, albeit commanding low salaries. In any case most professors made a point of keeping their noses clean by operating within the norms of so-called value-free knowledge. They were generally recruited from the lower middle class and for the most part they regarded their betters with deference and respect. In the final analysis, professors were indirectly intellectual retainers or subordinates of the capitalist class who were employed by universities to do intellectual work.

Despite the generally favorable situation of the elite of the professoriate the pressures on the more humble among them led to the founding in 1916 of an actual teachers union, the American Federation of Teachers, under the aegis of the American Federation of Labor. The main appeal of the latter was to high-school teachers but it soon recruited members from non-elite institutions of higher learning as well. The new union mainly concerned itself with job security and employment conditions in public schools but soon felt impelled to join the struggle for academic freedom in colleges and universities. This was partly a defensive response to the jingoistic patriotism that had marked American entry into World War I and the phobic hostility to the Russian Revolution on the part of the large and powerful American middle class. Despite this opposition, sympathy for socialism and anti-war sentiment rose sharply among faculty in high schools and universities during the period, which was generally one of sharply increased working-class militancy. It is no wonder then that espousal of socialism, pacifism, or neutralism provoked hysterical right-wing attacks and the dismissal of teachers and university faculty.[15] Perhaps the most notorious case of the latter was that of socialist Scott Nearing, who was fired from the faculty of the University of Toledo in 1917 for his opposition to American entry into the war.[16]

Interference in faculty appointments and what was taught in public institutions intensified in the immediate post-war period.[17] The wave of industrial strikes and the consequent Red Scare was especially fraught and led to numerous dismissals of faculty who were sympathetic to workers and the left. Despite this repression, interest in joining the American Federation of Teachers increased in the short run. The faculties of Howard University and the University of Illinois put themselves in the vanguard in this respect, and all told some 20 union locals were created on university campuses in the immediate post-war years. Interest receded in the late 1920s in the face of the ongoing hostility of university administrators and anti-socialist propaganda.[18]

From time to time there were purges in response to public outcries or suspicion of scandal or subversion. In 1923 seven faculty at the University of Tennessee were fired for teaching evolution, criticizing administrators, and talking about local political issues.[19] In 1929 two faculty at the University of Missouri were disciplined for inquiring into student attitudes about sexuality and the economic status of women.[20] Two years later it was the turn of a sociologist from Ohio State University, Herbert Miller, who was taken to task for championing the Indian freedom struggle led by Gandhi, speaking on forbidden topics in Japanese-controlled Korea, and encouraging fraternization between black and white university students.[21]

The Depression revived radicalism on campus, with the American Federation of Teachers able to expand recruitment, even opening branches in elite institutions like Harvard and Yale as a result of sympathetic faculty. On the other hand, the strong communist influence in the union made some members blanche and caused friction with the anti-communist American Federation of Labor.[22] Campus purges against leftists meanwhile intensified. Granville Hicks, literary editor of *The New Masses* and considered America's leading communist man of letters, was dismissed from Rensselaer Polytechnic Institute in 1935 because of his unacceptable political opinions.[23] Hugh DeLacy was canned from the English department of the University of Washington by the president in 1936, ostensibly for his candidacy for a seat on Seattle's city council. In fact he was fired for his radicalism, including involvement in a union local affiliated with the American Federation of Teachers. In 1937 there were complaints that Paul Sweezy and J. Raymond Walsh had deliberately been given terminal contracts at Harvard, in part because of their involvement in union activity and their Marxist opinions.[24]

The most notorious instance of outside interference and of a political purge occurred at City College in New York in 1940. The Board of Higher

Education offered a professorship to the British philosopher Bertrand Russell, renowned for his intellectual powers, iconoclasm, and atheism. The furor that surrounded his appointment led the populist Mayor of New York Fiorello Laguardia to step in and refuse to fund Russell's chair. The controversy that ensued then ignited the issue of communists on the faculty at City College and in other academic institutions.[25] New York City had become a bastion of Communist Party influence and nowhere more so than among the students and faculty at City College, where a strong faculty union had developed and communism had become rife among students. In the wake of the Russell affair and an outburst of anti-communism following the Hitler-Stalin Pact in 1939, a special state legislative committee organized hearings on suspected communists in high schools and colleges in New York. The committee subpoenaed testimony from over 500 faculty and staff in the New York area. City College faculty were especially targeted in what were more often than not extra-legal proceedings. As a result of the hearings and subsequent administrative actions by the Board of Higher Education, 50 faculty and other staff lost their jobs. This became the single largest political purge of an academic institution in the history of the United States, exceeding anything that happened in the McCarthy period.[26]

A more militant activism than could be found among faculty emerged among students who had become politically conscious at City College, Columbia, Wisconsin, Michigan, and Berkeley as a result of the Depression. Student organizers who reached out beyond the world of learning to labor unions and the poor extended their influence into the hinterlands, including states in the South such as Kentucky, Virginia, Arkansas, Texas, and North Carolina.[27] The question arises as to whether the mobilization of students was the result of indoctrination by radical faculty. In fact, left-wing faculty refrained from proselytizing among their students for fear of losing their jobs. Faculty overall across the United States were mainly liberal in their opinions, eschewing radical ideas. Academics, it can be said, had little influence on left-wing student politics.[28]

World War II

During the Depression higher education was starved for money. World War II marked a striking change as government funding for war-related projects poured into universities for the first time. Over 300 million dollars was provided, largely for weapons research including the development of radar and nuclear weapons. The Manhattan Project, which was largely staffed by university scientists, demonstrated the capacity of federally sponsored research to produce dramatic results.[29] Among students the influence of the military was reinforced by the permanent presence of ROTC programs which trained future officers on campus. Prior to the war, university administrators had looked to private enterprise to fund research and were suspicious of government. Business funding continued but government largesse during the war decisively changed the attitude of university heads. The enormous amounts of government money available for research made them fearful of being left behind by competitors in attracting outside funding. As a result, administrators, although themselves firm devotees of the free market, began to actively seek government support. Given the prevalence of the laissez-faire ideology, ongoing federal support to universities could only be justified initially by way of the notion of patriotic support for the military. The more so as now private corporations had likewise become dependent on military contracts.

By the close of the war a new set of values began to emerge. The transformation of Stanford, a private California university, during the Cold War has recently been studied in depth. Long closely controlled by its founders the Stanford Family, and deeply committed to the private enterprise system, the efforts of Stanford's presidents and deans to become a major university and to come to terms with the National Security State makes it particularly interesting because it exemplifies what was to happen to universities across the United States. At the end of World War II the Stanford administration and many of the science and technology faculty were of the opinion that the concept of the university as an ivory tower divorced from the economy or the concerns of society overall was obsolete. Many declared openly that research was more important than teaching. Those in administrative posts expressed the view that universities ought to be run like efficient business enterprises.[30] Administrators whose numbers were expanding gained power at the expense of departmental and faculty autonomy. They began to collect data on departments and individual departmental members including reports on research output, numbers of graduate and undergraduate students, and the amount spent on each student, which eventually gave them decisive leverage over faculty.

Between 1938 and 1948 university enrollment rapidly expanded, helping to swell university coffers. Very important in the immediate post-war period was the GI Bill of Rights (1944), which funded an influx of veterans into the universities initiating the expansion of higher learning and an increase in university budgets courtesy of the federal government. Universities prospered, basking in prestige and popularity. More than two million GIs had enrolled in universities by the mid-1950s.[31] By 1949–50 total student enrollment stood at 2.7 million, an increase of 80 percent over the decade. Ten years later it stood at 3.6 million. In the meantime, funding by the states for universities likewise expanded in response to the spectacular growth of enrollment.

During the 1950s and '60s recruitment into the universities was extended for the first time to much of the lower middle class and even into the working class. The growth of the community college or public junior college system was an intrinsic feature of this expansion. In the public mind, attendance at university became closely tied to the powerful notion of upward social mobility, which was put forward as a panacea by liberal apologists and enthusiastically embraced by the public. Extending higher education to millions of lower-middle and working-class students amounted to an enormous step forward for political and social democracy, necessitated both for economic reasons but also to fight the Cold War against the threat of communism. At the same time, it made possible putting to bed New Deal populism with its commitment to leveling the playing field in American life.

Growth in higher education reflected the remarkable success of American capitalism during these golden decades. Following the launch of the Russian Sputnik, expanding the number of science and technology students became a priority. The National Defense Education Act (1958) was designed to provide loans and grants toward this end. Taken together these public initiatives gave birth to the mass university of the post-war period, closely tied to government. Government research funding to science and technology still dwarfed that accorded to the humanities and social sciences but nonetheless became increasingly important in disciplines like psychology and political science. The emerging university of the post-1945 period was recognizably connected to the university of the past, but the scale of its operations and its increasing economic and social role transformed it into a qualitatively different institution. The large corporations and the military had become the most important institutions in American life but the university ran them an increasingly close second.

Immediately following the war, funding for research sharply declined. But despite the cuts the army and navy sought to maintain funding for select scientific and technological as well as social science projects. As early as April 1946, in what is considered the founding document of the National Security State, General Dwight Eisenhower, then the chief of staff of the army, issued a memorandum to the heads of the war department and to military commanders. In this directive on scientific and technical research as military resources he called for the closest possible contractual relationships between scientists, technicians, universities, private industries, and the military.[32]

The onset of the Cold War saw the reimposition of the draft in 1948 and the reinvigoration of the ROTC on campus. The outbreak of the Korean War in 1950 led to a dramatic reversal as the spigot of government funding of university research was suddenly reopened. From that point onward universities began to receive unprecedented amounts of cash from the military, and as a result the universities became an integral part of the emerging military-industrial complex. Indeed, government expenditure on the military, including military-related research, became a means of keeping not merely the universities but the economy as a whole afloat. Universities became the primary source of research for the government as well as private business while the militarist influence on campus became overpowering. The universities became an integral part of a triad consisting of the military, industry, and institutions of higher learning.[33]

What occurred was the birth of the National Security State, whose purpose became permanent military and ideological mobilization to ensure the interests and power of the capitalist class and to ward off another economic depression. World War II had proved a boon, enabling the revival of the capitalist economy and the extension of American power worldwide. The National Security State was designed to perpetuate the success achieved during the war through carrying on the Cold War while ensuring the permanence of big government. Socialism being the enemy, the gigantic American garrison state became a substitute while at the same time ensuring the power of private enterprise and the capitalist class. The universities willingly joined this new structure. Part of the price they paid was that the limited autonomy enjoyed hitherto by institutions of higher learning was seriously undermined.

The Onset of the Cold War

The direct influence of the military and military-funded research projects and the presence of the CIA on university campuses pullulated after 1950. But the cost proved to be even higher than a loss of autonomy or the permanent military presence on campus as McCarthyism and Cold War mobilization helped to create a permanent climate of secrecy, suspicion, and conformity. The depoliticization of faculties based on intimidation and fear of dismissal was reinforced by growing employment opportunities, higher pay, and the increasing professionalization of academics coinciding with rapid university expansion. As the demand for professors soared, tenure, which had been relatively rare prior to World War II, now became the norm. Scholarship was increasingly defined by professional and departmental boundaries and was more and more pursued as an end in itself in compartmentalized disciplines with teaching relegated to second place. Learning was increasingly fragmented and its social meaning neutered. The divorce of learning from social concerns was celebrated in the name of value-free learning. Accompanying these changes was a continuing restriction of faculty autonomy and decline of involvement in governance in favor of hierarchical administrative management. There was sporadic faculty resistance but it was ineffectual in the long term. At the same time, the pursuit of professional success led to the emergence of the academic entrepreneur who relentlessly sought outside funding, graduate students, and consultancies. An arriviste mentality that sought advancement based on so-called cutting-edge research and an ideology of the "newness of the new" increasingly prevailed as a norm.[34]

Left-wing ideas that fundamentally and critically scrutinized the existing order of things were increasingly unpopular, and became irrelevant in a corporate milieu different from but nevertheless strongly shaped by the private corporation. Whereas in the Depression some faculty had identified with Marxist ideas, the arrival of consumerist capitalism and the corporate university with their illusions of upward social mobility for both faculty and students caused interest in Marxism to wane. The political opinions of faculty mirrored those of much of American society moving rightward and finding a resting point in one or another variety of liberalism.

Given the growing embrace of the National Security State, universities, it is true, tried to maintain some autonomy. The issue of the extent of control over university researchers by government was resolved by the establishment of a policy of contracts to individual researchers as a way of somewhat limiting government control. A parallel struggle in Washington between elite institutions and less prestigious universities for access to government funding was settled in favor of the former, owing to the influence of the science mandarin and Harvard University president James Conant, backed up by members of the corporate and financial elite. The latter favored the centralization of power in academe as naturally as they supported the concentration of capital in business. By 1960 federal government spending on university research was close to 1 billion dollars per annum, disproportionately shunted to 20 top universities. Over the next decades the number of institutions involved in serious research gradually expanded, spreading to every region of the country.[35] Given the enormous number of higher educational institutions, the trained manpower and research activities of these institutions greatly boosted the American economy. Government spending on research orientated mainly toward science and technology dwarfed that of private business, while supplying the latter with an increasing flow of innovations at minimal cost. The state thereby assumed greater control while providing itself and business at large with a constant flow of new knowledge and techniques that fostered the productivity and competitiveness of American industry. University research thus became an integral part of the expansive American economy.

Despite the growing presence of government, the role of private foundations with respect to the social sciences, especially the Ford and Rockefeller Foundations, if anything increased. From 1948 until 1956 foundation support for the social sciences amounted to 85 million dollars, almost half of which went to Columbia, Harvard, and Berkeley, reflecting the overwhelming prestige and power of these elite institutions. Between 1959 and 1964 political science received some $100 million from the foundations, half of which went to the same institutions.[36] The amounts advanced did not compare with the funds eventually made available by government, yet it turned out that the same powerful people often sat on the boards which controlled financial funding in both the government and the foundations. Indeed, it is difficult to determine where the line was between those at the top of the private sector and the government elites. Meanwhile, private foundations, of which there were scores, became prime instruments through which the CIA funded and laundered its operations. Bona fide and prestigious foundations like the Rockefeller and Ford Foundations were considered the best and most plausible cover for the Agency. From the early 1950s CIA funds flowed through them as well as some 150 other foundations to universities as well as youth groups, labor unions, and publishing firms.

The tie between big business, the CIA, other governmental institutions and the foundations was characterized as follows in a 1952 report by the general counsel of a congressional investigating committee: "an unparalleled amount of power is concentrated in the hands of an interlocking and self-perpetuating group. Unlike the power of corporate management, it is unchecked by stockholders; unlike the power of government, it is unchecked by the people."[37] Many of the same people moved easily from posts in the CIA to positions in business and the foundations. The CIA's relationship to the Ford Foundation was the most important. By the 1950s it was the largest of the private foundations funding a broad range of philanthropic, research, and cultural activities both inside and outside the United States. Richard Bissell, a Yale alumnus, worked at the Ford Foundation in the early 1950s and established a close working relationship with the spy agency before becoming a senior CIA official later in the decade. Bissell was in charge of the U-2 spy program and later directed operations aimed at toppling the Cuban Revolution, including the fiasco at the Bay of Pigs.

Bissell's unofficial linking of the Foundation's activities to the CIA was formalized by the creation of a special committee when John McCloy, former High Commissioner for Germany and chairman of the Rockefeller's Chase Manhattan Bank, became the Foundation's head in the mid-1950s.[38] Winning the Cold War—or, as it was expressed, the promotion of social adjustment to change, the prevention of unrest and the fostering of peace, democracy, and growth—became an important aspect of the Ford Foundation's programs in support of the social sciences.[39] In shaping that support, the head of the Rand Corporation H. Rowan Gaither played a key role. Named director of the Foundation in 1953, Gaither came to rely on the advice of sociologist Hans Speir, head of the social sciences division at Rand, and social psychologist Donald Marquis, chairman of the psychology department at the University of Michigan, both of whom had been deeply involved in government psychological warfare programs during World War II. Both were members of the State Department-sponsored and top-secret Project Troy, established in 1950 in collaboration with administrators at MIT and Harvard to provide guidance in the conduct of psychological and political warfare. Speir and Marquis then drew up a series of recommendations to guide the Foundation's Program V. They recommended that emphasis be placed on studying the nature of totalitarian regimes and the factors promoting stability and instability within them. They also advised that research be directed toward the social psychological aspects of the Cold War in Western Europe. Based on these recommendations the Foundation backed the creation of MIT's Center of International Studies (CENIS), headed by Spier. The latter appointed Ithiel de Sola Pool, a political behaviorist at Stanford's Hoover Institution, to direct research.[40]

The Rockefeller Foundation was used as a public front to conceal CIA funding of Hadley Cantril's Institute for International Social Research at Princeton. Cantril specialized in carrying out survey research into political opinion and ideological orientation among the populations in France, the Soviet Union, Latin America, and the United States.[41] The institutionalization of these communication and psychological warfare studies in U.S. higher education and research has also been traced to Rockefeller funding at Columbia University. The Bureau of Applied Social Research established in 1944 at Columbia by Paul Lazarsfeld became particularly influential. Following the end of the war the social psychologist Leonard Cottrell, head of the sociology department at Cornell and president of the American Sociological Association (founded in 1950), served the Russell Sage Foundation as its chief social psychologist (1951–67) and one of its main spokesman. He simultaneously became chair of the Defense Department's advisory group on psychological and unconventional warfare (1952–3), a member of the scientific advisory panel of the U.S. Airforce (1954–8) and the U.S. Army's scientific advisory panel (1956–8), and a longtime director of the Social Science Research Council. Within the social science community he was one of the most enthusiastic supporters of psychological warfare operations, calling for "a new club dedicated to the task of bringing the full capability of our disciplines to bear on this field."[42] The techniques developed played an important part in fighting the Cold War but were also used in helping to provide psychological techniques to promote mass consumerism.[43]

While the foundations played a major role in fostering research in social science directed at winning the psychological aspects of the Cold War and shaping public opinion, they also helped to determine the direction of the more traditional disciplines. Funding from the foundations and also the government served to establish national standards in the pursuit of knowledge while research became the most important criterion in judging the worth of professors in traditional academic pursuits and assessing the excellence of universities. As the award of research grants lay in the hands of established scholars at elite institutions, this tended to ensure that existing paradigms of scholarship were reinforced.

The production of such knowledge required specialization, which reinforced the role of the department as the fundamental unit of university organization. Such a division of labor tended to isolate fields from one another and block an integrated view of learning or of society on the part of academics as well as students. Historians, for example, did not really understand what political scientists let alone professors of literature were up to. Indeed, Jack Hexter, a prominent Tudor historian of the period, counseled his fellow historians to eschew the role of active citizen since they were concerned with and lived as much as possible in the past and did not have real knowledge of the contemporary world.[44] The departmental organization of learning largely precluded, if it did not entirely block, the ability of academics to see the forest for the trees. It encouraged a kind of tunnel learning and an uncritical pursuit of specialized knowledge largely separated from other disciplines, and disregarded any kind of historically founded, systematic perspective that would allow scholars to conceive of their discipline as part of a larger whole. The goal was to know more and more about less and less. At the same time, the compartmentalization of knowledge within departments reinforced a hierarchical and undemocratic organization enhancing the power of university administrators whose overall vision increasingly resembled that of the managers of other national corporations.

Kees van der Pijl has explained the function of departmental specialization as follows:

> The academic division of labor itself has proved a crucial mutation in Western intellectual life. By setting the parameters of legitimate speculation about society for the cadre trained in higher education, it is a key transmission-belt by which the dominant order of society is being reproduced. Obeying the strictures of the disciplinary division of labor is a precondition for the hegemony of the liberal order ... The emergence of the "disciplines" through which a more comprehensive, class-discipline is maintained (ever more so as the middle-class cadre, whose allegiance to Western pre-eminence and the capitalist economy is primarily ideological, grows in number) was itself a response to the rise of the labor movement, Marxism, and the spectre of socialist revolution.[45]

In other words, the dividing up of the disciplines into specialties under the control of academic departments helped to block the aspiration toward a holistic understanding of society and culture which loomed up through the rise of the working class and Marxism. The fundamental move in this direction occurred at the end of the nineteenth and the beginning of the twentieth century through the splitting of political economy into two distinct disciplines of political science and economics as a result of the marginalist revolution in economics led by Alfred Marshall and Max Weber's licensing of an autonomous science of society.[46] Cloistering and dividing up learning in separate departments was a way of turning one's back on the wider development of society.

The Marxist theoretician Antonio Gramsci can help us to understand the overall political position of American universities at the beginning of the Cold War. Universities, along with other educational bodies, churches, and newspapers, constitute parts of civil society through which the capitalist ruling class tries to obtain consent to its hegemony by a process of persuasion and indoctrination. Exercising its hegemony through such institutions, the capitalist class ties together those who belong to this class while subordinating those who do not. On the other hand, the realm of the political or the government strictly defined is that of direct command—

of the juridical apparatus and the means of policing and coercion. Both civil society and the political realm constitute the realm of the state, the political sphere and civil society co-existing with one another in a position of dialectical tension.[47] In the case of the United States, a parliamentary democracy of the classical kind, the institutions of civil society started out at arm's length from the state proper. Admittedly this was not entirely so, as demonstrated by the importance of the federal endowment of institutions of higher learning through land grants in the nineteenth century, military officers training on college campuses, and the relationship of professional schools like law and medicine to the licensing bodies of respective state governments. Moreover, the budgets of the state universities were under the control of the same state governments who could and did interfere with the universities as they saw fit. Nonetheless, we can say that until World War II the presidents and governing bodies of universities sought outside support from business and looked askance at too close a tie to government. This balance was upset temporarily during World War II and then permanently with the onset of the Cold War, after which the federal state encroached on the universities and they fell into its embrace. Research funds made available by the federal government, while only a fraction of university budgets, nonetheless exercised extraordinary leverage. Obtaining outside funding carried with it enormous prestige and enabled the state to set the agenda for the production of new knowledge. Universities tried to cushion this influence somewhat by insisting on peer review and the adoption of the individual contract system. While not completely entering the political sphere in Gramsci's sense, there can be no question that in the post-war period universities were more closely subject to it.

The political sphere or the government's presence on university campuses was amplified by the direct, wide-ranging if largely covert activities of the CIA. This tie had developed during the war when the Office of Strategic Services under William Donovan recruited hundreds of academics into the organization in order to defeat fascism. The link between the clandestine services and academics continued after the war when many of the latter returned to university campuses. Following the founding of the CIA in 1947 the Agency used this network to recruit its staff, especially from Ivy League institutions like Harvard, Princeton, and Yale. The culture of the early CIA was shaped by tweedy big men from these elite university campuses. In 1951 the Agency formalized these arrangements by constituting its University Associates Program establishing a network of covert contacts with professors at 50 top universities. Its primary aim continued to be the recruitment of promising students into the CIA. But with the agreement of the officers of the American Association of Anthropologists, for example, the Agency also compiled a dossier of hundreds of members of the Association detailing the expertise of anthropological fieldworkers upon which the Agency might draw. The Russian Studies Centers at Harvard and Columbia, as well as Henry Kissinger's International Summer School at Harvard, whose students were largely recruited from Europe, were all funded by the CIA. Historians, political scientists, anthropologists, sociologists and literary critics were put on the Agency payroll as well. In addition, the travel costs of hundreds of American students to international conferences were paid for by covert money from the CIA. The critically important Michigan State University program in police and counter-insurgency, designed to train the security forces of the Diem dictatorship in South Vietnam, was financed by the CIA between 1954 and 1959. The program also provided cover for CIA agents at work in that country. Eager for support, the patriotic administrators of Michigan State University enthusiastically welcomed the program.[48]

The most remarkable propaganda initiative taken by the CIA during these early Cold War years was the Congress for Cultural Freedom. Its primary goal was to try to organize the non-communist intelligentsia in Western Europe against the communist threat while tying it to the Cold War foreign policy of the United States. It was initiated at a conference held in West Berlin, June 26–9, 1950, and for the next decade organized seminars and conferences, and sponsored books and periodicals, espousing an anti-communist perspective. Most of the participants in these activities were unaware of the source of the money and patronage they received. Organized by private individuals with the support of the CIA and the U.S. military authorities, the initial gathering in Berlin represented in many ways a "grand coalition" of individuals and viewpoints from a wide cross-section of post-war intellectual life. The intention from the beginning was to solidify and maintain an anti-communist consensus among the Western intelligentsia. In terms of occupations, those present in Berlin were mainly philosophers, historians, writers, editors, politicians, and union leaders. Arthur Schlesinger, the Harvard consensus historian and liberal activist, played a key role in organizing the Congress and was one of the central players in the attempt to use it to unite intellectual thought on both sides of the Atlantic under the aegis of the United States.[49] Schlesinger had outlined the political space for a militant liberalism of the "Non-Communist Left" in *The Vital Center* (1946), and helped to put his ideas into action within the United States through the highly influential Americans for Democratic Action (ADA), of which he was a mainstay. For Schlesinger the Congress of Cultural Freedom was an attempt to internationalize this effort. He had had significant stints in Europe during the late 1940s, working with Averell Harriman on the European Recovery Program while occupying a post as guest professor at Leiden University in 1948–9. As a key organizer of the Congress, Schlesinger worked hand and glove with the CIA.[50]

Perhaps the most important intellectual input into the early conferences of the Congress of Cultural Freedom were those of a trio of American sociologists, Edward Shils, Seymour Lipset, and Daniel Bell, who attempted to spread the idea that Marxism had become irrelevant to the modern age, which according to them was characterized by the end of ideology. The growing complexity of Western society had made the reductive class analysis of Marxism passé. From their perspective the fundamental political problems of the industrial revolution had been solved: the workers had achieved industrial and political citizenship; the conservatives had accepted the welfare state; and the democratic left had recognized that an increase in overall state power carries with it more dangers to freedom than inequality and poverty. This very triumph of the democratic social revolution in the West ended the role in politics for those intellectuals who were wedded to ideologies or utopias to motivate the masses to political action.[51] While Europe was the principal battleground for the Council for Cultural Freedom, its activities extended into the underdeveloped world as well. Here Shils, formerly of the OSS and a professor of Weberian sociology at the University of Chicago, took the lead. He appears to have been the principal organizer of a series of conferences during the 1950s in Bombay, Rangoon, Milan, Rhodes, and Ibadan. Shils played a major part in these meetings, denouncing those in the underdeveloped world who saw democracy and economic development as necessarily interlinked, expressing indignation toward those who demanded compensation from the advanced capitalist countries for the consequences of imperialism, and insisting that modernity in the underdeveloped countries entailed the inculcation of secular rationality as in the West.[52]

In the 1930s and during the war the United States had opened the door to European and especially German academics fleeing fascism, many if not all of whom were leftists. American universities benefitted enormously as a result. The coming of the Cold War saw a retreat from such cosmopolitanism. Indeed, the creation of the Cold War university did not merely involve increased government influence over the university mobilizing its resources and personnel to fight the Soviet threat. It also involved purging and inoculating campuses against Marxism. Ordinary professors like Hexter, cloistered in their disciplines, knew little of the high politics of university presidents and administrators. But they did know about the purging of leftists from university campuses, a major feature of campus life in the early Cold War period. While the influence of Marxism in the rest of the world increased in the post-war years, and its intellectual power grew, the United States, for all its rising scientific and intellectual influence, cut itself off from these currents and retreated into a kind of intellectual cocoon. The Iron Curtain, it turned out, worked both ways.

Marxists

Prior to the Cold War, Marxism had a limited if not inconsequential presence in American academe. Before the onset of McCarthyism, communists, fellow travelers, and Marxist scholars were to be found in American universities and some acquired considerable academic reputations. The profundity of the crisis of the 1930s, the prestige of the Soviet Union, and the political and intellectual influence of communism were such that Marxist ideas penetrated even the essentially middle-class precincts of the American academy. In response to the economic crisis, the rise of fascism and the influence of the Soviet Union, a popular front embracing a wide spectrum of the left came into being in the United States as elsewhere. The Communist Party was the most important component in this front and its members were key activists in a wide variety of movements and institutions, including cultural ones of which the universities were a part. The Communist Party had about 60,000 members in the second half of the 1930s, its influence extending to perhaps another 500,000 sympathizers.[53] It enjoyed its maximum influence in the popular front period, which extended through World War II when the United States was allied to the Soviet Union. During this phase the Party was under the control of Earl Browder, who deliberately muted its earlier revolutionary program in order to extend its influence under the New Deal. This line has to be understood as part of the overall strategy of the communist parties of the Stalinist Third International in the light of the threat of fascism. In the short run it gave the American Communist Party unprecedented influence while it largely abandoned its revolutionary aspirations. The Party essentially went over to an evolutionary politics based not on revolution but on the deepening of democracy. Opting for the one against the other instead of combining revolutionary objectives with a deepening of political and social democracy made little sense, especially in the light of the repression of the Party after 1945. No doubt it enjoyed wide influence under the popular front, but at the same time it virtually disarmed itself. Given the evolutionary strategy pursued by the Communist Party, the post-war purge of communists from academe and other parts of American public life seems all the more unfair.

Spearheaded by the Party, the popular front that emerged during the 1930s constituted a historic left bloc made up of a broad if fragile alliance of fractions of the subaltern classes that sought to gain influence and aspired to hegemony in American life. It formed part of the broader political coalition of the New Deal while creating an immense variety of cultural institutions. The cultural left constituted a key part of this coalition, which included leftist writers, journalists, artists, movie directors, entertainers, actors, folk singers, song writers, students, teachers, and academics who animated these organizations.[54] As we have noted, communist influence was substantial among students, faculty, and staff in New York universities, especially at City College during the 1930s and '40s. Thousands more were attracted to Marxist ideas in the New York area. The faculty union movement in New York and elsewhere, which was part of the American Federation of Teachers, was clearly strongly influenced by activists who were Communist Party members.[55] Party activity was also evident at such intellectually and culturally dynamic centers like Harvard, Michigan, Wisconsin, Washington, and Berkeley. During the war, the Manhattan Project, largely staffed by university scientists, attracted figures like David Joseph Bohm, Theodore Hall, Robert Oppenheimer, Frank Oppenheimer, and Joseph Weinberg who were strongly sympathetic to Marxist ideas and the Communist Party.[56] Moreover, a number of Marxist academics like Sidney Hook, Moses Finley, Meyer Schapiro, Ashly Montagu, Merle Curti, W.E.B. Du Bois, F.O. Mathiessen, Paul Sweezy, Leslie White, Karl Wittfogel, and Owen Lattimore were distinguished academics. The presence of the Frankfurt School, which took refuge in the United States during World War II and included Max Horkheimer, Theodor Adorno, Herbert Marcuse, and Erich Fromm, helped to increase the influence of Marxist ideas. The onset of the Cold War and the McCarthy purges abruptly crushed the influence of the Marxist approach these distinguished scholars espoused.

The attack on Marxist influence in the universities was part of the more general offensive against the left and especially the Communist Party that coincided with the onset of the Cold War. At the heart of the Cold War was renewed U.S. hostility to the Soviet Union and the threat of third world revolution, which were seen as a menace to the American way of life at home and abroad. The end of the wartime alliance with the Soviets meant an end to the official tolerance of communist influence within the United States, which had allowed the remarkable growth of the popular front and the Communist Party during the war. Populist anti-communism was a feature of this reaction manifest in the Catholic and other churches, veterans' groups, newspapers, and even conservative elements of the union movement. Moreover, the influence of the increasingly influential media—newspapers, magazines, movies, radio, and television—was extremely important to the anti-communist crusade. But the central role in this anti-communist crackdown was played by the state, and especially by J. Edgar Hoover's FBI, the congressional investigating committees, and the executive arm of the federal government. With its overwhelming power, the American state came down hard on the Communist Party and those who sympathized with it or its ideology.

The assault on the Communist Party and Marxist influence was a completely unwarranted attack on political and intellectual freedom. It deeply wounded American democracy and cultural life—wounds from which they have scarcely recovered. Moreover, the idea that the Soviet Union and the American Communist Party were bent on revolutionary change in this period is false. The Stalinist conversion to a popular front, as we have noted, was no mere tactic. It represented for better or worse a profound change in the nature of the communist movement, one which no doubt also reflected a conservative transformation within the Soviet Union, namely the liquidation of the old communist political and cultural vanguard. The popular front and its deepening during World War II meant that the Soviet Union and the American Communist Party had committed themselves to a long-term strategy of evolution rather than revolution as the path to socialism. It reflected itself in Soviet attitudes toward the politics of post-war Germany, Italy, Greece, and China. In the United States in the post-1945 period, it meant extending the influence of the Communist Party by deepening the New Deal. The sudden hardening of American policy with respect to the Soviet Union and labor unrest under Truman took communist leaders aback.

McCarthyism

In the immediate post-war period there were communists within the universities but there was little organized political activity among left-wing faculty. Professors who were Communist Party members kept their affiliation to themselves for fear of dismissal. But significant numbers of returned war veterans increasingly in evidence on campus as a result of the GI Bill actively participated in politics, most notably through the communist-controlled American Youth for Democracy. And it was precisely against this group, named by J. Edgar Hoover as a communist front, that the anti-communist attack began. As the Cold War gained momentum with the issuance of Harry Truman's loyalty-security program in March 1947, university administrators revoked the campus charters of the American Youth for Democracy organization, banning it from campuses where it was an established student group. For the most part this was the work of administrators, but at Queens College the faculty held a special meeting and proscribed the organization themselves.[57] As the anti-communist campaign gained momentum the chill on student activism was reinforced by growing demands from university administrators for the membership lists of student organizations. Communist Party leaders and, incredibly, leading figures like Paul Robeson and Howard Fast, were banned from speaking in many universities.[58]

Anti-communist investigations focused not so much on actual communists as on sympathizers or ex-members of the Party. One of the most glaring and significant cases was the McCarran House Committee attack on Owen Lattimore of Johns Hopkins University, and the Institute of Pacific Affairs which he directed. In the early 1950s the McCarran Committee singled out the Institute as a communist front that bore a large responsibility for the loss of China to the communists. The consequences of this particular attack were serious in that it crippled open-minded and critical academic study of East Asia including, fatefully, Vietnam and China.[59] Universities demonstrated their allegiance to the Cold War policies of the government by initiating their own loyalty investigations. They exchanged information on suspected left-wing professors with the FBI and other intelligence bodies. They joined a blacklist refusing to hire faculty members who had been penalized at other institutions because of their political sympathies.[60] Following passage of the McCarran Act (1950), travel by scientists suspected of left-wing sympathies as well as visits by suspect foreign researchers were sharply restricted.[61] The complicity of universities with congressional investigations into communism on campuses climaxed with the issuance in 1953 of an official statement by the American Association of Universities in which the presidents of most leading universities reiterated that those who adhered to the worldwide communist movement were disqualified from holding an academic position, and that full compliance and cooperation with congressional committees investigating threats coming from that quarter were expected from faculty.[62]

In the fall of 1947 the AAUP meanwhile rejected the view of Truman's loyalty program and officially took the position that membership in the Communist Party, as a legal political party, should not be grounds for dismissal. That did not stop the University of Washington from dismissing two faculty members precisely on those grounds, an action which proved to be precedent-setting.[63] Moreover, it was the view of the philosopher Sidney Hook, by now a leading academic anti-communist, that membership in the Communist Party—as a conspiratorial organization which demanded intellectual conformity from its members—disqualified such members as academics. Hook's argument became the line taken by university administrators and most liberal faculty as a standard rationale.[64] The majority of American academics, it is fair to say, were in fact liberal in their politics and accepted the Cold War consensus. On the other hand, it is notable that Arthur Schlesinger did not accept Hook's argument, although on somewhat specious grounds. Hook had argued that members of the Party were inherently inflexible and therefore disqualified themselves as seekers of the truth. Affecting to ignore the repression that was all around him, Schlesinger argued that the fact that so many academics had left the Party in recent years proved that they were not after all that dogmatic.[65] For good measure, most states imposed loyalty oaths excluding Communist Party members and required signing such an oath as a condition of employment in most public universities.[66] The proscribing of active communists in this way exposed the limits of American democracy and its supposed political and intellectual openness. In fact there were few communists in academe by 1950, nonetheless the witch-hunt of ex-communists, Marxists, left-wingers, and even civil libertarians by congressional committees, the FBI, and the media carried on into the mid-1950s. It was coupled with an academic blacklist which made it more or less impossible for those accused of communist sympathies or Marxist opinions to find employment. Like the inquisitorial proceedings in early modern Spain, U.S. government repression helped put a damper on political activity and academic thought that did permanent damage in limiting what was thinkable and sayable in American public life then and now. That, of course, was part of their purpose.

It is important in conclusion to take a closer look at Hook's rationale for excluding Communist Party members from academic life. If one looks at the Soviet Union in the Stalin period not only was there no free discussion in the Party but all aspects of intellectual life were closely controlled under the aegis of a dictator who thought of himself as a working-class philosopher-king. On the other hand, this was not the policy that the Comintern attempted to enforce on the other communist parties in the period of the Common Front or afterward. Nor could it have imposed such a policy even if it had wanted to. In fact, the intellectual life of the Italian, Indian, and British communist parties, and even of the more closely controlled French

Communist Party, was quite interesting and intellectually fruitful within its limits. And this despite repeated unsuccessful attempts by Communist Party dogmatists to impose a political and intellectual line on intellectuals. Certainly, with its admittedly fraught relationship to the likes of Jean-Paul Sartre, Henri Lefebvre, and Louis Althusser, the intellectual life of the French Party was more open and interesting than the life of the mind on American university campuses at the height of the Cold War, where a fearful conformity reigned. Can one seriously compare American historiography of this period with the work of the British Communist Party historians—Rodney Hilton, Christopher Hill, E.P. Thompson, and Eric Hobsbawm—of the same period?[67] Indeed, if we look at the history of the communist movement from the time of Lenin until the 1980s, its intellectual debates, to say nothing of the arguments between members of the Party and Marxists outside it, were in fact an unrivalled school for those who participated. In this regard the testimony of Marcus Singer, a professor of zoology at Cornell University, before the House Un-American Activities Committee in the spring of 1953 is illuminating. Asked about the communist group at Harvard-MIT, of which he had been a member during the war, Singer talked about himself and the group's discussions of Marxian philosophy and how it applied to the contemporary world. But he refused to testify about other members of the group. Pressed by the Committee that because the Party was a conspiracy prepared to use force and violence he ought to testify, Singer responded: "We did not conspire. We did not do anything subversive ... We were intellectuals. We were scholars."[68] Nor is it likely that such people could have been anything else. Admittedly the issue is complicated and requires some sense of political philosophy and historical context. On the other hand, it has to be said that in retrospect Hook's argument seems like a kind of deductive syllogism about Leninist organization, and one that he imposed with remarkable success on American academe. But in doing so Hook played the role of intellectual commissar within a fear-driven institutional setting that was prepared to accept his formulation without much scrutiny. The parallel with the situation in the Soviet Union under Stalin is obvious. The price to be paid was of course the intellectual and political conformity that crippled American university life for decades to come.

2

The Humanities and Social Sciences in the Cold War (1945–1960)

As we saw in the last chapter, in the aftermath of World War II colleges and universities became integral parts of the military-industrial complex. The wealth generated by American capitalism provided the material foundation for the achievements of higher learning, contributing to the growth of the economy, the stability and conformity of political life, and the extension of U.S. imperialism. A vast expansion in the size and research activities of universities took place, and research became an important component of the programs of the top-flight universities. Public universities were for the first time in the vanguard. Faculties of the humanities and social sciences were one of the core components of higher education and as such constituted an informal part of the state apparatus in the Gramscian sense. Marked by a shared commitment to liberalism and hostility to communism, the humanities and social sciences made a notable contribution to strengthening the American state using a mixture of positive knowledge and liberal ideology to help the government shore up the economy, impose control over society, and justify imperialism overseas.

Research and the production of new knowledge in faculties of science, engineering, and agriculture had an immediate impact on rising productivity and sustained profitability in post-1945 America. Likewise, new techniques of psychological warfare devised by social scientists, and the recruiting of CIA agents among professors and students, helped to fight the Cold War in a direct way. Support from government or private funding bodies for the humanities or social sciences during the Cold War was less obvious, but at least as important. It was in the humanities disciplines—economics, history, literature, philosophy, anthropology, sociology, psychology, political science, and geography—that hegemonic ideologies and knowledges were created which justified the continued dominance of the capitalist system under overall American command. The denial of world history and the rejection of class struggle were the most salient features of most of these disciplines during this period. The inculcation of these attitudes into university students and by extension into the broader public proved centrally important to maintaining the loyalty of the population. Reviewing and criticizing the knowledge created in these disciplines and demonstrating their relationship to anti-Marxism and fighting the Cold War is the main purpose of this chapter. Through the critical analysis of these disciplines we can illuminate the role that universities played in the political economy of the United States.

By 1950 there were about 2.3 million students being taught in some 2,000 institutions of higher learning by some 390,000 professors and teachers. These numbers would more than double by 1965. Total expenditure on higher education in the United States was already 2.3 billion dollars and this would rise to over 7 billion 15 years later. Many of the students enrolled were pursuing arts degrees or took arts courses as requirements in the pursuit of other degrees, where the additional training in arts subjects helped students entry into professions like education, law, and medicine and into managerial-level positions in the bureaucracies of the public and private sectors. Students were expected to develop a degree of literacy and critical acumen and even exhibit some imaginative capacity—but only up to a point. The social sciences, such as economics, history, sociology, and political science, assumed a perspective in which reconciliation between the classes, with the upper class remaining in control, was both possible and desirable. Fundamental criticisms of liberal democracy and capitalism were unwelcome and made less likely by the purging or suppression of Marxist thought. Indeed, references to capitalism, class antagonism and even the notion of a working class were considered impolite in classrooms at the height of the Cold War. The intellectual atmosphere can be described as stifling in the sense that certain things could not be spoken of. Here and there schematic explanations of Marxist ideas might be offered in history, sociology, or political science only to be dismissed as tendentious, dogmatic, and outdated, having been superseded by changing times, new empirical research, or cutting-edge theory.

Value-free knowledge on the model of the physical and natural sciences was considered *de rigueur*. Basic to this outlook was the idea that there was no limit to the accumulation of more and more positive knowledge in each discipline, which developed largely in isolation from other disciplines, and that the pursuit of such knowledge was an inherently worthy goal. Methodological individualism tended to be the preferred approach, and where there was a more systematic view it was biased in favor of equilibrium rather than change or crisis. Historical and materialist analysis was slighted or dismissed all together. The perpetuation of the division of labor among disciplines became an institutional end in itself as well as discouraging a more comprehensive understanding of society and culture. This approach to knowledge was undoubtedly congruent with the dominance of American capitalism, which had already been remarkably successful and was now entering its heyday. But we also conclude that the emphasis on such neutral, specialized, and cumulative learning was an attempt to stifle and repress the expression of left-wing or critical ideas. Contrariwise, those professors who defended liberal or capitalist values against subversive ideas, especially those who could do so creatively, were singled out and handsomely rewarded.

Pierre Bourdieu points out that the field of culture is itself differentiated and institutionalized. Therefore, in analyzing cultural production, including that carried on in universities, it is a mistake to view ideas simply as direct reflections of underlying social, economic, and political currents. Ideas and creative works must be viewed not just as mirroring such underlying trends but as refracted through the prism of the specific norms of a given field of culture and its institutional context.[1] The interpretation of the bombing of Hiroshima, for example, would be viewed differently in the discipline of political science from the way it was viewed in literary criticism. In this study we accordingly attempt to study the effects of the Cold War on the humanities by examining the way it made itself felt as refracted through the specific norms of the different disciplines. Even so, it is remarkable how quickly the humanities and social sciences as a whole fell into line with the opinions and demands of the U.S. state. The disciplines rapidly and across the board redefined the norms and the substance of their teaching in accord with such demands which were taken as working assumptions. There was of course dissent from a minority of scholars. But what is astonishing overall is the degree of intellectual conformity in the shadow of the emerging National Security State.

Gramsci has been useful to us in understanding the evolving relationship between American universities and the state. His ideas can also be helpful in understanding the history of the humanities and social sciences, especially his conception of the role of organic intellectuals.[2] Writing with eyes fixed on Italian history, Gramsci posited the existence of two types of intellectuals—the traditional and the revolutionary. The social classes whose opposition to one another is produced by their different relationship to the means of production create distinctive groups of intellectuals who base their activities on the interests and outlook of opposed classes. Traditional intellectuals operating under conditions of relative intellectual autonomy constitute the representatives of the dominant class who carry out the function of producing intellectual justifications for the existing social and political order. Although they enjoy a limited autonomy, the essential role of these organic intellectuals of the ruling class is nonetheless to defend the hegemony of the capitalist class.

In rivalry to these are the proletarian organic intellectuals who base themselves on the organizations of the workers, engage in a battle of ideas to challenge the intellectual and cultural hegemony of the ruling class, and foster the revolutionary project of the working class.[3] In Italy the historic role of landlords, rentiers, and legists was much more important than in the United States, and the influence of traditional intellectuals in the Church, universities, and newspapers was correspondingly greater. Such strata were not unknown in the United States, but the explosive development of capitalism and the transformation of the universities and mass culture from the 1920s makes the use of the term "traditional" anachronistic in the American context. A whole new stratum of intellectual apologists for the existing order was created in the United States, which included academics but also advertising executives, newspaper columnists, and radio and television commentators. The term establishment intellectuals, rather than traditional intellectuals, is more useful in the light of these sweeping changes which transformed American higher education and society from the 1930s onward. Within the universities those academics in the humanities and social sciences who served as effective apologists for American capitalism in the Cold War were selected out by the powers that be and rose to the fore as establishment intellectuals. Those who were critical or aspired to become what Gramsci referred to as organic intellectuals of the left were part of the so-called cultural front created in the 1930s and which included some academics. But as we have noted, these were marginalized, silenced, or purged altogether in the early years of the Cold War. As we shall see, the major disciplines in the humanities and social sciences, whatever their differences in subject matter and method, were unified by their common ideological orientation. By analyzing each of these disciplines in turn we can gain insights into their shared premises and their function in the political economy of the United States.

History

The denial or downgrading of history was the most common feature of the humanities and social sciences after 1945. Economics turned away from a once traditional historical approach in favor of one which aimed to eliminate crises by means of a quantitative and individualist method which sought the ideal of permanent equilibrium. English rejected a social and historical perspective on literature in favor of aesthetic formalism. Philosophy turned its back on its own historical development and its roots in society and retreated into making itself a handmaiden of pure science. Under the leadership of Franz Boas, anthropology rejected the historical evolution of societies in favor of cultural relativism based on an idealistic understanding of culture. In sociology Talcott Parsons imposed structural functionalism as a universal paradigm which excluded historically rooted class struggle and revolutionary change in favor of a model of static social equilibrium. Like economics, political science sought to become an ahistorical science as much as possible. Alternatively, it sought to defend Western democracy by assimilating both fascist and communist ideologies to the abstract model of totalitarianism. Or else it stressed the irrational nature of politics and subordinated internal social conflict to the overarching importance of international relations based on the balance of power. Psychology in this period overwhelmingly focused on the scientific study of individual human behavior and eschewed consideration of how culture and history might affect individuals. Geography, in which the difficulties of overcoming space are given priority over the possibilities latent in historical development, sought to make itself useful to American imperialism through the development of area studies in relation to the exercise of American power. The discipline of history was itself constricted by a sense of American exceptionalism and a rejection of the importance of class struggle and revolution to the historical process, including that of the United States.

Prior to 1945 European and Eurocentric history had occupied a primary place in the curriculums of arts faculties, shaping the way subjects like politics and literature were taught.[4] The great pedagogical innovation in the post-war period was the widespread adoption of Western Civilization as a course which became the primary introductory history course throughout the United States. It signaled a decisive break with American isolationism, and the wholesale conversion of professional historians to internationalism; or, in other words, to the expansion of American influence into Europe and the rest of the world. First developed at Columbia University immediately after World War I, it became prevalent in the arts curriculums of many universities after the onset of the Cold War. This was wholly in accord with the turn in American foreign policy under Roosevelt and Truman toward internationalism under the hegemony of the United States. At Harvard, for example, the Western Civilization course was strongly recommended by the highly influential General Education Committee in 1945 as part of the effort to promote the principles of a free society in a world of totalitarianism

46

and the need to present a consistent image of the American experience, the meaning of democracy faced with totalitarianism, and the strengthening of the heritage of Western civilization. Its manifest political aim was to ideologically mobilize students in behalf of liberal and capitalist values linking the United States with the fate of Western Europe.[5] At the same time, in a characteristically peremptory Eurocentric move, the Western Civilization course managed to annex the histories of ancient Egypt, Mesopotamia, Greece, and Rome and transform them into foyers of the Western heritage.[6]

But in studying history the investigation of social conflict and revolution was unavoidable. The French Revolution was, after all, central to the emergence of modernity with its notions of equality, individualism, and rational thought. Moreover, the Russian and Chinese Revolutions in the twentieth century only magnified the importance of understanding revolutionary change, not only in the West but globally. Questions of political and economic crisis and class struggle were central to history as a subject and could not be ignored. In the emerging Cold War the strategy of establishment historians came to be one of stressing the damaging effects of such upheavals and minimizing their influence on American history.

The field of history, especially European history, had traditionally been dominated by a WASP elite that controlled the history departments in Ivy League bastions like Harvard, Columbia, Yale, and Princeton. Its members presided over the American Historical Association, the major professional body of historians during the first half of the twentieth century, and held sway over the publishing houses and journals that published historical research. It was in the graduate schools of these prestigious institutions that most PhD graduates were trained, especially those who could expect employment in major universities like Berkeley, Chicago, Michigan, and Illinois. European historians of this type were especially prominent in the OSS during the war and later played an important role in the development of the CIA.[7] The conservatism of this WASP elite was reflected not only in their hostility to political radicalism, but also in their resistance to the admission of Jews, women, blacks, and other ethnic groups to the ranks of historians. As the president of the AHA in 1984, Arthur S. Link, described the situation for Jews:

although the AHA had Jewish members from the beginning of the association, their numbers, until the 1950s, were infinitesimal compared to the total membership. In some extenuation, this was true because the AHA increasingly drew its members from the ranks of professional historians, and the unwritten but nearly ironclad rule against the employment of Jews in all except a few colleges and universities made it foolhardy for many Jewish undergraduates to contemplate a career in the historical profession.[8]

The post-war period saw an enormous increase in both the number of historians and the range and depth of research in an increasingly professionalized discipline.[9] Patrician influence gradually declined and, as in other disciplines, the ranks of historians were filled with aspiring if insecure members of the lower middle class, including Jews. The turn of women and black people would arrive only in the 1960s. The introduction of cosmopolitan Western Civilization courses reflected the attempt on the part of the conservative historical elite of the United States to come to terms with the emergence of American global dominance. In order to focus the discussion we will concentrate on two historians whose works figured large in shaping American consciousness at the height of the Cold War: Crane Brinton and Richard Hofstadter.

The Harvard historian Crane Brinton was himself the author of a textbook on Western civilization. He was very much a member of the WASP elite, had close connections to the CIA, and specialized in the important subject of the French Revolution. The Revolution of 1789 in France, which ushered in modern times and aroused passions on both left and right from the beginning, helped to inspire the revolutions of the nineteenth and twentieth centuries, including the Russian Revolution. With the latter and the subsequent creation of the world union of communist parties or the Communist International (in 1919), the spread of revolution was seen as directly threatening the future of the U.S. economic and political system. Indeed, the United States and other capitalist states intervened militarily in Russia to try to quash the revolution, and in failing to do so tried to impose a political and economic blockade on the new regime.

Accounting for revolution using the tools of scholarship became a priority for American academics defending the status quo. Brinton, who served first in a senior position in the OSS and then again in 1962–66 as deputy director of intelligence in the CIA, had authored serious scholarly works on the Jacobins and on Talleyrand and was named president of the American Historical Association in 1960. His most famous work, *Anatomy of Revolution*, first published in 1938 and republished several times thereafter, aspired to be a definitive comparative history of the phenomenon of revolution based on the English, French, American, and Russian examples. The fundamental assumption of Brinton's work was that revolution is a pathological condition or a fever rather than a characteristic feature of modernity.[10] Revolution from above or sweeping reform from on high seemed a better option to Brinton, whose work was premised on the notion that popular revolution was a disease to be avoided. According to him, the major reasons for revolution included a decline in the confidence and capabilities of the established elites, financial crisis, and the alienation of the intellectuals. So the keys to avoiding revolution were maintaining the moral and intellectual vigor of the ruling class, ensuring a sound economy, and securing the loyalty of intellectuals. Revolutions when they happened passed through three stages, from moderation to radicalism and then to "Thermidorean" reaction, which saw the consolidation of the new order. Written in the heyday of enthusiasm for the Soviet experiment and popularized during the Cold War, Brinton's analysis was hardly neutral. For him, revolutions invariably destroy those who make them, and fail to achieve their goals. Indeed, many revolutionary gains are subsequently cancelled by the inevitable onset of reaction. According to Brinton, revolutions engender not only mob violence but also aggressive nationalism and dictatorship.

While Brinton's study is suggestive and has remained influential (indeed, has recently been up-dated[11]), his comparative method tends to gloss over the deep-seated economic and structural reasons for revolution in the cases of England, France, and Russia, all three of which began as capitalist revolutions against the entrenched feudal order. Pointing to excesses or failures, he underestimates the achievements of these revolutions especially in the longer run. In the final analysis, revolution for Brinton is a result of elite failure rather than the agency or aspirations of the underclasses in society and the contradictions of a given mode of production. As such, Brinton fails to capture the global process of revolution based on class struggle which cannot be understood on the basis of revolution in one country, but rather is a unified historical process across space and time. The idea that humanity en masse has made its own future through a process of revolutionary change which progressively renews itself was anathema to Brinton.

Brinton may be taken as a representative albeit sophisticated member of the WASP historical establishment. As we have suggested, the latter monopolized elite positions not only in history but in the universities generally until the 1950s.[12] The American historian Richard Hofstadter, on the other hand, was part of the emerging wave of more or less assimilated Jewish academics who challenged WASP predominance after 1945. Following the war, the stratum of establishment intellectuals underwent a recomposition as academics of Jewish and other ethnic groups fought their way to prominence and were coopted willy-nilly into the academic establishment. Indeed, this reconstitution was but part of a more general refiguring of the American middle class in which Jews figured prominently. Like others who emerged from an ethnic-minority milieu, such scholars had been more exposed to radical ideas and were more open to using the social sciences in their historical work than were their Anglo-Saxon counterparts. They were more favorable to labor and civil rights than were Brahmin academics, and were eager to redefine liberalism in these more democratic terms.[13] At the same time their loyalty to the American economic and political system faced with the threat of global communism was unreserved. However uncomfortable he may have been in the role, Hofstadter put himself forward as an apologist for American capitalist democracy and as a result became the most important historian during the early Cold War.

A previous generation of progressive American historians—largely from the Midwest rather than the East, and led by Charles Beard—had stressed that American history had above all been marked by clashes between competing economic groups, primarily farmers, industrialists, and workers. In his *The American Historical Tradition* (1948), Hofstadter instead announced, through a brilliantly written narrative, that the story of America was fundamentally one of consensus rather than conflict. In a series of well-drawn portraits ranging from the founding fathers to Franklin Roosevelt, he demonstrated that the leaders of America shared a common belief in individual liberty, private property, and capitalist enterprise.[14] Beard had espoused a determinism which stressed the conflicting interests of competing economic interests but also rival sectional interests in explaining American history.[15] Strongly sympathetic to the reform impulse of populism if not to the working class, he championed the notion of the struggle of American democracy faced with the power of robber-baron capitalism. Hofstadter's subsequent work, *The Age of Reform* (1955), turned Beard's beloved populists into confused, xenophobic, and reactionary opponents of modernity. Hofstadter became the most outstanding member of a new school of American history dubbed the consensus historians, including Daniel Boorstin, Louis Hartz, and Arthur Schlesinger, who acknowledged but downgraded the influence of economic factors and conflicting class interests in American history.[16] Reluctantly embracing the New Deal, Hofstadter seized the high intellectual ground for liberal consensus at the height of the Cold War, thereby ensuring his prominence.

Hofstadter had been a member of the Communist Party in the late 1930s. But the purge trials in Moscow, the Hitler-Stalin Pact, and what he regarded as the crude dogmatism of rank-and-file communists soon led him to quit. While rejecting the excesses of anti-communism, Hofstadter distanced himself from his earlier embrace of communism, seeing it as a threat to intellectual freedom. Indeed, his first job at City College entailed replacing Philip Foner, a historian tainted by communist affiliation, and he refused thereafter to defend left-wing academics purged during the McCarthy period. At Columbia, where he taught for many years, he became an integral part of a tough-minded group of liberal and Jewish New York academics and intellectuals—including Lionel Trilling, Peter Gay, Daniel Bell, Fritz Stern, and Irving Kristol—who had been touched by Marxism but who were committed to defending liberal compromise and elitist governance as reflected in the New Deal [17] Equally threatening to them were revolutionary communism and fascism, in which the masses were mobilized in behalf of a nihilistic and authoritarian politics. Hofstadter viewed the phenomenon of McCarthyism as particularly threatening and did not hesitate to link it to populism in his 1964 essay *Anti-Intellectualism in American Life* as well as in his *Paranoid Style in American Politics* (1965).

Perhaps the most penetrating critique of Hofstadter's politics has been offered by Ellen Schrecker:

Hofstader ... viewed McCarthy and his allies as populists, situating them within an anti-intellectual strand of American politics that had traditionally expressed the resentment of the little people against the cultivated upper class. Such an interpretation cloaked considerable hostility to and suspicion of mass political action. It also delegitimized American Communism by indirectly identifying its celebration of the common man with the excesses of the far right. And it strengthened the elitism that was such an important component of the cultural criticism of the 1950s. The New York intellectuals were vociferous in their denunciation of the conformity of American life. McCarthyism, suburbia, television, tailfins, "kitsch," Communism and Nazism—they were all, in one way or another, products of mass society. Far better to leave matters of culture and politics in the hands of educated elites... [18]

The irrationalities of right-wing populism were linked somewhat implausibly to the excesses of an emergent mass consumer capitalism. As for Hofstadter's interpretation of American history, it has been criticized for being insufficiently grounded in archival research which might have forced him to look more deeply into social history. Certainly his work was refreshing insofar as it took ideas seriously especially as they related to politics. This was part of a trend of the 1950s in which the history of ideas enjoyed a vogue partly as an antidote to historical materialism. On the other hand, subsequent archival research has cast doubt on Hofstadter's view that liberal values were as hegemonic in the American body politic as he supposed. The ideology of the early republic, it has been discovered, was more colored by a communitarian classical republicanism than by Lockean individualism. Moreover, even when the liberal individualist ideology became dominant in the course of the nineteenth century, it was far from becoming the worldview of aboriginals, blacks, workers, and ethnic immigrants, not to speak of white southerners.[19] In other words, a deeper understanding of the processes of history put into question the notion of the liberal consensus. At best, from the Gramscian perspective, liberalism amounted to a hegemonic ideology.

Beard in his early years had sought to contextualize American history within an international context that he believed was moving in a democratic direction. Late in his career, in the shadow of the dictatorships of the 1930s, he retreated to the idea of American exceptionalism, especially with respect to political democracy. Hofstadter's liberal consensus view of American history echoed Beard's nationalism in celebrating the unique quality of American liberal democracy. But Hofstadter's contention that there was a link between McCarthyism and populism has been cast into doubt by further research. McCarthyism, it has been shown, was never a mass movement rooted in populism as claimed by Hofstadter, but rather found its appeal among traditional conservative groups.[20]

One should take time to refer also to the historiography of black slavery since it is today acknowledged that the black experience was at the core of American history, something which was not admitted prior to the 1960s. It is painfully obvious that blacks lay outside Hofstadter's supposed consensus. Indeed, American historians had long had difficulty coming to terms with the idea of black resistance to their own enslavement. Enslaved people were traditionally seen by white American historians as either contented dependents of whites or passive victims of exploitation and racism. It was an avowedly communist historian, Herbert Aptheker, who first championed the idea of black resistance in a path-breaking work entitled *American Negro Slave Revolts* (1943).

Yet in the United States the idea of revolt by an underclass was met with skepticism and rejection, the more so as this view was advanced by a communist scholar. Yet Aptheker's thesis of a continuous history of overt black resistance to slavery is today increasingly acknowledged as based on a scholarship which has stood the test of criticism and has become part of an ongoing research agenda.[21] But during the Cold War Aptheker's view was largely discounted or even castigated by most professional historians, and Aptheker himself as an avowed communist was blacklisted. Contrast this with the reception in England of the work of dissident communist and stormy petrel E.P. Thompson on the origins of the English working class, or of French communist Albert Soboul's path-breaking study of French revolutionary populism, and one has the measure of the repression and parochialism which marked American intellectual life at the height of the Cold War. As to the reasons behind Aptheker's proscription, Columbia University Professor of American History Eric Foner offered the following observation in an interview which was published in 2000: "I think it's fundamentally political. The Cold War drew a very rigid line around what was acceptable and what was not acceptable in politics, in art, in history, in many other areas, and the universities played their role in the Cold War … That's the fundamental answer."[22] As we have argued earlier, intellectual life in American academe was carefully circumscribed to exclude a historical materialist approach no matter how well founded.

To be a member of the Communist Party or even openly espouse Marxism was anathema to the American historical profession.[23] Communists could not write objective history. The historians policed themselves in this regard and in so doing turned their backs on perfectly sound research. The tone of things is exemplified by the case of Armin Rappaport, whose appointment at Berkeley in 1949 was held up by one of the members of the department, John D. Hicks, who was worried that Rappaport "might have some of the ultra left wing tendencies so common in the New York Jewish intelligentsia." He was won over by assurances that the young historian was not opposed to American foreign policy.[24] More nuanced was the Harvard historian John K. Fairbank's recommendation to the same department the next year of Joseph Levenson. In answer to Raymond Sontag's suspicion that Levenson might be a Marxist, Fairbank noted that Levenson "tends to be eclectic in his thinking about politics. His approach is an intellectual and aesthetic one and he is not especially concerned about politics."[25]

Economics

Meanwhile, the importance of history was increasingly overlooked by academic economists. Of the humanities and social science disciplines none was more central than economics. For while American global ambitions loomed large, the immediate and principal goal of the United States after 1945 was avoiding another Depression. During the 1930s the Roosevelt administration had used government spending to try to break out of the Depression, but to no avail. It was only during World War II, when the government assumed control of most aspects of the economy and especially of investment, that the Depression ended. At the conclusion of the war, when government controls over the economy were lifted and defense spending sharply reduced, there was much apprehension as to whether the economy would once again be plunged into depression. Fortunately, the pent-up savings of workers and consumers picked up the slack at least in the short run. But, significantly, the economy relapsed into a serious downturn in 1949, which was only relieved by a resumption of significant defense spending following the outbreak of the Korean War (1950). Military spending then became the cornerstone of Washington's economic and political policy and has remained so ever since, constituting the permanent core of the institutionalized National Security State.[26]

At the same time the outbreak of the Korean War became part of the simultaneous and deliberate extension of American political influence over Asia, Europe, the Middle East, and Latin America. While the war in Korea helped to consolidate America's grip on Japan and East Asia, this process of expansion had already been initiated in Europe through the Marshall Plan (1947) and the creation of the NATO Alliance (1949). The simultaneous expansion of American influence into the oil rich Middle East (the Turkish and Iranian Crises of 1946) and in Latin America (the Rio Pact, 1948) rounded off the rapid worldwide extension of U.S. economic and political power. This global expansion of the American sphere of influence, added to ongoing productivity boosts and higher wages for workers, enabled the United States to enjoy a period of unprecedented economic prosperity which continued into the early 1970s. Indeed, having put an end to the global wars between capitalist states that marked the first part of the century and having overcome the Depression, the U.S. as would-be empire ushered in a new stage of capitalist accumulation worldwide. The technological compression of space and time through the unprecedented extension of modern sea and air power and global telecommunication networks by the American military, rather than the imposition of direct political control, represented a novel feature of this assertion of worldwide influence. Paradoxically, it enabled the United States to impose its control by enforcing liberalization of trade through institutional frameworks like the World Bank, the IMF, and the GATT which were in effect controlled by it. Ideologically the United States entered the lists battling against international communism and the threat of radicalism in the third world by means of a policy of containment, a policy that provided the rationale for the expansion of American global power.

The universities played a major supporting role in this expansion of America's worldwide ambitions.[27] The most outstanding initiative in this respect was the institution of the Fulbright exchange program. Created in 1946 it was designed to facilitate travel to other countries by American students and professors, as well as artists and writers, and extended visits by foreigners to the United States. A fundamental premise of its creation was a recognition of future American political and economic hegemony in the post-war world. The Fulbright program—which was controlled by the International Institute for Education and directed by a group of carefully selected political appointees—was meant to extend that dominance intellectually and culturally by promoting American liberal values and the rule of law. Funded initially by the sale of war surplus materials abroad, its financial resources allowed it to fund international academic exchanges involving tens of thousands of Americans and foreigners, among whom were many students and academics during the 1950s and 1960s. Directed at politically important countries like Great Britain, France, Italy, Greece, and Nationalist China, the distribution of Fulbright funds lay in the hands of local foundations, which were controlled by the United States. Many other foreign exchange programs were subsequently established, designed to extend the influence of American higher education overseas as part of a program of extending American cultural and educational influence internationally. Most of these coordinated their activities with the Institute of International Education. By 1948 such international exchanges were closely vetted by the U.S. State Department as a result of the passage of the Smith-Mund Bill, which made the propagation of American culture abroad part of the Cold War.[28] In cooperation with the State Department private foundations like the Carnegie, Rockefeller, and especially the Ford Foundation played a major role in financing research and meetings on international relations and educational exchanges during the 1950s and 1960s. They helped bring into being a national bureaucratic infrastructure for international education geared to the advance of American foreign policy.[29] More sub rosa but of equal importance, the CIA by 1950 had penetrated the leadership of the newly created and anti-communist National Student Association and made it an important instrument in the ideological struggle against communism.[30]

Stabilizing the capitalist economy by avoiding serious economic downturns and stimulating growth in both imports and exports became a major preoccupation. In this light academic economists in the United States turned to the theories of the Cambridge economist John Maynard Keynes. In the wake of the economic crisis that began in 1929 Keynes took the view that, given the reluctance of private enterprise to invest in a depressed economy, the government should assume the task of driving the economy forward by becoming the leading investor. Furthermore, government should use exchange controls and both fiscal and monetary instruments as tools to regulate the ups and downs of national economies. In short Keynes advocated a mixed capitalist economy retaining the market and a place for business enterprise but within a context in which government henceforth played the major role and called the tune.

Keynesian ideas including a central role for the state were vigorously propounded during the Depression by the Stanford economist Lorie Tarshis. But his downgrading of markets in favor of public investment, along with his unabashedly progressive views, made him an early victim of McCarthyism.[31] A milder, more politically acceptable version of Keynes's ideas was advanced by Alvin Harvey Hansen of Harvard, who began his career as a committed exponent of laissez-faire. Following the relapse of the American economy into Depression in 1938 Hansen became a leading advocate of Keynesianism and as such became an important adviser to the Roosevelt and Truman administrations. According to him, technological advance and population increase as stimulants to growth had exhausted themselves and therefore more or less permanent government deficits were necessary to support the market. His 1953 text *A Guide to Keynes* explained and promoted a version of Keynes's thought to the general public. In a retrospective look at his career Hansen commented that "my main job was to expound Keynes ... Indeed my entire role as an economist has been primarily that of an educator, an expounder, not an inventor."[32]

Hansen's Keynesian approach was imparted to his famous pupil Paul Samuelson, whose best-selling textbook on economics (1948) became the Bible of the new Keynesian economic orthodoxy for the next generation of professors and students. Samuelson's most important contribution to the development of Keynesian ideas was the accelerator-multiplier business-cycle model, which rigorously demonstrated the ripple effect of increased investment on economic expansion. Samuelson was born into a middle-class Jewish family in Gary, Indiana, and attended public school in Chicago. Following his Ph.D. at Harvard, Samuelson became a professor at MIT, where, under his guidance, the economics department became the most prominent in the United States. Although never accepting a government position, Samuelson became a major adviser to Democratic presidents from Truman to Johnson. Throughout this period Keynesianism dominated the economic profession and shaped the thinking of the policy elites in the United States. The triumph of Keynesian thought in economics constituted a major break from the laissez-faire orthodoxy which had dominated the economics profession for generations. Those few who continued to abide by laissez-faire principles were marginalized in the universities as intellectual anachronisms.

Samuelson's view that government stimulus was required because markets did not naturally tend to equilibrium and growth represented a break from orthodox economic thought. However, it is important to underscore that this break occurred within the framework of the neoclassical approach to economics with its stress on methodological individualism, consumer choice, and quantitative deductive modeling. The historical and institutional approach to economics represented by classical political economy (Smith, Ricardo, Mill, Marx) and the German Historical School current in the nineteenth century had long since been superseded by the model-building mathematical approach. Moreover, Samuelson continued to believe that the primary agent of the economy ought to remain the market rather than state investment. Indeed, it was precisely because Samuelson was a master of neoclassical economics that he was able to advance the Keynesian approach so successfully across a broad range of subjects including finance, welfare economics and, significantly, international trade, to the theory of which he also made important contributions. As such it is not too much to say that he strengthened the hold of a quantitative neoclassical approach on the economics profession, a hold which grew tighter during the post-war period owing to the influence of business, among other reasons.[33] Indeed, it was precisely because of his successful adherence to what was considered a scientific approach that his version of Keynesianism gained credibility among fellow professional economists. A course in quantitative methods became obligatory in economics departments, while the history of economic thought, which included reference to Smith, Ricardo, Mill, and Marx (long a required course), tended to become elective.[34]

Samuelson's neo-Keynesian synthesis represented an attempt to overcome the fundamental instability of the capitalist order. In its very method it sought to deny the volatility of a system whose progress had been based on repeated economic and political crises. Recurrent instability or shakeouts constituted an intrinsic feature of the history of capitalism and were important to whatever success it had as a system. Keynesianism tried to turn its back on this history. Its assumption was that a quantitatively rigorous analysis of markets supplemented by government intervention could provide the means to bring the capitalist economy under control. This constituted an attempt to deny the central importance of the role of productive relations, crises, and conflicting social classes in economic life.

Underlying such a view was a denial of the basic character of economic life under capitalism, i.e., the fact that it is a system marked by crises which are necessary to the operation and progress of an economy based on the accumulation of capital.

Samuelson himself assumed that markets with some government direction could still find an equilibrium and were the best means of adjusting supply and demand. As we have noted, Samuelson was not the author of this approach. Rather it was rooted in the whole evolution of economics as a field since the time of Alfred Marshall in England and Léon Walras on the European Continent in the late nineteenth century, which saw the rejection of classical political economy. Faced with the rise of socialism, class struggle, and the possibility of revolution, both economists rejected an approach founded on a labor theory of value and class conflict rooted in the work of Smith, Ricardo and Marx, in favor of a mathematized model based on the analysis of the sum of individualized consumer preferences or subjective value. Given the subterranean forces of class, exploitation, and the tendency toward instability, it was only a question of time before the renewed outbreak of crisis would put the neo-Keynesian synthesis into question, as happened in the 1970s. In the short term, post-war prosperity and economic stability appeared to confirm the validity of Keynesianism and guaranteed its academic supremacy. The fundamental view was that control over the economy ensured that social conflict could be minimized if not eliminated altogether. Indeed, it was a fundamental tenet of intellectual life during the Cold War that economic and political instability were pathological conditions.

English Literature

Whereas Hofstadter became the iconic historian of the Cold War his friend and colleague at Columbia, Lionel Trilling, became its most important literary critic.[35] Trilling's masterwork *The Liberal Imagination* (1950) constituted a sophisticated apology for a liberal approach to both literature and politics which placed him in the forefront of literary criticism during the 1950s. Trilling was born in New York City into a lower-middle-class Jewish family marked by social conservatism and religious piety. His mother Fannie, who had spent time in England on the way to the United States, inculcated into Trilling a rather snobbish Anglophilia while fostering a powerful thirst for intellectual success. At age 16 Trilling entered Columbia University, beginning a lifelong association with that university. In 1925 he graduated from Columbia College and in 1926 earned an M.A. in English.

He then taught briefly at the University of Wisconsin and Hunter College. He returned to Columbia in 1932 to pursue a doctoral degree and to teach literature. In the midst of the crisis that followed the crash of 1929 he briefly drew close to the Communist Party, even writing several critical pieces from a socialist realist perspective. But he soon became disillusioned and drifted into the orbit of the socialist but anti-Stalinist *Partisan Review*, described by Trotsky as a journal marked by a Marxism which had lost its political bearings. By the start of World War II, Trilling had abandoned left-wing ideas and embraced liberalism.

Trilling had had difficulty getting into Columbia as an undergraduate and his quest for permanent employment there in the midst of the Depression testified to his persistence and brilliance, but also to his political caution. By 1933 his political hesitations and doubts began to be perceived by acquaintances like the Marxist art historian Meyer Schapiro as simply rooted in a fear of losing his job.[36] This was a charge which Trilling indignantly rejected at the time, insisting rather on his independence of thought. Despite Trilling's denial, Schapiro's accusation should be taken seriously, since unemployment was a possibility that everyone, and especially radicals, faced in the 1930s. It is an important factor in explaining the political behavior of many academics, then and now. Indeed, in 1936 Trilling was told by the English department at Columbia that as a Freudian, Marxist, and Jew he might be better off somewhere else. Such an attitude was not untypical. English departments, like history departments, were bastions of the WASP elite and played an important conservative role in excluding from access to the higher reaches of success those who were untrained to appreciate the aesthetic canons such departments upheld. In particular, they took an increasingly unfavorable view of texts that might throw light on the social and political inequalities in American life in favor of a literary and artistic transcendence of such considerations.[37]

Trilling longed for admission to such a snobbish club. After much procrastination he earned his doctorate at Columbia with a dissertation on Matthew Arnold in 1938. No less than the approval of the dissertation by the president of Columbia, Nicholas Murray Butler, secured his place as the first Jew in Columbia's English department.[38] Butler, a closet anti-Semite and admirer of fascism, liked what he read. According to Trilling, Arnold's thought revolved around the consequences of the French Revolution, whose ongoing importance was acknowledged. The Revolution ushered in modernity, including the problematical nature of modern politics. In Trilling's view, Arnold taught that a cultured and humane middle class could defend liberalism, holding off the madness of revolution. Supposedly neither for nor against the revolution, Arnold positioned himself like "a liberal of the future."[39] Arnold's perspective was applicable not only to the nineteenth century but also to the twentieth. In short, Trilling made Arnold's opinions his own, transforming them into a program of liberal Cold War anti-communism. For Arnold, the proletarian revolution could not be trusted with the heritage of Western civilization. Whatever its drawbacks, the middle class was the only segment of society that could create a civilization into which workers could assimilate themselves. In other words, it was possible and necessary for the ideological and economic power of liberal American capitalism to reverse the apparent advance of history toward socialism.

As we have noted, Trilling's dominant position in post-war criticism was assured with the subsequent publication of *The Liberal Imagination*, a collection of essays which espoused balance and moderation in politics and literature.[40] In both realms, Trilling argued, a continuing sense of complexity, ambiguity, and irony ought to govern the individual's approach. The political liberalism that issued from this view emphasized caution and moral limitation, renouncing the quest for social perfection and recognizing the intractable quality of art and politics. The essays in the collection had been put together in the 1940s, during which time Trilling saw his task as redefining "reality" so as to wrest it from the Stalinists and the social realists of the Common Front. More specifically, Trilling aimed to challenge the dull uniformity of Stalinized writing which he claimed pervaded American literary life under the influence of the communists. For Trilling, Stalinism became an umbrella term for everything that he disdained, a formula for condemning everything from bad writing to middle-brow vulgarity. Above all he rejected what he saw as the ideological in literary thought. Trilling staunchly championed the contemporary modernist aesthetic of expressionism, subjectivism, and high art that distanced itself from immediate social reality. In this light the American literary historian Vernon Partington and the realist novelist Theodore Dreiser, two champions of realism and progressive reform, were singled out for condemnation for their formulaic thinking, lack of independence, and inability to live with uncertainty and doubt in their approach to both literature and political life. With these essays Trilling succeeded in forging both a moral and aesthetic language for liberal anti-communism in the Cold War years—no small accomplishment. His rise to pre-eminence as the leading literary critic of the Cold War demonstrates like no other example the importance of establishment intellectuals and their ability to delineate the limits of acceptable public discourse and sentiment.

Trilling's espousal of a modernist aesthetic, his moral position and historical sense, placed him in the first rank of liberal ideologues. But the rejection of a realist literary aesthetic was taken a step further by the so-called New Criticism that dominated the academic study of literature in the United States during the 1950s and 1960s.[41] For the New Critics the literary object, whether poem, short story, or novel, was to be appreciated as a coherent object in its own terms, not really subject to analysis in terms of things external to it. Like the economists, the New Critics took little interest in history. The literary work was to be comprehended by means of a process of close reading which analyzed those factors that gave the text as aesthetic object its internal coherence and integration. In order to achieve this, the text needed to be rendered free of both author and reader, indeed, liberated from its historical and political context. The literary object—novel, story, or poem—should be criticized and appreciated as a self-contained aesthetic creation divorced from considerations of history, morality, reader reception, and even author intent. As Terry Eagleton has pointed out, such an aesthetic object became a kind of spiritual fetish that might serve as an antidote to the material fetishes of commodity capitalism.

The first New Critics—John Crow Ransom, Alan Tate, Cleanth Brooks, among others—were greatly influenced by the views of T.S. Elliot. The task of the critic was to reveal how the work of art resolved its own internal tensions, paradoxes, and ambivalences in order to achieve artistic integration. New Criticism emerged from the American South, a backward region undergoing rapid modernization under the command of northern capitalists. In its original form New Criticism was a full-fledged irrationalism, closely linked to religion and right-wing southern populism. For critics like Ransom, New Criticism represented an alternative in the realm of literature to the sterile rationalism of northern industrialism. For Ransom, New Criticism was the ideology of a displaced and defensive intelligentsia who found in literature what they could not find in reality. On the other hand, whatever protest it originally embodied was quickly assimilated into the increasing professionalized and apolitical approach to literature to be found in English departments from the 1950s onward. The technical language it developed, in its rigor and self-consciousness, made it a serious rival to the mathematical discourses found in the science or economics departments of the universities. Moreover, its depoliticized approach, which paralleled that in other academic departments, proved especially useful in avoiding uncomfortable social and political questions at the height of the Cold War. Indeed, its insistence on ambiguity, complexity, and irony echoed the posture of Lionel Trilling in providing a discourse not simply in terms of literary culture but in terms of justifying a personal aloofness from political engagement.[42]

Philosophy

Philosophy in the U.S. up to the end of World War II was marked by a pluralist approach based on the competition between pragmatism, logical positivism, and Marxism, all of which took their cue from science. There was even a neo-Thomist school at the University of Chicago, backed by its influential president Robert Hutchins, who along with his protégé Mortimer Adler insisted that morality had to be based on the inculcation of the values of Western civilization rather than scientific knowledge. But pragmatism was by far the most powerful trend, led by the venerable John Dewey at Columbia University. Pragmatism had emerged in the last decades of the nineteenth century under the tutelage of Charles Sanders Peirce and William James. Under the influence of Dewey it became closely associated with the Progressive Movement and eventually the New Deal. Directed by middle-class reformers, the Progressive Movement aimed at revitalizing American democracy by curbing corruption and limiting the power of monopoly capital. Hofstadter had an unfairly jaundiced view of the Progressives as well as the Populists, dismissing them as representative of a largely Protestant lower middle class which was in decline faced with the growing dominance of the American corporation and the rise of ethnic minorities. On the contrary, the political program of the Progressives widened into the program of the New Deal, which opened itself up to ethnic politics, unions, and the black population, while espousing the welfare state and a mixed economy.

Pragmatism, especially in the hands of Dewey, linked itself with the idea of democratic reform, championing the application of science to the resolution of social and political problems. According to Dewey, inquiry is a form of activity, and no sharp distinction should be drawn between theoretical and practical judgments. Indeed, the traditional dualisms between appearance and reality, the theoretical and practical, fact and value, needed to be rejected. All inquiry is practical, concerned with transforming and evaluating the features of the social environment that people find themselves a part of. The "logical forms" used in the course of inquiry were understood by Dewey as ideal instruments, tools that helped to transform things and resolve problems. Rejecting foundationalism, Dewey espoused the fallibilism that was characteristic of pragmatism: the view that any proposition accepted as an item of knowledge has this status only provisionally, contingent upon its adequacy in providing a coherent understanding of the world as the basis for human action.

Marxism was far less influential in the United States where—depression or not—capitalism continued to be very strong. Nonetheless, the Russian Revolution, the 1930s Depression, and the rising influence of the American Communist Party made Marxism attractive to some philosophers. Its influence on academic philosophy was above all due to the intellectual power of Sidney Hook. Hook was born in New York City of Jewish parentage, and attended City College. He received a Ph.D. in philosophy at Columbia in 1927, where he studied under Dewey. Subsequently, he made his career in the philosophy department at New York University. An ardent socialist and Marxist, his laudable ambition was to synthesize pragmatism and Marxism and in so doing domesticate the latter in America. In 1933 he published *Towards the Understanding of Karl Marx: A Revolutionary Interpretation*, a serious theoretical work that strengthened the claims of Marxism as a philosophical position. Having been close to the Communist Party and having spent time doing research in Moscow, he denounced Stalinism in 1933 after being brutally roughed up for ideological deviation by the leadership of the American Communist Party, still in the throes of the dogmatism of Stalin's Third Period. By 1940 he emerged as a leading intellectual and political opponent of communism and radicalism in the United States, taking an important part in the anti-communist purges that followed World War II.

Widely acclaimed at the time of its publication, Hook's study of Marx's thought, which he later attempted to disavow, was imbued with the influence of Dewey. Hook espoused an experimental intellectual method, with knowledge considered hypothetical, fallible, and provisional. Hook's view that knowledge was not merely received as sense experience but as something created and obtained by engagement with the world echoed Dewey but also Marx's conception of praxis.[43] Of course, a class perspective rather than an individualistic view of society, a stress on the importance of historical change, a philosophical realist or foundationalist approach to knowledge which included the dialectical concepts of totality, contradiction, and negation, and a commitment to revolutionary as against evolutionary change, pitted Marxism in opposition to the positivism and political moderation of pragmatism.[44]

In the post-war period Hook espoused a right-wing social democracy which was accommodated within the ranks of the Democratic Party. Traveling to Europe in 1949, Hook denounced what he called the cretinism of those intellectuals who supported communist tyranny and declared his support for NATO and the Marshall Plan.[45] He played a major role along with Arthur Schlesinger in organizing the founding meeting of the Congress of Cultural Freedom in Berlin.[46] At the height of the McCarthy period, as we have noted, he justified the dismissal of professors who were communists from their university positions because they were under the discipline of the Communist Party and unable to independently and objectively research and espouse truthful knowledge.[47] Hook's view on this matter proved extremely influential in American academia.

The evolution of Hook at NYU, and of Trilling and Hofstadter at Columbia, away from Marxism toward social democracy or liberalism was part of the more general drift of a group of influential New York intellectuals—including Irving Howe, Alfred Kazin, Irving Kristol, and Diana Trilling—away from communism. Their shift from revolutionary anti-Stalinism of the Trotskyist variety toward liberalism or social democracy was obviously a consequence of the Cold War,[48] but it was also the result of post-war consumerist prosperity and the overall embourgeoisement of New York academics, journalists, and intellectuals. In the battle of ideas between capitalism and communism during the Cold War, these progressive intellectuals occupied a key role, living as they did in New York City at the crossroads of the American media, communications, and financial system. The rightward move of these men and women of letters reflected the necessity for unattached intellectuals to choose sides in the Cold War. It also reflected the increasing integration of such figures into academe as the disappearance of Bohemia, the growth of suburbia, and the decline of independent journals deprived free floating intellectuals of an economic, social, and cultural foundation outside the academy.[49]

Both Marxist philosophy and pragmatism placed great importance on science as a criterion of truth and as the basis for human progress. Both saw scientific knowledge as a by-product of social activity and as a powerful ideological weapon with which to advance a progressive intellectual and political agenda. On the other hand, the logical empiricist or positivist school, which became prominent in the United States after 1945 and ultimately came to completely dominate American philosophy, insisted that the basis of scientific truth could be determined logically, divorced knowledge from its social surroundings, and assumed a decidedly apolitical position reminiscent of New Criticism in English. Both schools were marked by a flight from social and political reality as well as an indifference to historical context.

Logical empiricism or positivism was developed in Vienna, where a circle of philosophers, scientists, and mathematicians met regularly in the 1920s to investigate scientific language and methodology. The work of this group was distinguished by attention to the form of scientific theories in the belief that the logical structure of any particular scientific theory could be specified quite apart from its content. They also claimed that the meaningfulness of a proposition is grounded in experience and observation. For this reason, the assertions of ethics, metaphysics, religion, and aesthetics were held to be meaningless. On this basis, they concluded that what was scientific could be comprehended as a totality and that such knowledge could be considered part of a unified science. Thus no fundamental differences were held to exist between the physical and the biological sciences or between the natural and the social sciences.

The founder and leader of the Vienna Circle was Moritz Schlick, an epistemologist and philosopher of science. Other members of the group included Gustav Bergmann, Rudolf Carnap, Herbert Feigl, Philipp Frank, Kurt Gödel, Otto Neurath, and Friedrich Waismann. In an associated group in Berlin, known as the Society for Empirical Philosophy, the leading lights were Carl Hempel and Hans Reichenbach. A formal declaration of the Vienna Circle's intentions was issued in 1929 with the publication of the manifesto "The Scientific Conception of the World: The Vienna Circle." Most of the members of the movement fled to the United States during the second half of the 1930s as a result of the Nazi takeover of Germany and Austria. In the English-speaking world, the exposition of logical positivism by A.J. Ayer entitled *Language, Truth and Logic* (1936) became the classic text and presented logical positivism as mainly philosophy of science interpreted by Carnap as viewed through the lens of Wittgenstein's ordinary language philosophy. Philosophy's essential function was to assist the progress of science by offering clarifying analyses of scientific language.[50]

The above represents a conventional account of the early history of logical positivism. The recent publication of George A. Reisch's *How the Cold War Transformed Philosophy of Science: To the Icy Slopes of Logic* has transformed our understanding of these origins.[51] The received account leaves the impression that the logical positivists were a philosophical movement without connection to the grave political, economic, and social problems of the first part of the twentieth century. In fact, the Vienna Circle deliberately reached out to public opinion to promote their critique of traditional philosophy and to put forward their scientific world conception as a means to help solve the political and social crisis that was giving rise to fascism. Especially important in the development of the social and political program of the Vienna Circle was Otto Neurath, a social democrat with ties to the communists, who promoted the Unity of Science movement. The movement undertook the task of unifying the sciences so that they could become instruments for planning the improvement of society. Promoting an understanding of science and logical empiricism among the public at large was an integral part of this program in order to defeat metaphysics and obscurantism and actively enlist the mass of society in creating a new enlightened order. In the conception of its protagonists, logical empiricism and the Unity of Science movement were to fulfill the promise of the eighteenth-century Enlightenment—both enlightening and transforming society while taking advantage of twentieth-century advances in science, logic, social thought, and politics.[52] Despite ongoing intellectual disagreements there was significant dialogue, and even cooperation, between logical empiricists and Marxists, and Neurath for one saw his work as an extension of Marxism. He also sought alliances with the pragmatists and could sound positively Deweyan when speaking of the "anti-totalitarian" and "democratic" attitude of science. Phillip Frank of Harvard, who helped shepherd the Unity of Science movement after Neurath's death in 1945, supported "the idea that the evolution of logical empiricism, rightly understood, was a vector pointing directly to North American pragmatism."[53]

On the other hand, while admiring the empirical approach of the logical positivists, their insistence on a single logic of science seemed like a formalist straight-jacket to both pragmatists and Marxists. Marxists especially rejected the static quality of logical positivism's empiricism, which seemed to fetishize the existing body of scientific knowledge that it attempted to organize in terms of a rigorous logic. Logical positivism seemed bound to divorce the acquisition of knowledge from the dynamic movement of social relations. In contrast to Marxist philosophy it refused to see the acquisition of knowledge as part of a social process and to understand the logic of positivism as deeply embedded in the logic of capitalism. It should be recalled that Marx characterized the Aristotelian form of logic as "the money of the spirit," in that in the cases of both money and logic there is the same indifference to specific content. Indeed, philosophical logic arises from a process of growing rationality and abstraction which emerges in a society based on markets and money, the latter being its end point. This means that Aristotelian logic or the logic of traditional philosophy and science, including positivism, is the most abstract philosophical expression of the bourgeois spirit or consciousness of value. The logic of Marx's dialectic, which is one of movement rather than stasis, expresses the continuing contradiction between exchange value and use value and between exchange and production. For the Marxists knowledge was seen as arising within society conceived of as a totality in dialectical motion, which creates the basis for new knowledge both social and natural.[54]

Logical positivists were challenged from within the domain of philosophy itself by the Harvard scholar Thomas Kuhn in his *The Structure of Scientific Revolutions* (1962).[55] Writing from the perspective of history, Kuhn claimed that major advances in scientific thought were not the consequence of the gradual accretion of new knowledge. They were the result rather of scientific revolutions in which an existing conception of truth was repudiated and a new fundamentally opposed interpretation replaced it. According to Kuhn, the established paradigms that dominated scientific thinking and experiment in any epoch were, among other things, the product of a consensus in the scientific community. If in the course of time enough anomalies accumulated which brought into question the dominant paradigm; it would then be overthrown and replaced by a radically different interpretation—Newton's theory of universal gravitation, Darwin's theory of evolution, and Einstein's theory of relativity being cases in point. Kuhn's theory of scientific change was advanced from the perspective of the history of ideas. Its insistence on the importance of scientific paradigms as embodied in intellectual communities helped open the door eventually to the progress of a sociology and history of science, an approach which had been pioneered by European and Russian Marxists but which was discarded during the height of the Cold War. For could anyone seriously believe that the overthrow of the Aristotelian worldview in the sixteenth and seventeenth centuries by Copernicanism or Newtonianism was merely the product of a battle of ideas? Or that the assault on creationism by Darwin and his allies was simply an intellectual disagreement. Such conflicts were clearly the result of profound political, social, and cultural change. On the other hand, one should not take Kuhn's theory to mean that the existence of the external world depends merely on our historically evolving understanding of it.

But the challenge to logical empiricists in America came not from Marxist critique, but from the massive assault on left-wing politics and thought after 1945. In the immediate post-war period, leadership of the Unity of Science movement in the United States devolved to Phillip Frank, who lectured on physics and philosophy of science at Harvard. Frank insisted on the need for philosophy to engage with the scientific disciplines while being socially committed.[56] The fact that Frank's biographical study of Einstein was lauded by the communist *Daily Worker* was enough for an investigation to be opened against him by the FBI.[57] Although nothing subversive could be found, the investigation tied him to Rudolf Carnap, then at the

Princeton Institute for Advanced Study. In his own work Carnap insisted on separating the philosophy of science from political and social considerations, which distinguishes him from the Marxists. On the other hand, since his early days Carnap had sympathized with the left, including the communists. The FBI was outraged by his signing a petition in favor of clemency for Julius and Ethel Rosenberg.[58] He had already aroused the wrath of Hook, who in 1949 had denounced him for supporting the Waldorf Conference for World Peace as a Soviet front.[59] Meanwhile, in the face of the increasingly repressive political environment in the United States, important logical empiricists like Feigel and Reichenbach busied themselves distancing the logical positivist school from the political and social engagement of Frank. In particular, they disavowed Frank and his leadership of the Unity of Science movement. The last straw was the withdrawal of financial support for the movement by the Rockefeller Foundation, in which political considerations almost certainly played a part.[60] In the wake of this vacuum there emerged the apolitical professional agenda of logical positivism and eventually the analytical philosophy which now dominates American philosophy.[61]

Anthropology

In regard to the development of anthropology, Talal Assad has explained "that we need to see anthropology as a holistic discipline nurtured within bourgeois society, having as its object of study a variety of non-European societies which have come under its economic, political and intellectual domination."[62] In other words, the origins of the entire discipline are rooted in the history of Western colonialism and imperialism, an undeniable reality which throws a clear light on the relationship between institutionalized knowledge and political and economic power. Furthermore, the massive intrusion of the United States into the underdeveloped world after 1945 greatly increased the importance of anthropology, which became an important instrument advancing the interests of the American state.

Modern anthropology emerged in the early twentieth century in response to the administrative needs of the colonial powers. The origins of French anthropology, like those of the British version, were deeply enmeshed in the projects and institutions of the colonial state.[63] The founders of the British functionalist school—Edward Evans-Pritchard, Alfred Reginald Radcliffe-Brown, and Bronislaw Malinowski—were supported by the British colonial governments. These pioneer anthropologists were assisted in order for governments to learn more about the people under colonial control, who they were interested in governing through the method of indirect rule. The paternalistic defense of the traditional cultures of African people by these anthropologists, however well meaning, was then used to justify ongoing colonial government. By and large these founders accepted colonialism and in fact involved themselves in it by investigating the colonized peoples. They failed to appreciate the degree to which colonialism itself created colonized so-called native people as a result of the imposition of the structures of European domination. Significantly, rather than viewing such people as colonized, they referred to them as primitive and, as such, as people without a history. This failure to understand the ramifications of the overall colonialist context in which they worked was not simply due to the self-interest of these anthropologists. The inability of British anthropology to articulate a total conception of the colonial situation cannot be entirely understood in terms of a lack of reflexivity on the part of these pioneer ethnographers. Rather, it has been a characteristic of positivist British culture since the nineteenth century to be conceptually incapable of putting the whole of British society into question, let alone of grasping the imperialistic nature of its colonialism. The functionalism of the British school aimed to understand how stability was maintained within such primitive communities, which functioned by means of a presumably inter-related set of social processes that were minutely described but not integrated into an overarching systemic theory in the manner of Durkheim or Marx.[64]

Positivism was also championed by the anthropology that emerged in the United States. As a university discipline, American anthropology was created by Franz Boas (1858–1942), who dominated the field in the first part of the twentieth century.[65] From his perch at Columbia he successfully challenged the dominant evolutionary approach to anthropology which presumed a universal and law-like progression of all societies through determined stages—an approach enunciated by the pioneer American anthropologist Lewis H. Morgan. Boas instead championed the complex and diverse nature of cultural change that did not lend itself to systematization. Once again historical development was excluded.

Boas was born into a comfortable and liberal German-Jewish family in Minden, Germany, and took a Ph.D. in physics. He participated in an expedition to northern Canada where he became fascinated with the culture and language of the Inuit of Baffin Island. He went on to do fieldwork investigating the indigenous cultures and languages of the Pacific Northwest. In 1887 he emigrated to the United States where he first worked as a museum curator at the Smithsonian and in 1899 became professor of anthropology at Columbia. His hundreds of publications, organizational activities, and many graduate students including such leading figures as Alfred Kroeber, Edward Sapir, Ruth Benedict, and Margaret Mead, established anthropology as a university discipline. He was outspoken in attacking scientific racism, opposed U.S. entry into World War I as an imperialist conflict, and for a while was a member of the American Socialist Party. Transcending the paternalist assumptions of British functionalist anthropology his anti-racism and cultural relativism helped to undermine the colonialist view of the world based on notions of Western superiority, while undergirding theoretically the concept of the political equality of all citizens of the American republic. In espousing this position he advanced the universalist claims of American anthropology at the moment that the European colonial empires were beginning to crumble. One cannot but note the coincidence between Boas's anti-colonial position based on cultural relativism, which celebrated the equality of the cultures of different peoples, and the U.S. adherence to the policy of the Open Door and eventually that of worldwide national self-determination based on the principle of sovereign political equality. On the other hand, despite his socialist proclivities and his criticisms of racism and colonialism, Boas's avoidance of questions of global political economy involving the power relations of the colonized and the colonizers made his cultural relativism at best simply an intellectual posture and at worst an instrument for understanding and controlling third world peoples.

Indeed, Boas is remembered above all for championing cultural relativism. He claimed that the anthropologist could and should judge the people being studied in fieldwork through the lens of their own rather than the anthropologist's culture. Whatever the ultimate political and philosophical deficiencies of cultural relativism, one can hardly underestimate the long-term positive importance of this questioning of ethnocentrism. As understood by Boas, culture was conceived of as an assemblage of the language, religious beliefs and practices, food, social traits, music, and dance of a given society. Change came about through the diffusion of practices from one culture to another. Overarching theories of progressive development through stages, such as those proposed by Morgan and Marx, were rejected. Rather, Boas championed the idea of the particularity and variety of human societies. The Otherness of non-Western peoples, which has become so contentious since the writing of Edward Said and his postcolonial epigones since the 1970s, was naively championed by Boas and his followers.

Cultural relativism has been rightly attacked for posing a false neutrality by remaining aloof from the twentieth-century political and economic struggles between the colonial and imperialist states and third world peoples. Indeed, anthropologists, despite their protestations of sympathy for the peoples of the underdeveloped countries, are a privileged part of the first world, and the knowledge they obtain from their field excursions has been used to facilitate the maintenance of Western control over non-Western peoples. Some critics have furthermore complained that Boas wrongly downplayed the importance of technological innovation or environmental factors in favor of the overriding influence of culture, making him a kind of cultural determinist and an idealist one at that. Indeed, while he resisted the idea that cultures should be regarded as all-encompassing systems, others who followed in his wake tended to treat it as such and as a result made culture into a kind of intellectual fetish. Moreover, the complaint is made that the systemic and determinist conception of culture tends to turn peoples into prisoners of inherited practices bound to reproduce the inherited order. Boas's views were to be vigorously attacked in the post-1945 period, but remained influential to the way that anthropology was thought about and practiced in the United States. Boas's culturalism, we should note parenthetically, has had an unexpected revival in the form of the cultural turn that has marked many disciplines at the end of the twentieth century. Ruth Benedict and Margaret Mead, meanwhile, were among the most celebrated supporters of the systemic view of culture that developed in the wake of Boas's work. They were the two most well-known protégées of Boas while pioneering the entry of women into the higher reaches of academe through their work in this relatively new field. United by friendship and common intellectual interests, Mead's *Coming of Age in Samoa* (1928) and Benedict's *Patterns of Culture* (1934) became anthropological classics. Benedict became professor at Columbia while Mead worked mainly at New York's American Museum of Natural History. By the mid-1920s they were using the insights of psychoanalysis and Gestalt psychology to portray the forms of psycho-social integration of individuals in a given society and to explain the deeply held beliefs and attitudes of its members, which were called patterns. Culture was conceived of as an entity whose elements were integrated into a totality.[66]

The relationship between the new field of anthropology and the Federal government deepened. Already during the Depression anthropologists had begun to find employment with the government, working especially with the Bureau of Indian Affairs. The head of the Bureau, John Collier, appointed by President Franklin Roosevelt, was a Boasian, and he tried to reverse the assimilationist policies that had long prevailed in Washington with regard to the conquered aboriginal peoples. However, most of the federal bureaucracy and some anthropologists rejected attempts to revive what they regarded as defunct cultures. With the outbreak of World War II opportunities for anthropologists expanded. They were hired to work for military intelligence, the State Department, the OSS, the Board of Economic Warfare, the Strategic Bombing Survey, the Military Government, the Selective Service Organization, the Office of Naval Intelligence, the Office of War Information, and the FBI.[67] One of the most notorious aspects of government involvement was helping to oversee the removal of Nisei Japanese from California to internment camps in the Midwest. Mead served as executive of the National Research Council's wartime Council of Food Habits, a far from innocuous responsibility given the importance of the international politics of food especially in wartime. Benedict threw herself into the war effort authoring a widely disseminated pamphlet *The Races of Mankind* and an anthropological analysis of Japan eventually published as *The Chrysanthemum and the Sword* (1946). This was part of a government-sponsored anthropological series called National Character Studies. Like other important academics, Mead and Benedict were charter members of the Office of Strategic Services, the forerunner of the CIA. At the same time, it is noteworthy that as undersecretary of state for Latin America, Nelson Rockefeller, whose family had immense interests in Latin America, channeled both government and Rockefeller Foundation funds into anthropological research in Latin America.[68]

In 1937 Ralph Linton, a conservative, was appointed to the post of head of the anthropology department at Columbia after the retirement of Boas. Butler, the Columbia president, was eager to rid the anthropology department of unsavory progressive elements, which included women like Benedict. The Boasians had expected Benedict to be named Boas's successor and they opposed Linton, with whom they had never been on good terms. As head of the department Linton informed against many of Boas's students to the FBI, accusing them of being communists. This led to some being fired and blacklisted, notably the highly esteemed colleague of Benedict, Gene Weltfish.[69] The Columbia department under Linton was riven by conflict, which ended only with his departure for Yale in 1946.

Linton's departure set the stage for the emergence of a new academic star, Julian Steward, who seriously challenged the Boasian tradition by reverting to an evolutionary approach to anthropology. Steward took his degrees at Cornell and Berkeley, where he was exposed to Boasian ideas through the teaching of Alfred Kroeber and Robert Lowie. Between 1928 and 1930 he became the first lecturer in anthropology at the University of Michigan. Stints of teaching at Utah University and Berkeley then led to an appointment at the Smithsonian Institution and the Bureau of Indian Affairs (1935–46). He then became professor at Columbia (1946–52) and the University of Illinois (1952–68). Steward did an enormous amount of fieldwork, but in contrast to the Boasians, who eschewed overarching theory and notions of evolution, Steward searched for cross-cultural regularities in an effort to discern laws of culture and cultural change. His work explained variation in the complexity of social organization as being limited within a range of possibilities defined by the environment.

In evolutionary terms, he located his version of cultural ecology as multilinear in contrast to the unilinear typological models of Morgan and Marx. Steward believed it was possible to create theories analyzing a typical and common culture representative of specific eras or regions. He did not limit his analysis, as did the Boasians, to micro-cultures but also explored more complex forms of social organizations at various levels of development. He pointed to technology and economics as the decisive factors determining the development of a given culture, while noting that there are secondary factors such as political systems, ideologies, and religions. These factors can push the evolution of a given society in multiple directions at the same time. There is no necessary progressive evolution. Steward pursued a strongly empirical and materialist anthropology which he regarded as a scientific approach in contrast to that of the Boasians. Indeed, he was hired at Columbia to counteract what some regarded as the overly psychological approach of Benedict.

While at Columbia Steward attracted a great many graduate students who went on to brilliant careers while taking anthropology in a left-wing direction. Indeed, the influence of Marx's materialism on Steward is evident. But in the context of the Cold War in the 1950s Steward eschewed the politics of the left. It has been shown, furthermore, that he used his expertise to support the U.S. government's denial of aboriginal land claims on the basis of the primitiveness of these societies. In this respect he reinforced the tie between anthropology and colonialism.[70] Moreover he served as general editor of the Rockefeller sponsored multi-volume *Handbook of South American Indians* (1946–59) which, whatever its scholarly virtues, furthered the interests of the economic imperialism that became extremely powerful in this period as U.S. capital poured into Latin America.

Steward sharply differentiated his own version of evolutionism from that of his rival at the University of Michigan, Leslie A. White. The latter espoused a strict unilinear evolutionism that echoed Morgan and Marx and appeared to be quite distinct from Steward's multilinear approach. On the other hand, Steward's fear of political repression also had something to do with his intellectual position. At the height of the student unrest in the 1960s, Steward explained his ideological position in a letter to the cultural materialist Marvin Harris: "It was during the thirties that Columbia became a communist cell, far more than people knew, and curiously, many adopted the political and economic orientations of Marx yet remained relativists in their anthropological work. I too read Marx and the others but it was dangerous to proclaim a Marxist position."[71] Linton was no doubt an unpleasant character and an informer, but he may not have been that far off base in this regard.

Leslie White had replaced Steward as professor of anthropology at the University of Michigan in 1930 and remained at Ann Arbor for most of his career. There he was able to build the anthropology department into the best in the United States, surrounding himself with a group of outstanding and progressive scholars and students. But his style was 180 degrees from the reticence and conformity of Steward, at least on the surface. He became the most sought-after teacher in the university because, in the midst of the McCarthyite purges and overall intellectual conformity, he made himself famous for his iconoclastic attacks on religion and the political and cultural shibboleths of 1950s America.

After serving in the U.S. Navy, White entered Louisiana State University, but after two years transferred to Columbia which was then a beacon of progressive thought. He received his B.A. and M.A. in psychology from Columbia and his Ph.D. in anthropology and sociology (jointly) from the University of Chicago. He began his career at the University of Buffalo and subsequently moved to Michigan. In his early career White did fieldwork among the Keresan Pueblo Indians of the American Southwest. He was certainly outspoken on many matters, but as his biographer points out, White, like Steward, was largely silent when it came to Marx. In his two best-known works, *The Science of Culture* (1949) and *The Evolution of Culture* (1959), he mentions Marx and Engels only in passing. Yet, as early as 1922, in the wake of the Russian Revolution, White privately declared himself a revolutionary and a historical materialist, and he visited the Soviet Union in 1929. Until the late 1950s he maintained a secret membership in the revolutionary Marxist Socialist Workers Party, writing regularly for their newspaper *The Weekly People* under the defiant pseudonym John Steel (Joseph Stalin?).[72]

White started his career as a conventional Boasian. But at the University of Buffalo his students attacked cultural relativism and White in response began to seriously read Morgan, whose evolutionism and materialism greatly impressed him. Attacking the Boasian viewpoint in the *Weekly People* (1931) he thundered:

> It has been the fashion among American anthropologists for years to attack Leslie H. Morgan, the great exponent of social evolution ... Having torn Morgan to shreds, American anthropologists set to work on intensive local area studies. The result is a wealth of ethnographic material and a poverty of synthetic formulations of results ... they have little conception of all culture as an integrated, organically developing entity. Their microscopic vision is excellent, macroscopically they are all but blind [73]

Despite his hostility to Boas, White took seriously the view that culture must be understood as a historically evolving organic whole. Furthermore, the elements of different cultures, however similar in function and appearance, are invested with different symbolic meanings. Corn, for example, is undoubtedly a food, but its meaning varies depending on whether it is produced in pre-Columbian Mexico, eighteenth-century France, or the twentieth-century U.S. corn belt. On the other hand, in a decisive article entitled "Energy and the Evolution of Culture" published in the *American Anthropologist* in 1943, he argued that technological innovation led to the development of culture, that culture evolves as the amount of energy harnessed per capita per year increases, or as the efficiency of putting this energy to work increases. Technology, although decisive, was but part of humanity's capacity to externalize itself by means of what he called symboling, which allowed it to not only invent tools, but also develop an overall culture including ritual, music, dance, and other social practices.[74]

As critics have pointed out, White's theory leaves unclear how his general understanding of culture relates to his technological determinism. Some have complained that his view, based on the concept of symboling, tends to idealism, while others have seen his viewpoint as a kind of reductionist technological determinism. What appears to be lacking is an understanding of Marx's dialectical view, which insists on the importance of labor as both a physical and a conceptual process producing both things and meanings simultaneously, according to a given mode of production and in concrete historical circumstances. For Marx culture is not something that lies apart from material activity, but is interwoven with it. It entails the transformation of human needs into material objects in order to satisfy those needs while embodying within those objects the existing social relations. It is the locus of both practical activity and creativity as well as the theatre within which contradictory social relations work themselves out. Moreover, cultures are not static, but are in a constant state of evolution and development.[75]

Looked at from this perspective, insofar as those in the Boasian tradition (including those who adhere to the recent cultural turn) attempt to split culture off from material activity or try to view it as some kind of independent variable which drives society, they fall into idealism and, indeed, turn the concept of culture into a fetish. White was celebrated for his courage at the height of the McCarthy repression. On the other hand, one must underscore his reticence to proclaim his Marxism publicly. Given his penchant for iconoclasm, his reluctance to openly declare himself in this respect testifies to the fear that anti-communism induced among intellectuals in the United States in that period, a fear that even affected a fearless man like White.

After 1945 the U.S. strongly supported the decolonization process which involved the liquidation of the British, French, Belgian, and Dutch colonial empires. But it by no means renounced economic imperialism and especially the drive to control the resources and labor of third world countries. Indeed, its victory in the war, highly productive economy, and the weakness of the other major powers fueled these ambitions. One of the ways it advanced its efforts was through the technical assistance program known as the Point Four Program (1949), which was orientated toward the economic and social development of underdeveloped countries, as development was understood by U.S. capitalism. Generously funded by the U.S. government, applied anthropologists found opportunities to pursue their research within this framework.

The close affinity between the field of anthropology and the U.S. federal government had solidified during World War II. Yet the end of the war seemed to threaten future prospects as research funding from the government dried up. The situation is exemplified by the fate of Margaret Mead. Following the war Mead, at first none too successfully, attempted to maintain continued state support for her various projects. But once the Cold War started the taps of federal funding were reopened and she quickly tried to cash in. She and her team of associates made the case that Russian authoritarianism could be explained as the result of the swaddling practices of Russians, as contrasted with the liberal child-rearing practices of democratic America. As part of her efforts to extend this dubious line of research, which became something of a laughing-stock, Mead unabashedly pursued further funding from the Rand Corporation, the government-funded Cold War think-tank.[76]

Mead was just one of the many anthropologists who both overtly and covertly had their research funded by the state through the 1950s and 1960s. Some researchers actively collaborated with the CIA, while others unwittingly received money from front organizations. The correlation between anthropological research and U.S counter-revolutionary activity in third world countries is astounding when one considers the flood of ethnographies produced in these years from fieldwork conducted in Cold War Iran, Guatemala, Costa Rica, Syria, the Philippines, Indonesia, Greece, Egypt, Angola, Zaire, Nicaragua, Panama, and Chile states, where the CIA fought long and hard to subvert the progress of revolutionary political change.[77] The most notorious example of the liaison between an anthropologist and the anti-communist policies of the U.S. government is that of Clyde Kluckhohn, head of the Harvard anthropology department. A militant Cold Warrior with no expertise on Russia, he was made director of the Russian Studies Centre at Harvard which became, along with the Hoover Institute at Stanford, the leading center of right-wing Sovietology during the Cold War. Actively collaborating with the CIA and FBI, Kluckhohn took the lead in helping to ferret out communists and fellow travelers among academics in the Boston area. Meanwhile he served as president of the American Anthropological Association, helped with the creation of the CIA and Ford Foundation sponsored Human Relations Area File, represented the American Anthropological Association at the Social Science Research Council, and served on the Department of Defense's Committee on Human Resources and the U.S. Air Force's Committee on Ethics. Such was the Old Boys network.[78]

Sociology

While the separate disciplines were shaped by their distinctive disciplinary response to the development of the mass university and the Cold War, the lack of a more interdisciplinary approach was keenly felt. One response was the emergence of a multitude of distinctive social science approaches which combined political science and psychology with sociology and economics. Those who worked in these fields, notably at Harvard, Yale, and Chicago, placed stress on a scientific approach aimed at comprehending human behavior on its own terms, i.e. divorced from a sense of the effects of history and ideology. Their approach therefore emphasized political and value neutrality, the use of survey research and quantification and a focus on individual behavior upon which overall conclusions needed to be based.[79] Prediction and control rather than social change were the goals of such inquiries. This turn to behaviorism was in part the result of an attempt to emulate the success of natural science and in part the result of Cold War conformity and a desire to avoid McCarthy-like attacks. Certainly the enthusiastic endorsement and financial support of the private foundations and especially the Ford Foundation for such a behaviorist approach played a large role. The funds provided by the latter to the social sciences were explicitly earmarked to prevent social unrest and the questioning of basic political and moral principles, and to promote adjustment to change.[80]

Although clearly marked by the Cold War and the reaction against Marxism, anthropology during this period was an intellectually exciting discipline largely because the hegemony of the Boasian school was being challenged by supporters of evolutionary anthropology. In contrast, sociology was dominated to an astonishing degree by the thought of a single man, Talcott Parsons, whose theory was marked by behaviorism and aspired to all-inclusiveness and rigor. His system came to be called structural functionalism and amounted to a comprehensive and integrated non-Marxist sociological theory congruent with the Cold War emphasis on stability. It provided an all-inclusive and integrated view of American society from a conservative perspective. In this Parsons stands in the long line of sociologists including Auguste Comte, Vilfred Pareto, Emile Durkheim, and Max Weber who sought to understand and, in so doing, to contain the revolutionary forces of the nineteenth and twentieth centuries.[81] Parsons spent virtually his entire career at Harvard. There he exercised a commanding influence on the graduate program in sociology from out of which the major universities drew a disproportionally large number of influential academic appointments. In this way Parsons's theory came to dominate the field of sociology until the mid-1960s. The fact that he exercised such extraordinary power, it must be said, reflected not simply Parsons's intellectual eminence but the conformity and conservatism that marked this discipline at the height of the Cold War.

Parsons was born in 1902 in Colorado, the son of a Congregationalist minister and college administrator. He was educated at a private school in New York City and then Amherst College. Spending a year at the London School of Economics, he took a Ph.D. at Heidelberg and then received an appointment at Harvard. At Heidelberg he was exposed to the intellectual legacy of Max Weber as a result of his personal contact with Weber's widow and brother. Through Parsons's translations Weber's works were made known to an English-speaking audience. Indeed, Parsons's theories may be seen as an elaboration and interpretation of Weberian sociology in an American context. All of Weber's work on economy and society forms an immense if oblique contestation of the Marxism which had conquered the working-class movement in Imperial Germany. Both Weber's and Parsons's thought are directed toward minimizing or rejecting the central Marxist idea of social contradiction.[82]

Parsons's thought went through several permutations but by the 1960s had crystallized into an overall theory which analyzed society in terms of four basic functions: economic efficiency, administrative effectiveness, conformity to social norms at one level and at a deeper level faithfulness to cultural values. Parsons added that four mediums of interchange—money, power, influence, and value commitments—arbitrate between these analytical subsystems. Added to these factors were notions of systems theory, pattern, and maintenance of hierarchy.[83] Parsons left room for a certain amount of conflict within this theoretical construction but insisted that underlying tendencies toward integration inhibited the breakdown of social systems. Society bore within it inherent tendencies toward adjustment which overcame whatever factors led to social conflict. In this respect Parsons's sociology echoed the notion of market equilibrium held by laissez-faire economists. The conservative and apologetic bias of this abstract and cumbersome system, the foundation of which was meant to exclude the Marxist notion of class conflict, seems plain.

Abstract and cumbersome though it may have been, Parsons's conservative social theory served its purpose in the Cold War, shaping an entire discipline. Not only did it ensure Parsons's ascendancy in sociology it also garnered political influence. Like many other academics of the period who rose to prominence, Parsons may be described politically as a Cold War liberal opposed to communism. Advising the American government on the future of post-war Germany, he became a member of the executive committee of the newly established Russian Research Center at Harvard in 1948, which had Kluckhohn, Parsons's close friend and colleague, as its director. Throughout the Cold War Parsons cooperated closely with the CIA, Defense Department, and the FBI in formulating policy and carrying out their operations. A bizarre twist is that Parsons himself was under the surveillance of the FBI because of his inordinate power and political orientation, which was considered by some in the Bureau to be too liberal.[84]

One noteworthy outgrowth of Parsons's approach was the theory of symbolic interaction elaborated by Erving Goffman, who outlined his ideas in his 1959 work *The Presentation of Self in Everyday Life*.[85] In the dramaturgical sociology he pioneered, Goffman argued that the elements of self-identity are dependent upon time, place, and audience. In other words, for Goffman the self is both an internalized identity and a dramatic effect emerging from the immediate scene being presented.[86] Goffman employs a theatrical metaphor in defining the method in which one human being presents himself to another based on cultural values, norms, and expectations. Goffman's ideas would later impact cultural criticism, especially Stephen Greenblatt's new historicist notions of Renaissance self-performance and Judith Butler's ideas of social performativity. [87]

Psychology

Building on the pioneer work of John Watson and the subsequent quantified experiments of B.F. Skinner in positive reinforcement, psychology promoted itself as a rigorous and quantitative behavioral discipline focused on the individual.[88] Perhaps the most important research done in the post-war period from this perspective was Harry Harlow's experiments on attachment behavior carried on at the University of Wisconsin. Basing himself on the insights of the English psychologist John Bowlby on attachment, Harlow carried out thousands of experiments on the mother-offspring relationship on monkeys which he bred for these purposes. As a result of the success of these trials Harlow was elected president of the American Psychological Association. He would later be charged with systematic cruelty toward animals by animal rights activists. Harlow had a close relationship with the American state, serving as director of the human resources department of the army.[89] The link between psychology and the state was already old, dating back to World War I. The tie became much closer between 1941 and 1945, and psychology professors then showed themselves overwhelmingly patriotic in the subsequent Cold War. With few exceptions they enthusiastically and unabashedly participated in defense-related research, which of course was government funded. No other discipline showed itself so un-self-consciously and unquestionably loyal to the state. It is difficult to say why this was so. In addition to venality and opportunism, it may be that psychologists, whose methodology was strongly individualistic, were victims of their own political naivety and had little sense of the political and ideological stakes involved in the Cold War. It is worth recording that the experience of psychoanalysts was completely different. Often of European and Jewish origin, sympathetic to the left and interested in matters of sexuality and freedom rather than social control, many psychoanalysts came under deep suspicion from the FBI.[90]

The discipline as a whole underwent extraordinary expansion. In 1947, the American Psychological Association, the major professional society for psychologists at the time, had 4,661 members. Within a decade the APA had 15,545 members, and by 1967, 25,800. Psychologists deployed both behavioral and Freudian psychology to fight the Cold War, including the use of propaganda to ensure the patriotism of Americans toward the policies of the National Security state. During the 1950s all the types of work that psychological experts had done in World War II were further institutionalized and pursued on the premises of the Department of Defense or directly on university campuses: psychological warfare studies, intelligence classification, training, clinical treatment, and "human factors" or "man-machine" engineering. Even the mysteries of military and civil morale and other fields of human relations research were vigorously pursued on the theory that, however speculative in the short run, their potential military payoff was large enough to justify the investment. By 1960, by far the major part of Department of Defense spending on the social sciences went to psychological research.[91]

The Korean War gave special impetus to studies of sensory deprivation and techniques of ideological conversion. This followed widely publicized reports of brainwashing supposedly used by the Chinese on American prisoners-of-war, including some accounts of Chinese practices by reputable scholars. Indignation was widely expressed against the purported Chinese use of such techniques, and even more against the American POWs who buckled under psychological pressure. In fact, this seems to have been a case of psychological projection. In 1956 Harlow and other psychological experts authored a U.S. Air Force study which claimed that the Chinese were amateurs and suggested how most effectively to torture prisoners.[92] Indeed, it was the United States that extensively financed brainwashing experiments from the early 1950s until the early 1970s, in a vast and illegal CIA program known as MK Ultra, much of which was carried on in university settings.[93] Academic psychologists were involved in this program. Recent revelations of torture in Iraq, Afghanistan, and Guantanamo Bay indicate that university psychologists continue to be involved in such programs.

The notion that the Chinese used brainwashing in the psychological sense is dubious. Rather, Chinese ideologists inculcated prisoners with Marxism and anti-imperialism and had some success, partly due to harsh conditions of imprisonment and the curious psychological identification of prisoners with their inquisitors, but also because of actual political circumstances. What seemed to trouble right-thinking Americans was that some POWS might have rationally decided to denounce American involvement in the Korean War, announce their conversion to communism, and refuse to return to the United States. Incredulous that Americans could behave in this way toward God's country, some concluded that this could only be the result of brainwashing. The whole affair betrays a lamentable ignorance of the actual history of the Korean conflict, the responsibility for which lies mainly with the United States, according to the most definitive history of the war written by an American academic.[94] Most of the 22 Americans who refused to go home were in fact members of the white and black working class who had suffered oppression or exploitation in their homeland.[95] The refusal to acknowledge, and the cover-up, of their real stories reflects a blindness on the part of politicians and pundits, but also academic psychologists, to the basic realities of American society and its imperialist foreign policy. Indeed, it was possible to cash in on such ignorance, with Hollywood scoring a major success in screening *The Manchurian Candidate* (1962). So successful was this political fantasy it inspired a remake in 1988.[96]

Political Science

The most influential work of political theory of the Cold War years was Hannah Arendt's *On Totalitarianism*. A German Jewish refugee, lover of the philosopher and Nazi anti-Semite Martin Heidegger, and ultimately married to a Marxist professor at Bard College, the publication of this work assured Arendt an open door at leading American universities. Her insistence on the uniqueness of the political sphere represents her major contribution to liberal political thought. Its major ideological feature was the equation of Nazi Germany and the Soviet Union as totalitarian regimes. This was tantamount to justifying the pursuit of the Cold War as a continuation of the war of American democracy against the Nazi dictatorship, which was entirely consistent with the policy objectives of the U.S. state. In Arendt's view these regimes could be considered totalitarian because they turned classes into undifferentiated masses and used propaganda and terror as key means of ensuring total control over the population while pursuing dreams of world domination. Critics have since complained that Arendt had little real understanding of how Soviet politics based on interest groups really worked, and that actual hands-on control by the regime was rather weak. Furthermore, class distinctions were not abolished in Nazi Germany, on the contrary, they were reinforced. Come to that, the supposed efficiency of the latter regime itself was confused by a lack of clear lines of authority. Furthermore, to equate the *grosse raume* policy of the Nazi regime with the external relations of the Stalinist program of socialism in one country is unsupportable. Arendt's work overall lacks a historical grasp of the genesis and specificities of the Nazi and Soviet regimes, which are characterized more by what separates than unites them.[97]

Be that as it may, the equation of the Soviet Union and Nazism by the use of the label totalitarian which served to suggest their equivalence had obvious appeal in the United States. Indeed, this equation played a key role in mobilizing the American population behind the pursuit of the Cold War. It did not hurt Arendt's reputation among powerful Americans that in a subsequent work, *On Revolution* (1961), she claimed rather facilely that the American Revolution was a success because it ended in democracy, whereas the French Revolution failed because it concluded with the Napoleonic dictatorship. Arendt ignored the history of American slavery and Jim Crow and deliberately excluded the notion of economic democracy, disdaining the possibility of deeper popular participation in government. Furthermore, the United States did not become a political democracy immediately following its revolution—far from it—while France was highly democratic already in the Jacobin period and became a liberal democratic state in 1871.

Arendt was a political theorist hostile to attempts to transform politics into a quantifiable theoretical science. In sharp contrast, the main trend in the study of politics following the war was toward making it rigorous, mathematical, and theoretical along the lines of the study of psychology or economics. American political scientists incorporated as much as possible of the behaviorist approach pioneered in psychology. In its most extreme form the quest for theory and rigor took the form of the systems approach pioneered by David Easton of the University of Chicago. Easton utilized a five-fold scheme for studying the policy-making process: input, conversion, output, feedback, and environment. The concept of "system" was the most important concept used by the American political scientists who based themselves on Easton's work, which during the 1950s was considered cutting-edge.[98] As we have seen, the systems approach was also to be seen in sociology in the work of Parsons among others.

While some political scientists like Easton sought to make their discipline more rigorous and theoretically minded, most were content with a less systematic and abstract approach. Nonetheless, three major figures— Robert Dahl, V.O. Keys, and David Truman—investigated American politics through empirical and quantitative studies of interest group politics, public opinion, and local government to understand behavior at the political grassroots, while trying to determine the link between civil society and the liberal democratic state. All three constituted a school known as majoritarian pluralism, and saw their work as by no means detached from but rather as part of an effort to secure the future of the liberal order against the threat of communism. Dahl, who became the most well-known of this trio, was interested in how democracy, which he defined as rule by competing and overlapping minorities, differed from dictatorial rule, which he defined as rule by a single cohesive minority. Democracy, as seen by Dahl, included a special role for elites, distrust of the masses, a stress on procedures and the rejection of any simple notions of the public interest. All three had in common a neglect of the class-based inequality, to say nothing of the centrality of the issue of race, in American life—questions which would burst to the surface in the 1960s. Indeed, the political science espoused by Dahl and others, while undoubtedly highly sophisticated, was designed to help control and stabilize existing society by dwelling on questions of voting, public opinion, party organization, and interest groups.

In international relations the most important change was the influence of the realist school, as exemplified in the writings of the conservative diplomat and statesman George Kennan or the more liberal academic Hans Morgenthau. Morgenthau was one of scores of German academics who fled Germany in the wake of the Nazi seizure of power, a fair number of whom specialized in international affairs. Morgenthau, who taught for many years at the University of Chicago, proved to be the most influential of the group. As part of his intellectual baggage, he brought the influence of Nietzsche, Weber, and Carl Schmitt into the study of international relations. Each of these realist German thinkers stressed the notion of the fundamentally irrational nature of politics. Ultimately, the work of intellectual refugees from Nazi Europe like Morgenthau was incorporated into the Anglo-American academic infrastructure with its particular funding structures and links to the National Security State and transnational capital. State power and the balance of power among leading nation-states were central to this realist perspective on international affairs. A corollary to these concepts was the selective promotion of the idea of national sovereignty invoked since the time of Woodrow Wilson as a counter to the threat of international Bolshevism. The goal of this approach was the maintenance of Western and more specifically Anglo-American global dominance by invoking the ideas of self-determination and national sovereignty as sacred principles. Whereas the Communist International called for unity of the working class beyond the limits of the nation, Morgenthau and other realists took their stand on the perennity of the state system and the national interest in which England and the United States ended up controlling the balance of global power.

Geography and Area Studies

As we have seen, the end of World War II meant that the United States would dominate most of the world's land mass and seas. The question of the global future of this gigantic nation-state now increasingly came to the fore. The central figure in this respect was the geographer Isaiah Bowman. Bowman trained at Harvard and taught at Yale from 1905 to 1925. He was chief territorial adviser to President Woodrow Wilson during the Versailles Conference, and became a director of the new Council on Foreign Relations created by the Rockefeller Foundation. The latter became the major foreign affairs think-tank and the principal conduit of influence with respect to foreign affairs for the American business community. Bowman served as president of Johns Hopkins University from 1935 to 1948 while continuing his role as an influential academic adviser to the government. Before and during World War II he served on the Council of Foreign Relations as part of its territorial group and chairman of the Council's Committee on War and Peace Studies. From 1945 to 1949 he was a vice-president of the Council.

Bowman's influence was based on the rising power of the United States as reflected in the outcome of the two world wars. As he conceived it, builders of empires in the making like that of the United States must take into account questions of space as well as time. It was this perspective that he brought to bear on the intensive wartime discussions in the Council of Foreign Relations which envisioned the expansion of U.S. direct influence over a "Grand Area."[99] By 1943 Bowman had arrived at the view that a geographical extension of U.S. power over the globe in the post-war period was inevitable. The real "question was where it would stop."[100] While recognizing the need to create a new international framework for the maintenance of peace, Bowman stressed the urgency of securing American economic interests as paramount.[101] Indeed, at the conclusion of the war America's requirements for overseas markets and access to raw materials, and especially overseas oil, had become pressing. Although Bowman himself was skeptical, his geographical perspective set the stage for the emergence of the field of area studies in universities which sought to delimit those regions of vital concern to American strategic interests.

Geopolitical concerns tended to mesh with those of the field of international relations. The intelligence connections of international relations which had deepened during World War II were carried forward when peace arrived. When the CIA was created in 1947, out of the wartime Office of Strategic Services, centralizing the flow of information from the international relations discipline was one of its major tasks. In 1965, the president of the International Studies Association, John Gange, recalled that the OSS "was like a big university faculty in many respects—sometimes, staff meetings were just like faculty meetings." Prominent figures within the field of international relations such as Max Millikan, Klaus Knorr,

Robert Bowie, Philip E. Mosely (then director of studies of the Council on Foreign Relations), Hamilton Fish Armstrong (editor of its quarterly, *Foreign Affairs*), along with various historians and Soviet specialists, worked through the 1950s and 1960s for the head of the CIA, Allen Dulles. Nation-building expert and Asia specialist Lucian W. Pye, of MIT, joined this elite-body, known as the "Princeton Consultants," later in the 1960s. The director of the Carnegie Institution, Caryl P. Haskins, and Harold F. Linder, assistant secretary of state and chair of the Export-Import Bank, were also participants.[102]

Already during World War II, largely at the prompting of the U.S. government, there had developed so-called area study programs, a kind of hands-on interdisciplinary political science which played a still larger role in the Cold War especially with regard to protecting America's interests in the underdeveloped world.[103] As we have seen, in 1941 Donovan, the head of the OSS, decided to draw on the academic community to assemble a strong team of intelligence experts to contribute to the war effort. Donovan invited representatives of the Social Science Research Council (SSRC) and the American Council of Learned Societies (ACLS), dominated by establishment academics, to help him draw up a "slate of academic advisors" for this purpose. By the time he was done Donovan had compiled a list of hundreds of leading academics and young scholars. Many of these individuals went on to play a key role in intelligence activities during the fight against fascism and then returned to academe while retaining their connections with the CIA post-war.[104] In addition to cooperating with Donovan on intelligence in the narrow sense, the Social Science Research Council and the American Council of Learned Societies also began working collaboratively with the United States military and intelligence communities to expand the conventional meaning of intelligence beyond its normal bounds.

These academic councils argued that, in light of the direct responsibilities the United States was about to assume for the "well-being" of the entire planet, knowledge about other peoples and places in every corner of the globe should be considered a matter of "intelligence." Indeed, the intelligence function was always central to the development of area studies. Furthermore, the councils asserted, the United States was sorely lacking in the expertise necessary to gather this intelligence—as a result of which the country put its interests at great risk. The expertise then available took the form of anthropological and orientalist scholarship, which assumed the timeless character of primitive peoples or the subjects of "oriental" empires like China and India.[105] The SSRC was determined to remedy these problems and laid out its vision for doing so in a 1943 document entitled "World Regions in the Social Sciences." The Council's plan to resolve the country's crisis of intelligence and security was based on the deployment of a novel classificatory discourse—one that brought all the peoples and cultures of the world into a single ordering schema in which the constituent units were discrete, bounded cultural regions. "World Regions in the Social Sciences" prescribed the kind of intelligence that should be gathered about these regional units. It also provided a rationale for ranking the regions according to their geopolitical significance. Finally, the report advised on how to train experts who could generate the much-needed intelligence about these regions.

What emerges out of the "World Regions" document is a plan for the institutionalization of a new geography of knowledge and power. The report begins by arguing that the rapidly changing geopolitical concerns of the United States called for the production of a new kind of knowledge on an unprecedented scale. It went on to argue that the need for a greatly expanded corpus of knowledge about unfolding conditions around the globe was something which should not be limited to the period of the war itself. Rather, once the fighting came to an end the safety and security of U.S. interests abroad would depend critically on the continued production of such knowledge. Although the Council planners recommended that U.S. education as a whole be revamped to train the experts needed to manage imperial domains, the special focus of reform efforts should be the creation of new institutes in major universities that could provide advanced training in each of the world's major areas.

Discussions about the relation between area knowledge and the extension of American overseas power continued after the war. A combination of Cold War politics and decolonization movements in Africa and Asia appeared to threaten U.S. interests on all sides, and made it abundantly clear that knowledge about seemingly far-off people and places did indeed have a strategic dimension. In this context, in the immediate aftermath of World War II, high-ranking officials at the Ford and Rockefeller Foundations and at the Carnegie Endowment arranged a series of meetings to discuss what was to be done. In the late 1940s the foundations began to make good on this vision. In 1947 the SSRC published a new report reiterating the strategic importance of area knowledge. The following year, area studies got off to a modest beginning when the Carnegie Endowment helped the SSRC launch its first program of area studies research and training.

As the Cold War heated up during the 1950s, joint SSRC/ACLS committees focused on specific world areas came to dominate the funding activities of both organizations and continued to do so for decades. There were ultimately eleven joint SSRC/ACLS area studies committees: Slavic, Latin American studies, Near and Middle Eastern studies, contemporary China, African studies, Japanese studies, Korean studies, Eastern Europe, South Asia, Western Europe, and Southeast Asia. With generous financial support provided by the foundations, these joint committees were instrumental in making area studies the dominant perspective in the social sciences. It was the Ford Foundation, however, that was to take the lead role in creating a new post-war geography of knowledge. At the dawn of the Cold War, Ford embarked on a project of truly massive proportions to create a new infrastructure of training, research and publishing in the social sciences. Using the two SSRC reports on world regions/area studies as a blueprint, Ford's Division of International Training and Research (1952) began building interdisciplinary, advanced-degree-granting area studies institutes at major universities throughout the United States. By 1966, when Ford discontinued the program, it had succeeded in building institutes at 34 leading universities, including Columbia, Harvard, Yale, Princeton, Berkeley, Chicago, and Michigan. The Foundation spent $120 million dollars on the endeavor.

The Splendid Isolation of American Academe

Looking back at this decade and a half (1945–60) the record of American universities is impressive. They had become important national institutions, opening up the possibility of higher education and social mobility to the middle class and some elements of the working class, and in so doing deepening American political democracy. Faculties and departments rapidly expanded and for the first time the United States forged ahead of the rest of the world in research, not only in science and technology but also in the humanities and social sciences. Real advances were made in the creation of new knowledge across the board, and this new knowledge, however instrumental and ideological, was nonetheless quite real. Moreover, the humanities and social sciences offered a spirited defense of liberal democracy and capitalism. What made this possible was the tremendous economic growth and prosperity of the post-war U.S. economy, to which the universities contributed highly skilled labor and new knowledge. What is striking though is how fragmented that knowledge was, based on a division of labor between compartmentalized departments, despite efforts to develop interdisciplinary approaches at the level of area studies or the behavioral sciences. Likewise, the learning and research pursued had an instrumental and professionalized quality which put it at a far remove from the life of ordinary citizens. Indeed, much of it was designed to bedazzle and control rather than to empower them.

Marxism was strictly out of bounds. Even an iconoclast like Leslie White hesitated to proclaim his historical materialist outlook. To be sure there continued to be Marxist intellectuals in America like those around the journal *Science & Society*, some of whose contributors like Aptheker had ties to the Communist Party. The independent Marxist group that published the journal *Monthly Review* bravely pursued a historical materialist outlook largely outside of the academic mainstream. There was the outstanding maverick at Columbia, the sociologist C. Wright Mills, who in the middle of the 1950s produced a masterful analysis of American society, *The Power Elite*, which was Marxist in all but name.[106] Rejecting the consensus view of American society that dominated sociology and political science, Mills described all facets of American society as dominated by an integrated economic, political, and military elite whose power crushed the mass of the population. Indeed, as Mill approached his premature death from heart disease, he more and more openly espoused Marxism, defending the Cuban Revolution, and as a result came under FBI surveillance.[107] There was also the University of Wisconsin historian William Appleman Williams, who in 1959 produced a convincing Marxist analysis of the history of American imperialism.[108] The intellectual power of these works presaged the explosion of Marxism of the 1960s, but at this point they were marginal.

The United States remained isolated from the extraordinary explosion of creative Marxist thought in the rest of the world that marked the 1950s. The end of the decade saw the publication of *Culture and Society*, the first important work of criticism by the still unknown English literary critic Raymond Williams, whose major aim was to show how bourgeois society had turned culture or the life of a people into an abstraction and an absolute.[109] As a result of the Cold War, American intellectual life was also cut off from the explosion of new historiography being created by the British Marxist historians E.P. Thompson, Christopher Hill, Eric Hobsbawm and Rodney Hilton.[110] The great synthesis of French revolutionary history by the communist historian Soboul was openly derided by U.S. historians.[111] American academics knew next to nothing of the theorizing of the French communist philosopher Louis Althusser and the urbanist and theorist Henri Lefebvre.[112] The revival of the thought of Antonio Gramsci that was occurring in Italy was scarcely known in America, the first translation of his work coming out in 1957.[113] The German Marxist philosopher Ernst Bloch wrote his masterpiece *The Principle of Hope* in the Widener Library at Harvard as a fugitive from Nazism while working in complete isolation. Published in Germany at the end of the 1950s it appeared in English only in 1986. The thought of the great literary critic and theoretician Gyorgy Lukács remained beyond the ken of scholars in the United States until the beginning of the 1970s.[114] Acclaimed Soviet thinkers like philosopher Evald Ilyenkov, literary theorist Mikhail Bakhtin, ecologist V.N. Sukachev and social psychologist Lev Vykotsky were virtually unheard of. The insights of third world and anti-racist theorists like C.L.R. James—expelled from the United States—and Frantz Fanon were unknown to American scholars except perhaps those in the CIA. Not to speak of the thought of Mao Zedong, whose insightful analysis of the conditions for making third world revolution was more or less proscribed. Indeed, this closure reflected the essentially "reactionary" or "hear no evil" response of America to the threat of Marxist-inspired revolution globally, and especially to upheaval in the underdeveloped world.

Reviewing academic research in the United States during the 1950s one takes note rather of the tendency toward methodological individualism, positivism, and instrumentalism in the social sciences which tended to put weapons in the hands of those who wielded economic and political power. Professors, whether they knew it or not, worked for capitalism. Anthropology, political science, and sociology did take a systematic view of society, but the dominant schools tend to deny the reality of imperialism, class, and historical change. Sociology, in particular through the influence of Parsons, took on a scholastic and static quality. As the systems approach did not include a sense of contradiction it tended to view society atemporally or without a sense of historicity. The historical aspect of all these fields of study was largely omitted. The historians themselves likewise tended to minimize the importance of class conflict in America. The phenomenon of revolution could not be ignored, but it was viewed not as a feature of the global historical process but as an affliction whose symptoms should be treated. Literature meanwhile was essentially aestheticized and insofar as possible divorced from social relations and historical change.

The suppression of a sense of the historicity of society and knowledge is what is most striking.[115] Herbert Marcuse's *One Dimensional Man*, published in the early 1960s, best captured this state of affairs. Thoroughly imbued with Hegelian Marxism, Marcuse, who had become a prisoner of American academic life, was deeply pessimistic about the possibility of transformative change or change based on a critical negation of both consumerism and instrumentalized knowledge:

To the degree to which freedom from want, the concrete substance of all freedom, is becoming a real possibility, the liberties which pertain to a state of lower productivity are losing their former content. Independence of thought, autonomy, and the right to political opposition are being deprived of their basic critical function in a society which seems increasingly capable of satisfying the needs of the individuals through the way in which it is organized. Such a society may justly demand acceptance of its principles and institutions, and reduce the opposition to the discussion and promotion of alternative policies within the status quo. In this respect, it seems to make little difference whether the increasing satisfaction of needs is accomplished by an authoritarian or a non-authoritarian system. Under the conditions of a rising standard of living, non-conformity with the system itself appears to be socially useless, and the more so when it entails tangible economic and political disadvantages and threatens the smooth operation of the whole.[116]

According to Marcuse, these developments had led to the imposition of a form of totalitarian control and a complete repression of critical thought. Society seemed frozen in time with no apparent historical exit from the existing repressive order of things. It was ironic that Marcuse published this despairing work just as the revolt of the 1960s was about to get under way and Marcuse himself elevated to the status of its guru.

3

The Sixties

As the 1960s began, universities had become an integral part of an American society dominated by giant corporations and the military. Massive increases in student enrollment and government-funded research helped to swell the power and size of university bureaucracies. Their mission was primarily to mobilize the intellectual and technical resources of the universities to serve the interests of business and the armed forces, including the provision of plentiful supplies of educated managers, supervisors, professionals, teachers, and salaried workers. The new knowledge produced in science and technology and also in the humanities and social sciences was designed ultimately to serve and to bolster business and the National Security State. This knowledge included the ideologies, strategies, and tactics required to suppress radical change in the increasingly restless underdeveloped countries as well as at home. Domestically, Marxists or other dissidents within or outside of academe who might have challenged these goals had been purged or silenced.

Students, however, who had mainly stayed mute during the McCarthy period, suddenly abandoned their passivity and rebelled in large numbers against the corporate university while attempting to change society at large. Their uprisings were inspired in the first place by the civil rights movement, but were then reinforced by the anti-imperialist struggle in Vietnam and the anti-war movement at home. Student protest broadened as a result of the emergence of the Black Power and women's movements. As sites of corporate and academic power, the universities proved surprisingly effective launching platforms for ideological and social movements that resonated broadly in American society, challenging the existing political and social order. Black, women's, Chicano, Asian, and gay and lesbian study programs were introduced into the curriculum as a result of student demands. In a case of the return of the repressed, Marxism spread more widely than hitherto both in and outside the classrooms. The writings of third world Marxist revolutionaries like Mao, Ho Chi Minh, Fidel Castro, and Frantz Fanon, as well as the British Marxist historians and the Frankfurt School, were incorporated into the social sciences and humanities curriculums. Meanwhile a tide of demands for the liberalization and democratization of university governance was contained by a combination of concessions and repression.

The struggle of the students did not lead to the development of a broad-based revolutionary politics in the United States, but it did help to advance the civil rights struggle and frustrate America's imperialist ambitions in Vietnam. It also forced universities to liberalize their rules, broaden their curriculums, and become more inclusive with respect to women, blacks, and other identity groups. Contrary to conservative opinion bemoaning the campus radicalism, universities in the United States at the end of the 1960s were far more cosmopolitan and stronger institutions than they were at the beginning of that decade.

It is the contention of this chapter then that the campus unrest of the 1960s was based on an uprising from below coming from black and white students. In the course of this upheaval the foundations of American universities and indeed American society were threatened. The student revolt led to a more inclusive university and opened a space within which Marxist ideology and scholarship were able temporarily to enter the mainstream of American culture and higher education. In contrast to the scholarship of the 1950s, a Marxist-inspired history came to the fore affecting not only the discipline of history but spilling over into sociology, anthropology, and literature.

We take the view that the movement initiated by the events at the Berkeley campus of the University of California constituted a struggle over nothing less than the purposes of creating knowledge. In that sense the protests at Berkeley that spread to other campuses during the 1960s were of enduring importance. They prefigured the emergence of so-called cognitive capitalism toward the close of the twentieth century in which the accumulation of an ever increasing abundance of knowledge is at one at the same time vital to capital and constrained by it, i.e., forced to remain within the boundaries of commodification and profitability. Insofar as knowledge continues to be limited by the demands of capitalism, it is narrowed, distorted, and debased. In cognitive capitalism knowledge workers occupy a strategic economic and political position, while their social and economic condition is rendered more and more insecure as a result of the increasingly precarious situation of knowledge and other producers within the system. At the same time their education, skills, and increasingly strategic location within the capitalist accumulation process give knowledge producers significant and perhaps decisive political leverage.[1] It is our contention that the struggle at Berkeley in the 1960s foreshadowed this situation.

Berkeley in the Vanguard

California became the most populated state of the Union during the 1950s. That state had long been in the vanguard of social and cultural change in America. Its economy grew rapidly, sparked by government spending on defense, electronics, and aerospace industries. Economic expansion was accompanied by a massive increase in student enrollments and in research, much of the latter on projects funded by the military. At the leading edge of this expansion was the University of California, whose example was looked to by universities across the United States. When the liberal economist Clark Kerr became president in 1958, the university already comprised eight units—the Berkeley flagship, the campuses at Los Angeles, Santa Barbara, Davis, and Riverside, the San Francisco Medical Center, the Scripps Institution of Oceanography, and Hastings College of the Law. The system expanded with the creation of new general campuses at San Diego, Irvine, and Santa Cruz.

Kerr authored the Master Plan (1960) which called for universal and affordable access to higher education for citizens of California based on a three-tiered system of community colleges, state colleges, and universities. Although the system was surprisingly open in appearance, working-class and minority students who came from disadvantaged backgrounds were effectively consigned to its lower tiers. The apparent success of the Plan allowed Kerr to become a spokesman for university expansion nationwide, and the California Master Plan the model for similar state-wide systems of higher education in Massachusetts and the state of New York. Kerr's views became widely known through his celebrated book *The Uses of the University*, published in 1963.[2] According to Kerr, the future of the university across America, which the developing California system foreshadowed, would inevitably be that of a multi-university. Kerr pictured the future university as a city of infinite variety. It was a place in which there would be less sense of community than in the traditional institution of higher learning, but also a place that was less restrictive than the old university and in which there would be many more ways to excel.[3]

This new university was characterized by multiple sub-units and by the need to serve different constituencies. Marked by pluralism it lacked a unifying mission, but Kerr considered this to be its strength.[4] Knowledge had become central to society and the university as producer, wholesaler, and retailer of knowledge could not escape service to society at large.[5] Universities were now part of the knowledge industry, which already produced an estimated 29 percent of GDP, and its role was destined to become even more important. Indeed, universities were becoming more like certain segments of industry.[6] The university's ultimate purpose was to create useful knowledge. The American university had become the nexus of the "invisible product" of new knowledge that, according to Kerr's vision, would serve as a catalyst for social and economic development, raising the standard of living and transforming society. The university trained the experts and professionals who kept society running. Indeed, the university's production of knowledge affected everyone—to the point that, Kerr argued, it could even cause the rise and fall of states. Kerr's vision of the role and governance of higher education was premised on the reality that he himself served the elite that dominated the board of regents.[7]

In Kerr's view the role of students in the multi-university should be passive: they were at university to learn or to submit themselves to a discipline in order to acquire knowledge. But he held out to them the consoling fact that the elective system made it possible for them to act as consumers, helping by their choices to determine in which direction the university should grow and which professors should be rewarded.[8] Such a role, including the right to choose which products to consume, was of course entirely familiar to students from suburban and consumerist California. Students' passivity during their university years, it was suggested, would be rewarded by their future role as overseers of other people's labor or practitioners of highly skilled and relatively well-paid work. Kerr admitted that students in the multi-university were sometimes confused and had difficulty finding a sense of security and an identity in such a gigantic place. On the other hand, they had a vast range of choices and were able to enjoy "the opportunities and dilemmas of freedom." Admittedly "the casualty rate was high."[9] Kerr conceded that the undergraduates were restless as a result of too many rules and restrictions and neglect by faculty who were preoccupied by their research. The implication was that since academics were irresponsible about taking care of mundane things including the lives of their students, administrators reluctantly had to pick up the slack. But in passing, he noted disapprovingly that there were some students who even wanted to turn the university into a fortress from which to attack society.[10]

While Kerr noted a certain dissatisfaction among students experiencing the multi-university, what he had not foreseen was that the mass university at Berkeley and elsewhere—which was meant to serve the interests of capital and the Cold War state and which was controlled by a bureaucratic elite—held the potential to create a strong democratic movement composed of more or less politically conscious and alienated students. Unwittingly, the needs of capital and the state had brought together large numbers of young people at Berkeley with the curiosity, education, and energy to question the institutional structure they were enmeshed in and ultimately to cast into doubt the whole social order.

It was the student-based Free Speech Movement (FSM) at Berkeley that proved to be Kerr's nemesis. It broke through the silence and political conformity of students on American college campuses, the perpetuation of which Kerr took for granted. The Movement was provoked by a group of powerful individuals scarcely mentioned by Kerr, namely, administrators. As Kerr pictured them, university administrators were merely benign and discreet servants who assisted the students and faculty. In fact, the managers operating under Kerr's direction controlled the university.

Presidents or chairmen and advisers of student organizations received a letter from the dean of students, Katherine A. Towle, dated September 14, 1964, announcing that, effective from September 21, by order of the university's regents, tables would no longer be permitted in the 26-foot strip of university property at the Bancroft and Telegraph campus entrance and that literature and activities on off-campus political issues also would be prohibited.[11] This space at the gate of the university had long served as a kind of Hyde Park that made it possible for students to acquaint themselves with and to debate a variety of political issues. This was clearly an attempt to close down this political space and sanitize the grounds of the public university from contact with the politics of society at large.

A series of protests that led to the suspension of several students culminated on October 1, 1964. Mimeographed fliers appeared on campus that day calling for student and faculty support for the suspended students and announcing a "Free Speech Rally" at noon on Sproul Hall steps. At approximately 10 a.m. two tables were set up outside Sather Gate, and one at the foot of Sproul Hall steps. At 11:45 a.m. deans George S. Murphy and Peter Van Houten, along with university police Lieutenant Merrill F. Chandler, approached and spoke to a man who was soliciting funds at a table for an important civil rights organization, the Congress for Racial Equality (CORE), at the foot of Sproul Hall steps. The man, later identified as Jack Weinberg, a former student, refused to identify himself or to leave the table. Lieutenant Chandler arrested the man for trespassing. Weinberg went limp. Instead of carrying him into the campus police headquarters in Sproul Hall, university police moved a police car into the area where students were gathering for the noon rally. The crowd chanted "Release him! Release him!" About 100 students lay down in front of the police car, another 80 or so sat behind it. One of the student leaders, Mario Savio, removed his shoes and climbed on top of it, urging the gathering crowd to gather round. By noon, about 300 demonstrators surrounded the immobile police car; by 12:30 p.m., several thousand students were crowded around the car, which became the focal point and rostrum for the next 32 hours of student demonstrations. The subsequent protests, occupations, and mass arrests crystallized into the Free Speech Movement, which received the support of the majority of students at Berkeley and in one form or another initiated mass protest across university campuses in the United States.

The ensuing crisis at Berkeley led to an enormous outpouring of pamphlets. One of the more notable was by the long-time Trotskyist and freelance Marxist scholar and revolutionary Hal Draper, entitled "The Mind of Clark Kerr."[12] In it Draper castigated Kerr's vision of the university as that of a corporation at the service of business and the military, in which administrators control the institution as its managers. According to Draper, Kerr's conception of the university is that of a factory which produces knowledge in the same way as a sausage factory produces sausages. Indeed, in the *Uses of the University* Kerr had matter-of-factly linked the way the University of California operated and the way that sectors of private industry functioned. Draper denounced Kerr's regime as a tyranny over the students and faculty, and his critique became the common opinion among Berkeley students and their sympathizers. Important to the development of the confrontation was the axiomatic assumption of the administrators and the regents that the Berkeley campus was a form of private property closed off from society at large. The claim of the Free Speech Movement, on the contrary, was that as a public institution of higher learning it was or should be a form of common space or public commons. In this respect the struggle foreshadowed the struggle for the commons which was to become a feature of the 1960s and was to re-emerge in the Occupy Movement that marked the period 2011–12.

Calvin Trillin, whose no doubt well-intentioned speciality is to make light of serious matters, inadvertently makes this point in an article on the Free Speech Movement for *The New Yorker* (March 1965). As he entered the main gate of the Berkeley campus he recalls that

> by the time I had crossed the sidewalk to the tables, standup hawkers had presented me with a flyer announcing the picketing of Oakland restaurants by the Congress of Racial Equality, a flyer asking for contributions to raise bail for some earlier demonstrators from the Ad Hoc Committee to End Discrimination, and a homemade pamphlet called "Some Organizing Ideas: Excerpts from Idea Essay by Lee Felsenstein." The table at one end of the line was sponsored by the Young Socialist

Alliance, an organization that is ordinarily referred to as Trotskyist, though few people seem to know just what the implications of that position are in Berkeley, California, in 1965. The Y.S.A. table was being watched over rather casually by a collegiate-looking young man in a blue blazer; he was reading a book, but would glance up occasionally at students who stopped to look at his display, which included leaflets in Support of a local City Council candidate, pamphlets introducing the Y.S.A., and a number of booklets on the order of "Fidel Castro Denounces Bureaucracy and Sectarianism, Speech of March 26." The Y.S.A. table was separated from the table of Slate, a campus political party of left wing but non-sectarian views, by a cardboard sign announcing that placards for the CORE picketing of Oakland restaurants would be made on the steps of Sproul Hall, the administration building, the following afternoon. A young man wearing a lapel button reading "Free Oakland Now" was sitting behind the Slate table and calling out at intervals that he was selling the "Slate Supplement," a student critique of the university's courses.[13]

Clearly these groups each had their separate agendas which more often than not were in debate with one another. The way Trillin pictured the scene for subscribers to *The New Yorker*, the young activists at the Berkeley front gate were no doubt well-meaning but sooner or later ineffectual and useless in the face of the powers-that-be. As part of the Free Speech Movement, however, they collectively offered students a comprehensive critique of the existing political and economic order which in itself could be an education or the beginnings of one. By contrast, as Kerr admitted, the university for the most part offered an incoherent, fragmented, and instrumentalized form of knowledge which it controlled, designed to underpin rather than to understand and transform existing society. These very different forms of knowledge were at the heart of the Berkeley struggle.

Implicit in Draper's analysis was that Kerr was correct in pointing to the economic importance of the knowledge industry of which the University of California was a key part. Mario Savio, who emerged as the leader of the Free Speech Movement, in his famous speech at the birth of the Movement a few months later, at first described the university not as a private corporation but as the vital training ground and laboratory for private corporations. But, accepting the comparison between the university and the private corporation, he then concluded: "well I ask you to consider—if this is a firm, and if the Board of Regents are the Board of Directors, and if President Kerr in fact is the manager, then I tell you something—the faculty are a bunch of employees and we're the raw material!"[14]

In a certain sense Draper, Savio, and Kerr agreed with one another. The university had evolved into an institution which closely resembled a modern corporation. Knowledge was a productive force whose importance would only increase. The basic question that the conflict at Berkeley foreshadowed or prefigured was whether such knowledge would continue to be controlled by the existing economic and political elites, or would be democratized and put into the service of building a more egalitarian and peaceful society in which knowledge was no longer subject to commodification. Moreover, as subsequent developments are demonstrating, the insurgent student position was by no means destructive or disruptive. It foreshadowed the way forward both politically and economically, whereas the bureaucratized, instrumentalized, and eventually commodified knowledge under elite and capitalist control itself has become part of the impasse that blocks the further advance of society. The knowledge economy is the way forward. But because of capitalism's dependence on wage labor, commodities, and profit it produces an economy based on knowledge capitalism, which is a fundamentally constricted and even destructive form of knowledge.[15]

It has been argued that the development of student-led revolutionary protest as seen in the Berkeley Free Speech Movement and in so many other places across America and the globe reflected a weakening of the potential for socialist revolution based on the industrial wage worker of the nineteenth and early twentieth centuries. Students lacked the political punch of revolutionary movements organized by industrial workers.[16] Undoubtedly there is a certain truth to this in that it was to prove a weakness that student movements like that at Berkeley (if not Paris) could not extend their influence beyond a certain point in existing consumerist society, or connect with the traditional white working class *in the short run*. On the other hand, it has to be kept in mind that the worker-based revolutionary movements that were born in the revolutions of 1848—revolutions which also failed—were themselves new in their time, as the young Marx underlined. Moreover, like the students in the 1960s those movements were led by the most skilled and politically conscious craftsmen who themselves were profoundly troubled by the future implications of the unprecedented development of industrial capitalism. In fact, many who supported the 1848 revolutions had aspirations to upward social mobility, but were destined to become fully proletarianized as part of a fully developed industrial capitalism that eventually engulfed them. They were resisting further proletarianization in a way that resembles the struggle of academics today to hold onto the remains of their autonomy and professional status under the onslaught of neoliberal academic capitalism, or of students struggling to maintain their place in the middle class.[17] Viewing the upheavals of 1960s from the present it can be argued that the decade represented the start of a new phase of capitalism based on the labor power of knowledge workers, including academics who have come to assume increasing economic importance within the context of the late twentieth-century restructuring of capitalism. In this context the role of producers in universities, or those formed by institutions of higher learning, became more and more central to the economy, while the actual status and security of such well-educated producers has become increasingly precarious and their labor degraded by the dynamics of capital. Is it going too far to suggest that the students who revolted in the 1960s represented a prefigurative anticipation of these developments at least analogous to the fate of artisan workers in the revolutions of 1848?[18]

In the *Uses of the University* Kerr acknowledged the presence of those around Berkeley who wanted to turn the university into a citadel from which to attack the existing social order. Indeed, the student body and the town included a large number of leftist sympathizers including Communist Party, Du Bois Club, and Socialist Worker Party members who were to assume leadership roles in the FSM. Moreover, by the early 1960s the doctrinal differences separating the various leftist elements had softened, making possible a less ideological approach in the FSM, which included a minority even from the Goldwater youth wing of the Republican Party.[19] Meanwhile, activist students in recent years had protested the inquisitorial investigations of the California legislature's anti-American investigation committee as well as that of the U.S. House Un-American Activities Committee. The hearings of the latter had led to serious rioting in San Francisco in 1960. Also prominent in Berkeley was the Fair Play for Cuba Committee, defending the Cuban Revolution. Last but not least were the civil rights organizers especially those involved in the Congress of Racial Equality.

Kerr's memoirs take note of this radical element among students, but also signal the legacy of the loyalty oath controversy of the 1950s, which deeply alienated the more progressive elements of the faculty from the university administration.[20] Many of these professors were to be found in the humanities, which was losing ground to the sciences and technology in terms of power and influence, and these academics resented their declining leverage. Berkeley was also deeply involved in projects funded by the military, including the Lawrence Radiation Laboratory, which played a key role in the development of nuclear weapons. This body had itself become embroiled in politics as a result of the feud between the right-wing scientist

Edward Teller and the prominent leftist Robert Oppenheimer. As a result of these conflicts a significant portion of the faculty was alienated from the administration and prepared to lend their support to student protest.[21] The tactics of the FSM played on this alienation. The result was that the majority of the faculty supported the students on the question of free political speech on campus. As a result, the administration was forced to give way. The outcome of the free speech protests at Berkeley led to the widening of the space for politics and activism there and on other university campuses, especially in the wake of the large-scale U.S. invasion of Vietnam in 1965. Enough of the faculty, disgruntled by their treatment at the hands of the administrators and sympathetic to some of the political demands of the students, stood with the student protestors to ensure victory. But what is notable is that throughout the campus upheavals of the 1960s faculty either stood back or tailed the initiatives taken by students. There were of course a minority who were prepared to throw their lot in with the student radicals. But most followed in their wake or held aloof.

The Civil Rights Movement

Undoubtedly the Free Speech Movement and the nationwide student protests that followed were a product of the contradictions and frustrations of student life in the corporate university and the revolt against Cold War political conformity. But the spark which ignited the revolt lay in the civil rights movement which galvanized students both white and black into activism from the early 1960s onward. This was no prefigurative struggle, but an actual bitter fight for racial equality that engulfed American society in the late 1950s and 1960s. In the months leading up to the Free Speech Movement there occurred a series of desegregation protests that shook the San Francisco Bay area. The largest and most boisterous was a blockade of the Sheraton Palace Hotel in San Francisco for its discriminatory practices, in which many students from Berkeley took part and were arrested. These demonstrations which received wide publicity prepared the ground for the Free Speech Movement attuning students to the issue of civil rights and providing a precedent for action. The Bay area demonstrations were part of a response to the Birmingham protests led by Martin Luther King in the spring of 1963, which were echoed by almost 1,000 demonstrations in 115 cities nationwide.[22] Indeed Savio was himself a veteran of the civil rights struggle in the South in which white volunteers joined with blacks in Freedom Summer under the auspices of the Student Non-Violent

Coordinating Committee (SNCC). From the SNCC Savio learned the importance of both grassroots organizing and group decision-making.[23]

Contrary to general belief, the struggle for black educational rights did not begin with the Brown versus the Board of Education Decision of the U.S. Supreme Court in 1954. That decision was the culmination of a much longer struggle based in the black community. The civil rights movement had several roots including ties to the black churches, the NAACP, the Communist Party, and the black colleges. By the 1950s there were over 100 historically black colleges located mainly in the segregated southern states. Deprived of resources though they were, these institutions provided young students with a distinctive black consciousness which paralleled that found in black churches throughout the South. During the first part of the twentieth century, black student groups protested against white paternalist control of these colleges, which essentially normalized segregation imposing a highly moralistic code of conduct and a Eurocentric curriculum on students. Despite the great difficulties under which the black population of the United States lived, during the 1920s student enrollment in black colleges and universities increased by 50,000 annually, quintupling over the decade.[24] In the 1930s the civil rights struggle became increasingly politicized as a result of the activities of the communist-led American Student Union and Southern Negro Youth Congress as well as the NAACP and the CORE.[25]

The post-war period saw a further surge in black enrollment into both black and white institutions of higher learning. Growing impatience with the restrictions of official and unofficial segregation became apparent particularly among the increasingly large educated black population. As part of the global black diaspora American blacks were aware of the rise of the anti-colonial movement in the West Indies and Africa. The Brown versus Board of Education decision then was immediately followed by the Birmingham Bus Boycott led by the seamstress Rosa Parks, who was secretary of the local chapter of the NAACP (1955–6) and a veteran political activist. The next year saw the foundation of Martin Luther King's Southern Christian Leadership Conference (SCLC). King's organization, based on a highly organized grassroots network of black churches throughout the South, took the lead in organizing the desegregation movement south of the Mason-Dixon Line. The year 1957 saw the Little Rock High School crisis which forced the national government to send troops into that city in order to enforce desegregation. But this crisis, which became the focus of national media attention, came in the midst of a developing wave of sit-ins throughout the South and Midwest between 1956–60.[26] The sit-in at the

Woolworth's counter in Greensboro, North Carolina, by four local college students from the North Carolina Agricultural and Technical College in February 1960 was the culmination of this ascending wave. Within a week, protests and sit-ins spread rapidly across the South and into the North.[27]

The techniques of Gandhian non-violent resistance which marked the sit-ins were pioneered by a black seminarian, James Lawson, who had encountered them on a visit to India. Hired by Martin Luther King, Lawson taught them to black student volunteers in workshops in Nashville and elsewhere in the South.[28] The black churches were closely tied to the SCLC and worked in concert with the black colleges. Many of those who joined the sit-ins were students in the black colleges. The Greensboro protest quickly drew in hundreds of students from the neighboring area, in which there were ten black colleges. Many of these students were also members of church congregations. In North Carolina ministers were often alumni of the theological faculties of these colleges and a similar pattern existed across the South.[29]

In the wake of the Greensboro protest, Ella Baker, a former student activist and now first executive secretary of SCLC, called a conference at her alma mater Shaw College in Raleigh, North Carolina, to begin organizing the burgeoning student movement. It met on April 15–17 with 200 students from 50 colleges and high schools in attendance. In her introductory speech Baker encouraged the students to create their own organization based on group-centered rather than personal leadership. The meeting then formed the Student Non-Violent Coordinating Committee (SNCC), which dedicated itself to non-violent activism and grassroots democracy. Along with other civil rights organizations it then joined the Voter Registration Project sponsored by the Kennedy administration in 1961. The Washington administration hoped that the Voter Registration Project would shift the focus of the black students away from demonstrations and more toward the support of voter registration.

The SNCC was particularly active in trying to register black voters in Mississippi where white resistance was most intense. Friends of SNCC groups and other new campus civil rights groups based on university campuses in the north and west raised money for southern campaigns, sponsored speakers, and protested against de facto segregation outside the South. A bitter desegregation struggle at Albany, Georgia, in which the SNCC played a leading part, ended in failure and the first signs of tension between the SNCC leaders and Martin Luther King appeared. In the fall of 1962 James Merideth, a grandson of slaves, successfully enrolled at the University of Mississippi as thousands of troops occupied the campus in order to protect him from the fierce resistance of large numbers of white protesters.[30] During 1963 black college students, angered by growing white resistance to desegregation in the South and North, moved toward campus activism and black power with campus protests at Jackson State, Alcorn State, Norfolk State, and Howard University. A meeting in early May organized by the Afro-American Student Movement, an offshoot of the SNCC at Fisk University, proved a catalyst in the transition from civil rights agitation to black power.[31]

Students for a Democratic Society

The black civil rights movement powerfully affected white activists. We have already noted its impact on Mario Savio and others at Berkeley. It had a similar impact on student activists at the University of Michigan who created the Students for a Democratic Society (SDS), the signature organization of the New Left and the focal point of anti-war protest. From its founding, SNCC activists began to visit northern college campuses to gather support for its desegregation campaign. The early leader of SDS was the Michigan political activist Al Haber, who for some years had been a member of a small group known as the Student League for Industrial Democracy, an off-shoot of the League for Industrial Democracy, a pro-labor and strongly anti-communist organization supported by the organized labor bureaucracy. Haber became exasperated by the inertia and lack of vision of the Student League for Industrial Democracy. Already in 1960 he had created a new organization on the Michigan campus which took the name Students for a Democratic Society. Associated with him was Tom Hayden, activist and editor of the influential student newspaper *The Michigan Daily* and increasingly involved in the fight against segregation. Haber called a conference in the spring of that year to strengthen the relationship between white student activists and the SNCC. A key figure in this process was a white woman from the University of Texas, Sandra "Casey" Cason. Of a religious and philosophical bent, she joined the SNCC and with others, notably Hayden, began to create links between that organization and students in the North.

In the spring of 1962 several dozen activists debated a proposed statement of principles for SDS at a UAW educational camp at Port Huron, Michigan. The ensuing declaration became the founding document of the SDS and of the New Left. Largely written by Hayden, its major inspiration was C. Wright Mills. In 1960 Mills had published a "Letter to the New Left" in the British journal *New Left Review* which was later republished as an

SDS pamphlet. In it Mills challenged the residual Marxist belief that the industrial working class would necessarily be the main force leading the way to progressive change. Rather he claimed that young intellectuals all over the world including in the Soviet bloc were emerging as the leading force.[32] Indeed, the Port Huron statement's preamble asserted that the new generation of students were being forced in conscience toward activism as a result of the southern struggle against racial bigotry and the constant threat of nuclear annihilation. The failure of America to live up to its democratic ideals and the outbreak of revolutionary struggle in the third world added to the sense of urgency. As an alternative the SDS proposed a participatory democracy that would include an economy in which individuals might do meaningful work and be allowed democratic participation in economic decisions in a context of overall public regulation. Such a program fell short of plans to nationalize industry and so may be considered social democratic rather than socialist.

The Port Huron analysis of the condition of the students within the university system is of great interest as it accurately sketches the negative impact of the Cold War and the mega-university on individual students. It begins by taking note of recent student involvement in civil rights and anti-war activity and demonstrations against HUAC. These, it says, are encouraging signs that students are finally breaking through the crust of apathy and alienation that for too long has dominated university campuses: the campus up to now has been a place of private people, engaged in a notorious "inner emigration." It is a place of commitment to business-as-usual, getting ahead, playing it cool. Almost no students value activity as citizens. University control over students as a result of the doctrine of *in loco parentis* and manipulation of student government by administrators have rendered students passive and alienated. A powerful indictment of the mega-university follows:

> There is, finally, the cumbersome academic bureaucracy extending throughout the academic as well as extracurricular structures, contributing to the sense of outer complexity and inner powerlessness that transforms so many students from honest searching to ratification of convention and, worse, to a numbness of present and future catastrophes. The size and financing systems of the university enhance the permanent trusteeship of the administrative bureaucracy, their power leading to a shift to the value standards of business and administrative mentality within the university.[33]

The Port Huron statement then indicts the huge foundations and other private financial interests that shape universities, making them not only more commercial, but less disposed to diagnose society critically, less open to dissent. Many social and physical scientists, it says, neglecting the liberating heritage of higher learning, develop "human relations" or "morale-producing" techniques for the corporate economy, while others exercise their intellectual skills to accelerate the arms race. A bitter denunciation of the military-industrial complex dominating American life then follows.

While the Port Huron statement makes clear its opposition to Soviet authoritarianism, there is also an unprecedented and courageous rejection of what it describes as paranoid anti-communism: An unreasoning anti-communism has become a major social problem for those who want to construct a more democratic America. McCarthyism and other forms of exaggerated and conservative anti-communism seriously weaken democratic institutions and spawn movements contrary to the interests of basic freedoms and peace. In such an atmosphere even the most intelligent of Americans fear to join political organizations, sign petitions, and speak out on serious issues. Militaristic policies are easily "sold" to a public fearful of a democratic enemy. Political debate is restricted, thought is standardized, action is inhibited by the demands of "unity" and "oneness" in the face of the declared danger. Even many liberals and socialists share static and repetitious participation in the anti-communist crusade and often discourage tentative, inquiring discussion about "the Russian question" within their ranks—often by employing "Stalinist," "stalinoid", "Trotskyite" and other epithets in an oversimplifying way to discredit opposition. Much of the American anti-communism takes on the characteristics of paranoia.

In the next few years SDS tried various strategies to expand its influence. Some members moved into northern urban slums in an effort to create an inter-racial movement of the poor in a way analogous to what SNCC was doing in the South. Relations with the League for Industrial Democracy became increasingly strained as the trade union leaders of the latter complained that SDS was not sufficiently anti-communist. In 1965 the relationship between the two came to an end.[34] This rupture coincided with the invasion of Vietnam, beginning with the landing of 30,000 American marines at Danang in March 1965 which set the course of SDS from then on. The invasion was sparked by the near collapse of the puppet Republic of Vietnam in the face of ongoing political crisis and a powerful rural offensive of the communist-led National Liberation Front. The first college teach-in on Vietnam took place on the University of Michigan campus, the home turf of the SDS, later that month. It spread quickly to over a hundred other campuses and led to a national campus radio teach-in in April. That month the SDS sponsored an anti-war march in Washington that attracted 20,000.

The role of students in the civil rights and anti-war movements marked a turning point in the history of universities. Whereas up to this point the fiction—and it was a fiction—of the ivory tower and student hi-jinks still held sway, from this point on students en masse became involved in trying to change society. Moreover, there can be doubt that their activity had enormous impact on American society at large. Looking back, it is clear that this upheaval emerged above all from the ranks of students galvanized by idealism in the fight against racial oppression and imperialism as well as the lack of democracy in the university and American society as a whole. But it is also true that an important catalyst for their protests was the ever present threat of conscription into the armed forces and dispatch to Vietnam.

The invasion of Vietnam was a direct response to a threat to American imperialist control over the underdeveloped world, a hegemony that had been taken for granted since 1945. But the Cuban Revolution of 1959 and the rapid spread of revolutionary and anti-colonial movements in its wake set alarm bells off in Washington. Coupled with the growing strength of China, the prospect of a communist triumph in Vietnam was intolerable to American policy elites, who feared a communist avalanche in South East Asia. In their eyes the suppression of communist revolution in Vietnam would provide a clear demonstration of the power of the American Empire over the underdeveloped world. Moreover, such a venture could provide a welcome distraction to the problem of spreading unrest among the black population within the United States. The U.S. was already primed to employ counter-insurgency methods against the communist-led insurgency in Vietnam. It had a long history of counter-insurgency operations in its Indian wars during the nineteenth century and in the Philippine Islands, Nicaragua, and Greece in the first half of the twentieth century. Since 1952 it had deployed units of its special counter-insurgency forces or Green Berets into various third world conflicts including in Indo-China. British techniques used against insurgents in Malaya and countless other places were assimilated by MIT professor of political science Lucien Pye.[35] The sophisticated tactics used by the French against Algerian rebels were brought to the United States through the appointment of David Galula, a veteran French officer and scholar who had fought in Algeria, as an associate of the Harvard Centre for International Affairs.[36] Under the Kennedy administration the expanding American program of counter-insurgency in Vietnam became tied to the doctrine of flexible response, which included the concept of gradual escalation—both intellectual products of academic think-tanks during the 1950s.

The overarching framework for such armed and imperialist interventions was laid down by academic theories of third world development and modernization which the U.S. government generously funded during the 1950s. Among the more notable figures in the field were Shils and Pye, but also Gabriel Almond, Sidney Verba, Daniel Lerner, and Samuel P. Huntington. These academic theorists were committed to the idea that change in the third world ought to be compatible with the expansion of capitalism, and they assumed that the experience of Western democracy was necessarily linked with capitalism. They shared a fear of mass politics, and a methodical approach that stressed the psychological and cultural factors involved in controlling society. Parsonian sociological theory, with its omni-disciplinary and descriptive theory of social action, was axiomatic to the thought of these theorists who applied it to the third world.[37] Echoing 1950s American political science they associated democracy with elite control, and formal support of democratic institutions with management and manipulation from on high.[38] The purpose of development was to transform traditional societies into modern ones characterized by rationality, cosmopolitanism, secularism, social mobility, and openness to change. Such a transformation involved the imposition from above of these norms on the mass of the population in the underdeveloped states. Indeed, for these theorists the end point of development was the creation of a society which mirrored that of the United States.[39]

From an economic perspective these modernization theorists depended on the work of Walter Rostow. Rostow was born in New York City to a Russian Jewish immigrant family who were socialists. Their son made a rapid upward ascent. He entered Yale University at age 15 on a full scholarship, graduated at 19, and completed his Ph.D. there in 1940. During the war he served in the OSS. In 1945 Rostow became assistant chief of the German-Austrian Economic Division in the State Department. In 1946–7 he was Harmsworth Professor of American History at Oxford. In 1947 he became the assistant to the executive secretary of the Economic Commission for Europe and was involved in the development of the Marshall Plan. He was professor of economic history at MIT from 1951 to 1961 and a staff member of the Center for International Studies there. In August 1954, Rostow and fellow CIA-connected MIT economics professor Max F. Millikan convinced Eisenhower to massively increase U.S. foreign aid for development as part of a policy of spreading American-style capitalist growth in Asia and elsewhere, backed by the military in those countries. He became an influential adviser to Kennedy and Johnson during the Vietnam War, consistently advocating no compromise.[40]

The work that recommended Rostow to Kennedy was his *The Stages of Economic Growth: A Non-Communist Manifesto* (1960).[41] It was intended as a rejoinder to Marx's claim that the future lay with communism not capitalism. Based on his interpretation of European and American history, Rostow postulated a five-stage modernization process: traditional society, the preconditions for take-off, the take-off, the drive to maturity, and the age of high mass consumption. Rostow's model was a liberal one emphasizing the efficacy of free trade and laissez-faire, while accepting the necessity of government intervention in the early phases of modernization. Rostow's work is hardly a theoretical answer to Marx's intellectually powerful analysis of the development of capitalism, but rather a conceptually thin rationale for U.S. imperialism.

Based on the strategic and tactical posture of modernization theory and counter-insurgency war incubated in universities, the Johnson administration plunged ahead, in three years escalating the number of troops sent to Vietnam to more than half a million men. In reaction to the U.S. escalation, the Democratic Republic of Vietnam, backed by its allies in China and the Soviet Union, developed an astute and powerful political and military response which climaxed in the Tet Offensive that began in January 1968. In the meantime, internal dissent to the war, led by students, turned into a serious challenge to the policy of escalation of President Johnson and his administration. Campus unrest grew and became the basis for an anti-war movement that spilled out into the cities. A two-day protest and teach-in against the war took place at Berkeley in May 1965. Out of this campus event there emerged the Vietnam Day Committee of student, labor, religious, and pacifist leaders, which took protest from the university to the streets. In November it organized a march through the city of Oakland despite attempts on the part of the police and national guard to block it. Over 10,000 people marched in the first of many such demonstrations on the West Coast, which spread across the rest of America and reflected the capacity of campuses to engender protest throughout society. Universities revealed themselves to be focal points of intellectual and social revolt capable of shaking up the rest of society.

In response to the escalation of the war, SDS membership mushroomed from 2,500 in December 1964 to 25,000 by October 1966. Its spectacular growth was directly fueled by rising indignation on the part of the idealistic young at the deception underlying American foreign policy, which professed to be defending democracy but was revealed to be in the business of blocking political self-determination and national liberation in order to defend its own imperialist and strategic interests. As the escalation continued, many students who had begun by questioning the war policy as liberals ended up rejecting the legitimacy of capitalism. SDS chapters sprang up on scores of campuses, and at the 1966 national convention a new generation of revolutionary leaders pushed aside the old SDS elite. More and more of the expanding rank-and-file membership came from non-elite schools.[42] The new leadership tended to be younger, having entered politics through the anti-war movement. Whereas the old leadership had come mostly from a handful of traditionally liberal—often upper-class—schools, the new leadership tended to come from state schools, often in the Midwest. The new forces in SDS, grouped around what was known as the "Prairie Power" faction, combined a critique of the national office with demands for a more decentralized structure for SDS and a greater focus on campus organizing and war resistance.[43]

The growing militancy in SDS was paralleled and extended by the radicalization of the civil rights movement. The 1965 Voting Rights Act, which legally ended Jim Crow segregation, shifted the focus of the civil rights movement away from the South to the northern cities. The move was highlighted by a series of urban rebellions beginning in 1964 in Harlem and most strikingly in 1965 in Watts, Los Angeles. Members of SDS began to debate how best to relate to the revolutionary potential within the Black Power movement. Starting in 1967, SDS organized a series of direct actions aimed not just at protesting the war, but at disrupting the "war machine." One such action took place at the University of Wisconsin-Madison in 1967, where the local SDS chapter organized a demonstration to prevent Dow Chemical, the largest producer of napalm, from recruiting on campus. They distributed leaflets and on October 17 activists led several hundred students into the university's commerce building where Dow was recruiting. University administrators called in the police, who attacked the demonstrators, breaking windows and hauling students out through the broken glass. The front steps were covered in blood. Suddenly, after the initial shock, the students fought the police in large numbers and many were arrested. At Wisconsin and elsewhere the split between students and university authorities widened into a chasm.[44]

In the months that followed, SDS chapters on dozens of campuses protested their administrations' involvement in defense research, military recruitment on campus, and the draft. Students discovered that, far from being noble institutions of debate and free thought, their universities were corporations deeply involved in military research, and that students were thought of as little better than cogs in a machine or even as law breakers. Suddenly they were confronted with the huge gap between the myth of the university as a place for the free exchange of ideas and the reality of their school's involvement in the war. They were also confronted with the often peremptory and violent reaction of administrations when students began questioning the established order, including the complicity of the university. Many activists began to see their schools as part of a single system that put the expansion of profits and its own global power before the needs of ordinary people. SDS's arguments for a student power movement resonated with a growing number. Student anti-war groups increasingly began to see the war not just as a mistaken policy, but as an outgrowth of a social system based on competition and profit.

The New Left, and SDS in particular, moved from being anti-war to anti-imperialist. The slogans on anti-war demonstrations changed from "For a Negotiated Peace" and "Bring the Troops Home" to "U.S. Out Now!" and "Victory to the NLF" (Vietnamese National Liberation Front). At the beginning of 1968, the Tet Offensive inspired the student left to adopt more radical tactics. Propelled both by the escalating crisis in American society and by the manifest bankruptcy of its earlier social-democratic reform-oriented approach, SDS politics went through a very rapid evolution to the left, from peaceful protest in 1964 ("Half the Way with LBJ"), to anti-imperialist resistance in 1967, to varieties of anti-capitalist and often Marxist revolutionism.[45] What began as an idealistic movement to save the world was becoming increasingly serious and militant.

Columbia University, located in Manhattan—the focal point of the U.S. financial and media system—became a key site of contestation in the spring of 1968. A member of the SDS discovered documents uncovering the secret connection between Columbia and the Institute for Defense Analyses (IDA), a think-tank funded by the Defense Department. This set off campus protests in which SDS played a leading role, resulting in the suspension of six students. Meanwhile a dispute between the university and residents of Harlem over the university's plans to build a swimming pool on a piece of land that had become campus property came to a head. Roger Kahn, a critic of the university and its development plans, noted that Columbia was one of the largest and most aggressive real-estate developers on the planet, and that half of its assets were in land, buildings, and mortgages, much of it in Harlem. In pursuing its projects, the university had already displaced nearly 10,000 Harlem residents.[46] In response to the administration's attempts to suppress student protest over the swimming pool and the university's secret ties to the military, black and white radicals held a second demonstration on

April 23, 1968, which happened to coincide with the assassination of Martin Luther King. The students seized an arts complex, Hamilton Hall, but then the black students demanded that the whites leave. The latter retreated and took over Low Library, which housed the president's office. After a week the police retook the buildings. The black students evacuated quietly, while the buildings occupied by whites were violently cleared: approximately 132 students, four faculty members, and 12 police officers were injured, and over 700 protesters were arrested. The end of the academic year was disrupted, with the university meanwhile abandoning its plans to build the swimming pool and severing its ties to the IDA.[47]

The issue of the university as urban developer resurfaced dramatically in Berkeley in April 1969. The university there owned a small piece of property adjacent to the campus whose use whether as a parking lot, student residence, or sports field had not definitively been decided. Students and townspeople inspired by the Free Speech Movement of five years earlier, by simmering anti-war feeling, and by the rampant and exuberant Berkeley counter-culture, invaded the property declaring it a People's Park and free speech commons. At a protest march at the end of May there were "antiwar protesters, Hell's Angels, senior citizens, Black Panthers, Free Speech Movement veterans, hippies, women's liberation advocates, rich people from the hills, poor people from the flats and delegations from all over."[48] Governor Ronald Reagan had been critical of university administrators for tolerating student demonstrations at the Berkeley campus, and had received enormous state-wide support for his 1966 gubernatorial campaign promise to crack down on what the public perceived as a generally lax attitude at California's public universities. Reagan considered the creation of the park a direct leftist challenge to the property rights of the university, and saw the establishment of the People's Park as an opportunity to fulfill his campaign promise of harsh repression. He ordered in massive numbers of police and finally the National Guard to quash the increasingly large and militant demonstrations. But despite the repeated attempts to stifle them, the demonstrations continued into the 1970s and the site was eventually turned into a city park. At Berkeley and elsewhere across the United States demonstrations like this by students and others often took on the air of revolutionary festivals.

At Berkeley and other campuses the purposes of the university, including its research activities whose goals were largely to serve capitalist or military interests, were challenged. Indeed, for a time, the values of the counter-culture deeply affected student attitudes toward competitive and performance-orientated learning. On many campuses activists attempted to create alternative universities with more political and "relevant," or even "irrelevant," courses. A trivial affair in itself, the matter of the People's Park highlighted the role of the university as a corporate and urban developer—an issue which was to loom larger and larger as the function of the university as an integral part of neoliberal capitalism expanded.

The People's Park confrontation also reflected the polarization of public opinion in the United States by the late 1960s. The debates of the Old Left—reform versus revolution, racism and the consciousness of the working class, and the need for a revolutionary party—now took on new significance. In the fall of 1968, more than 350,000 students said that they strongly agreed with the statement that some form of "mass revolutionary party" was needed in America. According to one poll in 1969, more than 1 million students considered themselves revolutionaries or socialists of some kind or other. By then, more than 300 out of 2,000 campuses had experienced sit-ins, building takeovers, riots, and strikes. Between January 1969 and April 1970, young radicals bombed hundreds of police stations, corporate offices, military facilities, and ROTC buildings. Twenty-six thousand out of a total population of 10 million college students had been arrested.[49]

SDS reached a peak of 100,000 members and then collapsed almost as quickly as it had risen. It needed to tie itself politically to an insurgent white working class but was unable to do so organizationally or even theoretically. The white working class was still enjoying the pleasures of post-war consumerism, bemused by Cold War propaganda, and dominated by an anti-communist trade union bureaucracy. As a result, the student movement aborted. At its national convention in 1969, SDS split into two rival factions, one dominated by the Maoist-turned-Stalinist Progressive Labor Party (PL) and the other called the Revolutionary Youth Movement (RYM), which itself promptly split into two. Important to the splits was the issue of race and class, or how SDS as a Marxist and revolutionary organization would relate to the nationalism of the Black Power movement. Some RYM members later organized themselves into the Weathermen and resorted to urban terrorism, vainly trying to destabilize the system.[50]

University administrators attempted to deal with student unrest partly through concessions. They abandoned the role of *in loco parentis* as rules and regulations governing sexual and other behavior on campus were relaxed. Discussion of politics both inside and outside classrooms widened, especially in the wake of the Berkeley Free Speech Movement. Students were given minority representation in departments, faculties, and university senates. On the other hand, as the cases of Berkeley, Wisconsin, and Columbia made clear, harsh repression was used against students to put them in their place when necessary. The most notorious example of repression was of course the killing of four students at Kent State University in the spring of 1970 by the Ohio National Guard, in the wake of the U.S. invasion of Cambodia—an event which was followed by the closing in protest of most universities and colleges across the United States.[51] Significantly, the coincident killing of two black students protesting the war and racism at Jackson State University by Mississippi state troopers passed virtually unnoticed.[52]

As we have mentioned, during the protests at Columbia in 1968 black students had separated themselves from white student protesters. This reflected the turn that black student activists had taken three years earlier toward black nationalism. The catalysts for the change came with the Selma March, the assassination of Malcolm X, and the Watts riots of 1965. In March of that year a large force of police brutally dispersed a march from Selma to Mobile, Alabama, by black integrationists led by the SNCC. The killing of ex-Black Muslim Malcolm X, purportedly by fellow Black Muslims, that same year was interpreted in the black community as a deliberate provocation by the U.S. government. The Watts riot meanwhile bespoke the awakening of the masses in the ghettoized black communities across the United States. In the wake of these dramatic events the charismatic Stokeley Carmichael assumed control of the SNCC, espousing the idea of black power or self-determination.[53] Carmichael's message deeply resonated on black and other college campuses among black students. It was reinforced by the rise to national prominence of the Black Panther Party in 1968, which likewise recruited many of its members from black university students. Inspired by the SNCC and the Black Panthers, to say nothing of the growing urban riots, unrest grew among black students. Black revolutionaries succeeded in linking with the mass of poor and ghettoized members of their communities in a way that white student revolutionaries could not. Inspired by third world Marxism, the goal of the Black Panthers was the creation of armed and autonomous revolutionary black communities.

San Francisco State

Nowhere did black protest on campus assume greater significance than at San Francisco State College in 1967–8. Black students took the lead in an alliance with other ethnic groups in a major uprising which combined demands for the creation of black and ethnic studies with protests against the Vietnam War. Unlike elsewhere, in the course of the San Francisco State struggle ethnic student groups developed a common front. Moreover, these ethnic groups had real connections with their largely working-class local constituencies. Their common working-class vision and their ties to local communities deeply threatened the Bay Area elites.

A large urban college which was part of the California system, San Francisco State attracted a big Black, Asian, and Chicano population as well as the offspring of the white working class. Eighty percent of the 18,000 students worked to pay their way through college. The movement at San Francisco State reflected like nowhere else the fact that by the late '60s protest in the United States had spread from elite institutions down into universities and colleges with a student body recruited from the working class. Because of the Vietnam War the matter of the draft had become a question of life and death for students across America. At the beginning of May 1967, 60 San Francisco State students staged a sit-in at the office of the president demanding that the college stop sending reports to selective service offices on students' academic standing. Academic failure by students was tantamount to an end to their exemption from the military draft, but the administrators refused the students' demands.

By the late '60s black school enrollment in colleges and universities across the United States was skyrocketing. Many of these students, including those in the historically black colleges of the South, were affected by the ideology of black power. Conflict between black students and the police had led to the shooting and deaths of black students at Houston Texas Southern University and at South Carolina State University in Orangetown.[54] In California, demands for admission to university by blacks were increasing while academic restrictions on admissions were tightening. Meanwhile in Oakland intense community organizing was taking place, including by the Black Panthers.[55] In November 1967 black students attacked the white editor of the campus newspaper who had written a racist editorial calling on the Carnegie Corporation to abandon its plan to fund service programs which included Black Student Union programs. The Carnegie plan was part of a broader educational initiative by business and government to co-opt black student protest.[56] Six of the students involved in the assault were booked on felony charges and the college suspended others pending an investigation. At the beginning of December, protesting students occupied a college office and the president closed the campus rather than call in the police. Dr. Walcott Beatty, chairman of the Academic Senate, observed that campus demonstrations and disturbances would not end due to their underlying causes, including Vietnam and racial tension. He concluded that the campus was a microcosm of society.

In the wake of these events the president of San Francisco State announced his resignation, thereby deepening the crisis. At the end of February 1968, 300 high school and junior college minority students came to the campus to ask for waivers of admission requirements. Sociology professor Juan Martinez was influential in inviting the high school students to come forward. The students were refused admission and Martinez's contract with the college was not renewed. The next month Black Panther Party minister of defense Bobby Seale spoke in the main auditorium of the college, telling the audience that "blacks need to defend themselves with guns."[57] On March 23 a newly formed Third World Liberation Front (a coalition of the Black Students Union, the Latin American Students Organization, the Filipino-American Students Organization, and El Renacimiento, a Mexican-American student organization) occupied the office of the YMCA on campus. The outgoing president of the college then ordered the Third World Liberation Front to evacuate. The protesters demanded an end to Air Force ROTC on campus, retention of Juan Martinez, programs to admit 400 inner-city students in the fall, and the hiring of nine minority faculty members to help students. Police forcibly cleared the occupiers and 26 of them were arrested. On May 23 students again protested, demanding campus reform. The demonstrations were led by the SDS and the Third World Liberation Front. On June 1, Dr. Robert Smith, a professor of education, became the new president of the college. In September a graduate student in English was hired to teach special introductory English classes for 400 special students who were admitted to the college, and the creation of a black studies department was announced.

California State College trustees voted to ask the president to reassign Black Panther George Mason Murray, a member of the faculty, to a non-teaching position. At the campus of a neighboring college he had allegedly stated that "we are slaves and the only way to become free is to kill all the slave masters." Back at San Francisco State he was quoted as saying that black students should bring guns to campus to protect themselves from racist white administrators. President Smith refused to fire Murray and was forced to resign amid further student and faculty strikes. Another faculty member, S.I. Hayakawa, a conservative linguist, replaced him and took a hard line, to the acclaim of California conservative opinion.[58] After months of further protest, on March 20, 1969 an agreement was signed between representatives of black and third world students' organizations and the university, in which the establishment of a range of ethnic study programs was conceded.

Politics and Sexuality: Marcuse and Chomsky

One of the most widely read works among radical students of the 1960s was Marcuse's *Eros and Civilization* (1955). This Freudian-Marxist work asserted that advanced capitalist society imposed work discipline and concomitant sexual repression far beyond what advanced civilization required. Whereas in earlier periods disciplined work required repression and control of sexual expression, humankind had reached a stage of development in which such excessive restriction had become redundant and tyrannical. Revolt against surplus sexual repression was inherent to the struggle against capitalism, and the overthrow of capitalism would entail freer self-expression of an overflowing libido. Marcuse's views, as well as those of the earlier Freudian-Marxist psychoanalyst Wilhelm Reich, greatly influenced left-wing students in the 1960s. Like C. Wright Mills, Marcuse looked to student protest as the most important liberating force in contemporary capitalism. Marcuse and Reich helped inspire the much more open attitude toward sexuality characteristic of the students of the 1960s, opening the door to the fusion of political revolution and sexual liberation. During that decade the role of the university as *in loco parentis* collapsed under student pressure.

By far and away the most popular intellectual among the student movement was the MIT linguist Noam Chomsky. Politically Chomsky was a convinced anarchist but he had hitherto kept his views to himself. Until the American escalation of the war in Vietnam in 1965 Chomsky quietly pursued an increasingly successful academic career in linguistics. In a way reminiscent of Immanuel Kant, who had insisted on the existence of inherent categories of thought in humanity, Chomsky insisted on the inherent human capacity for language. But with the escalation of the war Chomsky came to the fore politically. He eschewed theory, especially Marxist theory, in favor of an unrelenting empirical analysis through which he exposed and flayed America's imperialist foreign policy and its liberal academic apologists. In the spring of 1967 Chomsky published a scathing attack in an essay entitled "The Responsibility of the Intellectuals" in the *New York Review of Books*, a new journal that soon attracted a wide readership.[59] According to Chomsky, intellectuals have the material and intellectual means to seek truth and expose the lies of ideology and government propaganda. Instead, the academics close to presidents Kennedy and Johnson, notably Arthur Schlesinger, Walt Rostow, McGeorge Bundy, and Henry Kissinger, and others like New York intellectual Irving Kristol, systematically lied about the motives behind the American attack on Vietnam. But their misrepresentations were part of a deeper pattern among practitioners of social and political science in the United States, who have covered up America's imperialist past and who today practice an instrumental and technocratic rationalism in the service of those who wield power.

Chomsky further developed the idea of the betrayal of critical scholarship by American academia in *American Power and the New Mandarins* (1969). He attributed this sellout to access to power and money, a long tradition of passivity and conformism, as well as the cult of professionalism.[60] Above all he singled out the influence of the new mandarins, a technical and instrumental intelligentsia made up of psychologists, economists, sociologists, systems analysts, and political scientists. Indeed, Chomsky discerned the emergence of a new and privileged academic elite whose function was to carry out the subordination of the rest of the citizenry and, indeed, the rest of the world to an American counter-revolutionary project.[61] The liberal intelligentsia that dominates the universities essentially rationalizes and justifies American capitalism and state power as benign. Fundamental to the concern of this elite is an obsession with stability and order.[62] In its social science guise it seriously distorts what it considers to be scientific method and its theories are all too often deployed as a new coercive ideology.[63] Chomsky sounds the note of an Old Testament prophet as he rightly castigates the social scientists, political scientists, and historians for serving rather than criticizing power. His indignation demonstrates that within the university there were critical thinkers who could not be seduced by power. But in his critique he fails to come to grips with the historical role of the university as an establishment institution in a highly undemocratic society. The knowledge garnered by scholars should make humans more ethical and better citizens, as Chomsky and others within and without academe believe, but under capitalism it cannot. Many academics under such conditions serve the existing order. Still, the enormous influence that Chomsky gained humiliated many of the academic elite and showed that academics like himself could make an essential contribution to the transformation of society. The existence of scholars like Chomsky demonstrated that within the humanities and social science faculties, as elsewhere within the universities, critical scholarship, however threatened, nonetheless had a tenacious foothold.

The Decline of the Anti-war Movement and Birth of Identity Politics

The unrest at San Francisco State and on other campuses began to dissipate by the early 1970s. The decline of student agitation reflected the fact that the overall political context had radically changed. Under Nixon a program of Vietnamization of the war or the withdrawal of American ground forces and the end of conscription was promised. The student movement had grown out of deep concern over civil rights, consumerism, bureaucratic tyranny, and the injustice of the Vietnam War among a large minority of students. But the threat of the military draft was fundamental to mobilizing millions of students to campus demonstrations. Once that threat was removed by Nixon, along with the promise of an end to direct involvement in the conflict, many only marginally involved in politics lost interest in further protest. Radical students and others who attempted to form Leninist parties to bolster anti-capitalist protest failed to find a significant following. Many of those who were led in this direction had been at the forefront of the long anti-war struggle and their hopes of revolutionary change based on mass insurrection were disappointed. On the other hand, by helping to force the withdrawal of American ground troops, activists played an important part in changing U.S. policy in a direction that ultimately assured Vietnamese national liberation and unification and temporarily inhibited direct American intervention elsewhere. In the course of doing so they had shaken the institutions of U.S. society, including its universities, to their roots.[64] On the other hand, although the student left had challenged the stability of American society, the mobilization of conservative and reactionary forces behind the Nixon presidency revealed that ruling-class institutions were still intact. The resulting loss of momentum and the increasing frustration with the sexist and racist contradictions within the radical student-based movement led to the emergence of identity politics.

As at San Francisco State, the movement as a whole fragmented on the basis of identity politics—black first of all, then feminist, Chicano, aboriginal, Asian, and gay and lesbian. The first accredited women's studies course was taught at Cornell in 1969. The first two women's studies programs in the United States were established the next year at San Diego State College and SUNY-Buffalo. The first undergraduate course in the United States on gay and lesbian studies was taught at Berkeley in 1969 and was followed by similar courses in the fall of 1970 at Southern Illinois University Edwardsville and the University of Nebraska-Lincoln. Although never growing particularly large, the presence of these new departments served to widen the course offerings of many institutions in ways that would appeal to women and other minorities. They helped to permanently diversify and enlarge the curriculum to reach hitherto excluded or suppressed young people. Moreover, unlike older disciplines these departments tended to be more closely connected to students and more likely to engage in activism in their communities. The study of women's or black history was thus closely linked to the need to provide a past which would be useful in ongoing contemporary struggles for change.

In the meantime, caucuses of women appeared in many different departments across the disciplines, including science and engineering, calling for the hiring of more women and curriculum changes that would reflect a feminist perspective. Ongoing pressure by feminists forced open the gates of academic employment. Although never achieving parity in pay or numbers with their male counterparts, large numbers of women were hired by colleges and universities for the first time. In some places quotas were imposed by university administrations on male-dominated departments which proved recalcitrant. Gay and lesbian academics also found employment. At the same time, such new fields only confirmed the now resurgent post-1960s ideology of liberal diversity and individualism. While demands for class equality were spurned, concessions based on demands for equal treatment on the basis of identity were gladly made, following the logic of divide and conquer.

Perhaps the single most important intellectual achievement to emerge out of the new interest in feminist and gay and lesbian studies was the development of the concept of gender. Initially, second-wave feminist theory had tended to conceive of women in essentialist terms—women by nature were different from men. Now, as a result of postmodern questioning of foundationalism as well as the impact of gay and lesbian studies, the notion of gender as a social construction gained ground. The idea that sex roles were socially generated proved to be an exceptionally fertile one in both the humanities and social science, as important in its way as the concept of class. Indeed, in the longer term the turn away from class and toward an understanding of identity ultimately led to a deeper and more dynamic understanding of class itself.[65]

Ecological Science

The upheavals of the 1960s produced not only new identity-based programs but also environmental studies programs. As was said at the time, the environmental movement kicked off by Earth Day in 1970 was in part an establishment ploy to divert the attention of the young from the Vietnam War and from student and minority radical protest. Indeed, foundation and government money immediately poured in for the creation of university-based environmental teaching and research. On the other hand, the universities undoubtedly had the intellectual and scientific resources to develop new interdisciplinary programs in this field, which were urgently needed and of great value. But the administrative structures of universities were initially ill-equipped to pursue ecological studies, which demanded an integrated approach to knowledge. University faculties were largely made up of highly individualistic academics organized in departments that had evolved on the basis of the increasing fragmentation and specialization of learning. As we have argued, this was by no means accidental but reflected a commitment to professional specialization that tended to block a critical and holistic understanding of the world. Despite these obstacles, environmental programs mushroomed across university campuses during the 1970s, fueled by an apolitical belief in technological and scientific solutions to economic and political questions and by middle-class moral conviction.[66] It was a way of shifting the subject away from radical political and social demands.

Gradually a body of knowledge and expertise developed which, if properly applied, could assuage the increasingly serious environmental problems accompanying capitalist economic growth. On the other hand, there was general reluctance to admit that the most important barrier to addressing environmental problems was the unswerving commitment to profit-making and capitalist growth on the part of the ruling class. Indeed, a considerable body of theoretical literature was devoted to vainly trying to show that concern for the environment was compatible with capitalism, and indeed that the market itself was the mechanism through which ecological concerns could be addressed. Eventually a Marxist ecology was created centered on the journal *Capitalism, Nature, Socialism*, edited by James O'Connor of the University of California at Santa Cruz. Paul Burkett and John Bellamy Foster helped to revive Marx's own thoughts on ecology and in particular his key notion of the disastrous metabolic rupture between human society and nature which was an intrinsic characteristic of capitalism.[67] In any event, the recovery of this idea put an end to the ridiculous notion that Marx was an advocate of the idea of unlimited growth as conceived by capitalism. Marx favored the multiplication of use values instead of environmentally noxious exchange values, which would entail the restoration of an equilibrium between economic needs and the environment, demonstrating that this was only possible by eliminating capitalism and establishing socialism.

Marxism on Campus: The Return of the Repressed

As we have seen, the presence of Marxism was not particularly strong in American universities in the first part of the twentieth century. This reflected the class bias and insularity of American academe. Nonetheless, Marxists had established themselves in the academy and some of them were outstanding scholars. But the position Marxism had on campuses was virtually extinguished during the height of the Cold War in the 1950s. The 1960s saw an astonishing rebirth, or an unprecedented new birth, of the Marxist presence in U.S. academia. It was the students who rediscovered the importance of the Marxist tradition as part of their rebellion and in so doing forced open the gates of establishment learning. In the context of opposition to the Vietnam War, scholars opened themselves to and absorbed the texts of third world revolutionary Marxism and by extension the Marxist intellectual tradition. Marxism meanwhile supplied students with the main weapons for critiquing the university and society. Radical courses at free universities and counter-texts refuting received wisdom in the social sciences and humanities proliferated. The writings of Fidel Castro, Che Guevara, Mao Zedong, Ho Chi Minh, and Frantz Fanon were all popular, and increasingly also the Marxist classics—Marx, Engels, and Lenin. Marcuse, as we have seen, was also widely read. But now much of the entire corpus of Marxist writers of the twentieth century, including Lukács, Lefevbre, Gramsci, E.P. Thompson, Christopher Hill, Eric Hobsbawm, Rodney Hilton, Soboul, Bakhtin, James, and Fanon found enthusiastic American publishers and wide readerships. The influx of Marxism into the universities put an end to the insularity of U.S. academic culture.

It was the British Marxist historians who had the greatest impact. In certain disciplines like history, sociology, anthropology, and English remarkable advances in scholarship were made by young academics. Their materialist, unified, conflictual, and historical view of society fundamentally challenged the ahistorical, fragmented, consensual, and too often idealist view of society that characterized American social science and humanities. As such it provided a means to look toward the future. Indeed, the key trend in these fields in the 1960s was the movement toward history.

History

Marxism invaded American graduate schools nowhere more so than in history departments. Indeed, as the 1960s abated, many activists took refuge in academe and entrenched themselves in history and other departments in the lower-rung colleges and universities. Historical research initiated in that tumultuous decade began to appear during the quieter decades that followed. Powerful works of Marxist-based history were published, breaking through the anti-materialist and anti-historical bias of the social sciences and humanities in the 1950s. The most impressive piece of American historical scholarship came from Eugene Genovese. His masterpiece *Roll, Jordan Roll*, which was on a par with the work of the great British Marxists, appeared in 1976, but a decade earlier he had already published a preliminary study in the form of analysis of the political economy of slavery.[68] In it he had systematically analyzed southern plantation slavery as a mode of production, demonstrating its inability to compete with free labor. But in *Roll, Jordan Roll* he explored with the help of Gramsci the paternalist hegemonic ideology of the slave owners as well as the highly creative counter-ideology of Black Christianity. In doing so he demonstrated the capacity of Marxism to elucidate the complex relationship between the culture and the relations of production of a key American social and historical formation. On the other hand, it can be said that in insisting on the gap between the slave and capitalist modes of exploitation in terms of Marxist economic conceptions, Genovese fell short in explicating their actual interdependence under the conditions of the nineteenth-century global capitalism.[69] The incontestable brilliance of his work, however, assured Genovese the Bancroft Prize and the presidency of the Organization of American Historians. His achievement bespoke the emergence of Marxist historians from obscurity to sudden prominence. Marking the partial retreat of the establishment, some Marxists occupied posts in history departments at important institutions—Barton Bernstein at Stanford, Staughton Lynd at Yale, Gabriel Kolko at Pennsylvania, and Jesse Lemisch at Chicago.

Genovese held posts at Rutgers and then Rochester, where he became chairman of the history department. At a teach-in on the Vietnam War at Rutgers in April 1965, Genovese asserted: "Those of you who know me know that I am a Marxist and a Socialist. Therefore, unlike most of my distinguished colleagues here this morning, I do not fear or regret the impending victory in Vietnam. I welcome it."[70] The statement caused a political furor, but was in keeping with Genovese's revolutionary and internationalist attitude which had been shaped by his time in the Communist Party. But however nuanced and careful his scholarship, personally, Genovese was a deeply authoritarian and aggressive personality who was almost a caricature of the Stalinist dogmatist. Indeed, he traded on his communist past, assuming in quite inflexible fashion political positions which he put forward as the necessarily correct line.

This tendency reached its peak at the 1969 business meeting of the American Historical Association, at which young New Left historians tried to seize control of the organization while sponsoring a resolution condemning the Vietnam War. Not only did Genovese join with the establishment in defeating this insurgency, he took the lead in publicly opposing the resolution. Genovese claimed that passage of the resolution would lead to a purge of the AHA, as those who opposed it would be forced to leave. Such a purge had not occurred in other academic associations that had passed such resolutions. Nor did it occur at the American Historical Association either when a few years later it quietly passed such a measure. At the end of his infamous speech at the 1969 meeting, Genovese urged the AHA to deal harshly with those sponsoring the resolution "put them down, put them down hard, and put them down once and for all."[71] After spending some time teaching in Canada, Genovese moved to the South, ending up many years later as a political reactionary and an apologist for southern slave paternalism. Genovese's highly individualistic not to say idiosyncratic cursus no doubt reflected his own personal foibles, but it also reflected the failures of an academic culture that might otherwise have helped scholars better survive the rigors of the oncoming neoliberal age.

One historian whose life and work set more of a positive example was David Montgomery. Of middle-class background, Montgomery went to Swarthmore College in the immediate post-war years. After a stint in the army he completed a degree in political science and somehow became radicalized just as the Cold War closed in. In what some would describe as a quixotic choice, following graduation he went to work in a New York factory whose workforce was part of the left-wing United Electrical Workers Union, and joined the Communist Party. Moving to Minneapolis in the mid-1950s he drifted away from rather than broke with the Party. He took a doctorate at the University of Minnesota and received an appointment at the University of Pittsburgh, where he remained for several years before ending up at Yale. His influence in labor history and beyond derives from a large body of scholarship produced over many years on the history of workplace organization and conflicts, strikes and other protest behavior, ideology and political organization, and racial and ethnic relations in working-class American populations.

Montgomery was particularly important in documenting the role of the state in class relations and he was instrumental in bringing labor history into the mainstream historical narrative. But he also exerted his influence by training large numbers of doctoral students working on a wide array of topics and through his mentoring of countless other historians who were not his students. His editing of the journal *International Labor and Working*

Class History in its formative years, and of more than 70 volumes in the University of Illinois Press series *The Working Class in American History*, also proved highly influential. His masterwork *The Fall of the House of Labor* is a deep study of the complex origins of the American working class which coincided with the triumph of American industrial capitalism in the late nineteenth and early twentieth centuries. Some critics underline the influence of Edward Thompson, stressing the weight Montgomery gives to culture. On the other hand, unlike Thompson his work is remarkable for its structural understanding of the evolution of both organized labor and capital within the American state. Thompson's influence is present but so too is the influence of the other British Marxist historians, as well as the Marxist historians of the French Revolution.[72] Montgomery's significance is that he demonstrated that while the history of the American working class had to be understood in terms of its distinctiveness, it was by no means historically exceptional.

Another scholar whose work proved both creative and influential was Robert Brenner, a professor at UCLA. While pursuing his Ph.D. at Princeton at the height of the Vietnam War Brenner identified with the Trotskyist International Socialist tendency. Since 1974 he has been a member of IS/Workers Power/Solidarity and is presently the editor of the radical journal *Against the Current*. His doctorate *Merchants and Revolution*, which he worked on in the 1960s but which only saw publication in the 1990s, is a remarkable study of the key role of a new elite of colonial merchants who, Brenner demonstrated, were in the vanguard of the English Revolution.[73] Brenner's most celebrated work appeared in the 1970s in the form of a number of key essays on the origins of capitalism.[74] These pieces helped to spark off a renewal of the celebrated debate on the transition from feudalism to capitalism, a debate originally organized by the New York-based journal *Science & Society* at the height of the McCarthy period. It involved leading Marxist historians and political economists who differed over whether the prime mover in the transition to capitalism was trade or a breakdown of the feudal mode of production due to over-exploitation and class conflict.[75] Brenner sided with the latter group while deepening the debate by arguing that changes in what he called property relations between landlords and tenants during the late medieval period of breakdown set the stage for the sixteenth-century development of capitalism in England. Brenner's tightly organized arguments, which stressed the importance of competitive markets in advancing the productivity of capitalism, laid the foundation of a whole school of Marxist historiography known as Political Marxism.

Sociology

In sociology the principal development was the collapse of Parsonianism and the rising influence of history. Already in 1959 C. Wright Mills had published a withering attack on Parsons, pointing especially to his abstract and cumbersome language which covered up actual human behavior and societal relations with a wet blanket of structural-functionalist phraseology. According to Mills, Parsons was bent on denying social conflict and the degree of upper-class social control, and he concluded that "to accept his scheme is to read out of the picture the facts of power and indeed of all institutional structure, in particular the economic, the political and the military. In this curious 'general theory' such structures of domination have no place."[76] The upheavals of the 1960s then led to a widespread rejection of Parsons's theories which, being based on the notion of social equilibrium, now seemed irrelevant. More and more attacks were launched on Parsons's theory during the decade, culminating in a comprehensive critique by Alvin Gouldner in 1970 entitled *The Coming Crisis of Western Sociology*.[77] It was a sign of the times that in 1967 a professor of psychology, rather than sociology, at the University of California Santa Cruz, William Domhoff, produced a sociological study entitled *Who Rules America?* which empirically demonstrated that a political and social elite controlled the United States.[78] This surprising piece of news was grudgingly acknowledged by the academic establishment.

But it was the turn to historical sociology, the importance of which Mills insisted upon, that was the most impressive development of the period. Rivalling Brenner's treatment of the origins of capitalism was Immanuel Wallerstein's *The Modern World System*, the first volume of which appeared in 1974.[79] It was not an accident that the ambition of this American academic was nothing less than a theorization of the global history of capitalism. This universalizing goal reflected both Wallerstein's location at the heart of the global capitalist system dominated by the United States but also his deep-seated critical attitude toward this American imperialism. Wallerstein was a sociologist whose early work had dealt with Africa, and his work reflected both the globalization of capitalism and the growing impact of the underdeveloped countries on world politics. In contrast to Brenner's stress on changes in the relations of production at the heart of capitalism as key to unleashing the economic potential of social labor, Wallerstein stressed the importance of the simultaneous development of the world market and the extraction of surplus from the underdeveloped world. According to him, the exploitation of wage labor was only one aspect of the new capitalist world system in which the surplus extracted from slave, serf, sharecropping, and other forms of dependent labor fed economic growth in the West at the expense of the politically and economically weaker regions of the world. Historically, development and underdevelopment were simultaneous processes. In reality Brenner's approach and Wallerstein's were really two-sides of Marx's coin, which stressed the coincident origins of capitalist social relations of production and the world market. The rival theories of Brenner and Wallerstein nonetheless drove the capitalist transition debate to a new and theoretically more complex level.

Another outstanding work of historical sociology was Barrington Moore Jr.'s *The Social Origins of Dictatorship and Democracy*. From an elite background, Moore graduated from Williams College, Massachusetts, where he received a thorough education in Latin and Greek as well as in history. He became interested in political science and was elected to Phi Beta Kappa. In 1941 Moore obtained his Ph.D. in sociology from Yale. He worked as a policy analyst for the government in the OSS and at the department of justice. While at the OSS he met Herbert Marcuse, who became a lifelong friend. His academic career began in 1945 at the University of Chicago. In 1948 he went to Harvard, joining the Russian Research Center in 1951 as an independent but politically neutered scholar among a group of conservative researchers. Lenin's insight that capitalism develops according to two distinct paths—the American and the Prussian—was the inspiration for his own work. In the first instance the rural petty producers are either free or liberate themselves from landlord control and as a result are able to transform themselves into a progressive capitalist class. In contrast in the Prussian route the landlords continue to dominate the countryside, turning themselves into capitalists while remaining in political and social control and creating a truncated capitalism. Moore transformed these ideas into a political thesis, arguing that the elimination of the landlords by the petty producers and bourgeoisie together, or by the peasants alone by revolution, produced bourgeois democracy as in France and the United States, or communism as in Russia and China. In Japan and Germany, by contrast, landlords blocked revolution and retained control over the peasant farmers and the authoritarian state, and fascism was the outcome.

Anthropology

The historical approach also characterized the work of the most distinguished anthropologist of the period, Eric Wolf. Wolf was one of the coterie of students who developed around Julian Steward at Columbia in the

1950s. While Steward kept his Marxist proclivities to himself, his students, including Wolf, Sidney Mintz, Morton Fried, Elman Service, Stanley Diamond, and Robert F. Murphy, intensively discussed the implications of Marxism for anthropology. Wolf's dissertation research was carried out as part of Steward's "People of Puerto Rico" project. Shortly afterwards Wolf began teaching in the outstanding anthropology department created by Leslie White at Michigan. From 1971 he held a joint position as a distinguished professor at Lehman College and the CUNY Graduate Center, where he spent the remainder of his career. His *Europe and the People Without History* (1982) entailed a rejection of ideas such as historical versus non-historical peoples and societies, which had been common to both Marxist and non-Marxist scholarship up to that point.[80] History and sociology ignored these supposedly non-historic peoples while anthropologists failed to understand them as part of an evolving historical and global context. The focus of Wolf's work was on the relationship between European expansion and historical processes in the rest of the world—charting a global history, beginning in the 1400s through the twentieth century. As reflected in its title, his work is interested in demonstrating ways in which societies written out of European histories were and are deeply involved in the evolution of global historical systems and changes. While both Wolf and Wallerstein for the first time included the underdeveloped world in their analysis of global history, their approaches differed. Wallerstein saw the world system operating within a capitalist framework since the sixteenth century. Wolf believed that the non-European peoples remained part of tributary systems that were only fully integrated into capitalism during the Industrial Revolution.

Wolf's work was part of a deep upheaval in anthropology provoked by the Vietnam War.[81] The war in fact crystallized growing dissatisfaction because professional anthropology was deeply implicated with Western imperialism. Many were outraged by the exposé of Project Camelot in which some anthropologists had become involved in a Defense Department project to use social scientists to pre-emptively research and discover sources of unrest in Chile and elsewhere in the underdeveloped world.[82] Plans also surfaced to use anthropological research to counter insurgency in Thailand, which caused further consternation. In reaction, the meetings of the American Anthropological Association, like those of the American Historical Association, became sites of angry confrontation. A highlight was Kathleen Gough's 1968 article in *Monthly Review*, "Anthropology; Child of Imperialism."[83] Gough pointed to the colonial character of the countries in which anthropologists did their fieldwork, and the complicity of researchers with colonialism, calling upon them instead to serve the people they studied rather than serving the interests of the colonial rulers.

By 1971 a loose network of Anthropologists for Radical Political Action (ARPA) had formed. It organized workshops, raised political issues within the American Anthropological Association, and planned symposia for national meetings. Among other Marxist anthropological journals created during this period was *Dialectical Anthropology*. The women's movement greatly affected the field in the form of Marxist-feminism. Among the subjects dealt with were the reification of the family as an ideological support for female subordination; the relationship between gender, class, and race; the economic role of women's and child labor in the development of capitalism; and the effects of modernization on women globally. Very significant was the republication of Engels's *On the Origins of the Family* with an important introduction by Eleanor Leacock.[84] Indeed, the outstanding achievements and political activism of Leacock and Gough reflected the growing influence of women in anthropology.

The influence of French Marxist structural anthropology was also felt. In *Rationality and Irrationality in Economics*, Maurice Godelier addressed the question of how Marxist analytical methods applied to the study of non-stratified societies in which economic relations are often highly ritualized and deeply embedded in social relations.[85] Emmanuel Terray's *Marxism and Primitive Societies* re-evaluated the work of Morgan.[86] His discussion also built on the ethnography of the French Marxist Claude Meillassoux, analyzing the relations of production that existed among the Guro of the Ivory Coast at a time when their economy was still a subsistence one. These and other works generated an important discussion of the various components of Marx's notion of forces of production especially with respect to non-capitalist societies. Also significant was Marvin Harris's cultural materialism. Harris accepted but qualified Marx's notions of superstructure and base, means of production, and exploitation, stressing the importance of the means of reproduction among other things. On the other hand, he rejected the dialectic and the necessary unity of theory and practice while reviving a Malthusianism which stressed the effects of demography on sociocultural evolution.

Literature

During the early 1960s Leslie Fiedler was the most talked about literary critic in America. Fiedler was born of poor Jewish emigrant stock in New Jersey, took his degree in English at NYU, and received his M.A. and

Ph.D. at the University of Wisconsin. Following service in World War II he spent many years teaching at the University of Montana and then at the University of Buffalo. But despite his apparent academic marginality Fiedler managed to ingratiate himself with the anti-Stalinist New York intellectuals. In 1953 he published a rumination on the execution of the Rosenbergs for *Encounter*, the flagship journal of the Congress of Cultural Freedom, a piece which sold out the issue. While regretting the lack of clemency for the Rosenbergs, he savaged them as traitors who suffered from bad taste, among other sins. Even Sidney Hook blanched at the cruelty of Fiedler's article, urging the editor to publish a disclaimer to the effect that Fiedler's meditation "should not be construed as an attack against human beings who are dead."[87]

Fiedler showed himself to be the epitome of the upstart professor or the professor on the make so decried by C. Wright Mills. His flirtation with the New Left reflects both his characteristic cultural opportunism and the formlessness of the 1960s counter-culture. Nonetheless he proved to have considerable talent, which was reflected in his *Love and Death in the American Novel* (1960). Breaking with the aesthetic approach of the New Criticism that had dominated the 1950s, Fiedler engaged with what he considered the homoerotic nature of much of American literature, emphasizing the denial of sexuality and the entrenched racism that underlay it. Fiedler enthusiastically joined the counter-culture and the New Left, profiting from the celebrity that followed a trumped-up drug bust at his home by publishing *Being Busted* (1969). No doubt moved by his thirst for celebrity, Fiedler rejected the snobbery of New Criticism and broke new ground with essays that seriously engaged with popular culture, anticipating one of the features of the postmodern period which was to follow.

Fiedler illustrates the contradictions of the 1960s on university campuses. Unrest among the students and in society at large led some faculty like Fiedler to adopt radical postures which no doubt served careerist ambitions. At the same time their intellectual work served to challenge the elitism and social and sexual repression that characterized life in the universities during the 1950s. Even more influential in American academe and mainstream culture was another professor of English, Marshal McLuhan. McLuhan took a B.A. and M.A. degree at the University of Manitoba in Canada in the early 1930s. He subsequently gained a Ph.D. at Cambridge University, where he was inculcated with the New Criticism as espoused by F.R. Leavis. Holding posts at various Canadian and American universities he spent the greater part of his career at Saint Michael's College, a Catholic college at the University of Toronto. Indeed, having been born into an

austere Protestant milieu he converted to Catholicism in 1937. His faith
was but part of an early attraction to right-wing and irrational ideas. In an
article written for the University of Manitoba student newspaper in 1933,
which has been almost totally ignored, McLuhan exclaimed:

> I think most will be convinced that there is more of the substance of
> Democracy to be had in the corporate state than under outworn parlia-
> mentarianism ... The really impressive feature of the Corporate State
> is the miraculous manner in which it has, without curtailing individual
> initiative, harmonized the interests of labor and capital ... The whole
> of the Corporate State is based on these corporations, which have
> direct representation by nomination in the minister of corporations, the
> National Council of Corporations, etc. Each profession has its union
> and, like the medieval guilds (and like the Bar and Medical Associations
> in our country), has a system of self-discipline and administration. By
> pyramiding these, the state has a closely knit corporate character ... The
> political future of the 20th century belongs to the corporate state.[88]

This text was no youthful folly.[89] McLuhan's admiration of the corporate
state reflects his life-long belief in the virtues of not only Catholic but
also fascist collectivism, the latter projected into the notion of the coming
of a new tribalism which will supersede individualism and rationality.
For McLuhan it was not the anti-imperialist, anti-racist, democratic, and
socialist ideas of the 1960s that were attractive but the hippie communalism
and anti-intellectualism which anticipated the coming new age. Likewise,
McLuhan's stress on the medium rather than the message reflects not
only his appreciation of television and even the coming of the internet,
but his admiration for the arts of irrational propaganda as practiced by the
Catholic Church and Mussolini. Ignoring the progressive element in the
black, student, and anti-war struggles, McLuhan celebrated the important
irrational element in the counter-culture. In doing so he harked back to the
Italian futurists, whose aesthetic sensationalism anticipated Italian fascism.
Clearly McLuhan's celebration of the irrationalism of the counter-culture
demonstrates its amorphous character while anticipating the coming of
postmodernism's dissolution of the lines between high art, propaganda,
and advertising. Indeed, McLuhan himself became the darling of the
corporate media and the advertising industry, cashing in on the notoriety
of his not very precise ideas by offering his advice in major marketing
campaigns. In doing so he made an extraordinary leap from the ivory tower
aestheticism of the New Criticism to Madison Avenue. Indeed, his stress on

the emotional power and manipulation of key words and images opened up undreamed-of opportunities for the university-educated spin doctors of not only consumerism but also neoconservative politics.

In the meantime, student protest and the Vietnam War helped to radicalize many academics in departments of English. At the MLA Convention at the Americana Hotel in New York, Louis Kampf, chairman of the literature department at MIT, and several others were arrested for putting up anti-war posters in the hotel lobby. The protests were the result of the initiatives of what came to be called the Radical Caucus, in which Kampf played a leading role. The Radical Caucus was formed out of two prior groups called the New University Conference and RESIST. The arrests led to further protests during the convention itself, and calls for the democratization of the Association, which was dominated by English departments from the elite universities. A partial opening up of the MLA took place and in 1971 Kampf was elected its president.[90] The activities of the Radical Caucus focused on pedagogical and professional issues. The Caucus put out a journal, *Radical Teacher*, which, as its title indicates, was concerned with issues of teaching, language, and composition. In short, the Caucus was primarily interested in questions of the canon, of recovering women's and other literatures, along with the nature of the profession itself. It continues to exist as part of the MLA.

The Marxist Literary Group was formed by Fredric Jameson and a number of his graduate students, including James Kavanagh, Bill Langen, Gene Holland, June Howard, and John Beverley, at the University of California, San Diego in 1969–70.[91] It was originally part of the Radical Caucus. The two groups soon divided along the fault line of theory and praxis. The Jameson group, made up by a number of more patient, tenured members of high-profile departments, were addicted to theory. The main body of the Radical Caucus, on the other hand, was constituted by more imperiled inner city, community college activists, demanding more overtly disruptive tactics and abjuring the long-term as just another form of cooptation. The Marxist Literary Group was concerned with the development of theory, and specifically Marxist theory. In the late 1960s and early '70s, Jameson, along with others on the Marxist left, saw the lack of a firm theoretical foundation as one of the inherent weaknesses of the emergent New Left. Any real systematic change in American society required as a minimal first step the creation of a social-democratic movement. This, in turn, entailed two preconditions: the creation of a Marxist intelligentsia and of a Marxist culture or intellectual presence. Such a posture reflected no doubt Jameson's increasingly high status as against those in the Radical

Caucus. But it also was a reflection of the waning of 1960s radicalism and of a falling back into theorizing that recalls that of the Frankfurt School. On the other hand, it facilitated Jameson's work, which made Marxism in the long term the focal point of American literary criticism. Largely as a result of Jameson's intellectual leadership, the Marxist Literary Group became the largest affiliated group of the MLA. The political implications of the long-term ascendancy of Marxist criticism should not be underestimated. Jameson himself retreated into theory and emerged over the next decade as a towering philosophical and literary thinker. In this respect he resembles his mentor Karl Marx, who after the tumult of 1848 retired to theorize capital.

Jameson took his Ph.D. at Yale under the supervision of the philologist and literary scholar Erich Auerbach. The influence of Jean-Paul Sartre on his three key early works, *Marxism and Form* (1971), *The Prison House of Language* (1972), and *The Political Unconscious: Narrative as a Socially Symbolic Act* (1981), embody the development of Jameson's approach to literature—a criticism rooted in Hegelian Marxism as developed by Lukács.[92] In the hands of Jameson, Hegelianized Marxism opened the door to a non-reductive materialist analysis of literature. Not only did it provide fresh means for understanding the functions of culture and ideology, it offered new effective instruments for understanding the affective and symbolical valences of the concept of modes of production itself. The over-determination of the formal characteristics of modern art, with its drive for rational control over the contingent elements of art or of lived experience, for example, was linked to the increasingly centralized nature of economic life in advanced capitalism.[93]

Fundamental to Jameson's criticism is the need to historicize aesthetic production. The informing principle of his approach is the very Marxist conception that history is a unity based on a succession of modes of production and forms of class struggle. Social reality must be conceived of as a totality which develops dialectically. It is within this context that the creation of literature must be understood. Indeed, literary narrative is a privileged and enduring habit of human consciousness throughout history. According to Jameson historical criticism is not to be understood as an optional auxiliary to other forms of literary criticism. Rather it is the absolute horizon of forms of interpretation within which other approaches are to be understood as partial and subordinate. Accordingly, Marxism acts as the master code within which literary texts are to be rewritten through the work of criticism. Hegelian and Marxist mediation may be redefined semiotically as a transcoding operation whereby a single discourse can analyze and articulate two or more objects simultaneously, as for example text and history. Literary works are to be grasped not primarily as objective structures but as symbolic practices, strategies for providing formal or imaginary solutions to unresolvable social contradictions. The function of criticism is to show that a given text represents a rewriting of a prior historical or ideological subtext. The literary work embodies such a text while attempting to transcend it. The text must also be understood as what Jameson describes as a ideologeme, a particular form of class discourse or a symbolic move in a strategic ideological confrontation between classes. Such discourses should be situated within the organizing unity of a mode of production.

Jameson's originality lies in the fact that he does not posit the mode of production as an inert extra-textual object which is merely economic in character. The succession and synchrony of modes of production is also a sequence and composite of dominant orders or sign systems—including magical and mythical narrative, kinship, religion, politics, relations of personal domination, commodity fetishism—which fix the outer boundaries of historical genre. The individual text that forms part of a literary genre can be understood as a complex field of force in which messages emitted by sign systems peculiar to distinct modes of production enter into collision with one another. The notion of genre is an indispensable mediation between immanent textual analysis, the history of cultural forms in conflict with one another, and the evolution of social life. Jameson's insistence that the forms of culture need to be understood as part of an evolving mode of production represents a real advance in overcoming the chronic reductionism that has plagued Marxist thought. On the other hand, while, for example, capitalism as a mode of production can be analyzed in this way as part of a given social and historical formation, capital, by its abstract nature, can operate by transcending the particular historical and concrete features of a given mode of production. Jameson embraced cultural analysis of both text and society, but demonstrated how it could be convincingly linked with the abstractions of historical materialism.

It is fitting that we close this discussion of the 1960s with Jameson. Another, darker age soon arrived, dominated by postmodernism and neoclassical economics. But the power of Jameson's Marxist-rooted theorizing was able not only to ride out this barren period, but also to critically understand and transcend it. As a result, Jameson represents the most powerful bridge between the intellectual and social ferment of the 1960s and the current revival of Marxism.

4

The Retreat from History (1980–2008)

As we have seen, largely inspired by Marxism, students and workers in many countries challenged the legitimacy of the capitalist system during the 1960s. In the United States, at the height of capitalist post-war prosperity, students and the black and Chicano working class organized and protested war and capitalism. On the other hand, the white working class—its organized elements controlled by conservative union bosses, its mind policed by the Cold War media, and enjoying unprecedented prosperity—remained politically inert if not hostile to radicalism. Its political weight and passivity proved decisive, and eventually protest exhausted itself giving way to identity politics, environmental concerns, and careerist preoccupations.

By the 1980s the bureaucratic socialist system in the Soviet Union entered into crisis. China, which had gone through the radicalism of the Great Leap Forward and the Cultural Revolution, experienced its Thermidor with the death of Mao and the overthrow of the Gang of Four in the mid-1970s. Henceforth, the Chinese Communist Party moved to a Chinese "path to socialism." This entailed the muting of ideology and an economic and ideological restructuring that carried the country in the direction of a market economy. As a result, the popularity of Marxism as an ideology faded worldwide. In the United States it was virtually abandoned, with the exception of isolated groups of true believers and small numbers of academics who were mainly veterans of the 1960s and were now tenured.

Meanwhile, from the 1970s onward, the golden age of the U.S. economy faded away. More productive or lower-cost economies—Germany and Japan, then China and South Korea—began to challenge American competitiveness. This was part of the exodus of manufacturing from the Global North toward the Global South. At the same time the capitalist economy overall slowed, increasingly took on a financial rather than a productive aspect in the leading capitalist states, and eventually entered into a full crisis. The mass of workers in the advanced countries and especially in the United States suffered a steep decline in living standards in the next four decades. The export of industrial jobs to underdeveloped countries weakened trade unions in the West and even put into question, for some, a Marxist analysis of capitalist society based on the working class. Those at the top prospered through speculation, by extracting surplus from those below in the form of interest on consumer, housing, and educational loans as well as through rents or patents on intellectual property of all types, and by stepping up the exploitation of the Global South. Worldwide the polarization between the rich and poor dramatically increased. The prospects for strong capitalist growth seemed to dim as increasing fractions of the population lost out and came to question capitalism's legitimacy without being able to do much about it. The concluding decades of the century and the first years of the new millennium thus saw a dual crisis—a crisis of Marxism but also a crisis of capitalism. While the global economy sputtered, the collapse of the East European communist bloc facilitated the expansion of world trade and especially global finance under the aegis of the United States. Indeed, the dismemberment of socialist Yugoslavia and the increasing penetration of the Middle East by the United States signaled a revival of U.S. imperialism.

The universities during the height of the Cold War had responded patriotically by producing knowledge and ideological rationalizations that served the needs of capital and the U.S. government in fighting the communist threat. Many of these approaches, like New Criticism, Parsonian sociology, political systems theory, majoritarian pluralism, and modernization theory, had been discredited by social protest and critical scrutiny during the 1960s. At the same time, the tremendous expansion of the universities, their impressive research activities and the shake-up of their structures by student protests had enhanced the quality of higher education and given it a more cosmopolitan outlook. The expansion of curriculums, diversification of faculties, wider accessibility to minority and women's studies, and relaxation of the rules imposed on students, made universities more intellectually and culturally interesting and more open places than ever before. Moreover, with their enormous resources, American universities stepped to the forefront of an increasingly globalized hierarchy of institutions of higher learning, attracting growing numbers of foreign students. While not ceasing to be influenced by the limitations of American political culture, U.S. universities nonetheless increasingly opened themselves to intellectual currents from across the globe.[1]

The legitimacy of American capitalism had been seriously shaken by the upheaval of the 1960s and called forth an across-the-board political and cultural reaction from business, governments, right-wing academics, think-tanks, and foundations. Indeed, the imposition of austerity on workers, minorities, and students, while mainly economically motivated, was also founded on the determination to restore social discipline. With this in mind, from the onset of the 1980s a cultural offensive against the mixing of politics with the teaching of the humanities and social sciences and a demand for the restoration of standards issued from the right-wing, led by William Bennett, Alan Bloom, and David Horowitz. Accompanying these ideological attacks, public funding for universities, including research budgets, were sharply cut by the federal and state governments. This had mainly to do with the imposition of neoliberal austerity, including overall declines in health, welfare, and educational spending. But many right-wing politicians and business interests saw such cuts in university budgets as a means of disciplining academics and students who were considered radicals.

In the context of this right-wing ideological and financial counter-offensive, scholars in the humanities and social sciences were forced into retreat. Briefly moved by the student revolt and the breakthroughs of Marxist scholarship during the 1960s, the essentially liberal majority of aspiring lower-middle-class academics now distanced themselves from an increasingly unfashionable Marxism. From the 1970s onward new apologetics for the existing order came into vogue. It was this changed context that spawned postmodernism as a new cutting-edge academic movement. It constituted a wide-ranging attack on Marxism, couched in the form of a rejection of so-called meta-narratives.

Admittedly the motives behind the development of postmodernism were complicated. Many academics were affronted by what they considered the reductionism of Marxist thought. Also not to be discounted was the distrust felt by women, black people, and gays against a schematic Marxist sociology which effectively deprived them of recognition and a sense of agency. Be that as it may, almost instinctively internalizing the demands of the ruling class across the humanities, a mood of postmodern skepticism swept through academe, the effect of which was to cast doubt on knowledge which could inspire political action. Understanding the deep structures of society, which had been a preoccupation of previous decades and might have provided a springboard for radical political action, was rejected as intellectually impossible. Postmodernism became preoccupied with language, meaning, and interpreting what had hitherto been assumed to be the more superficial or superstructural aspects of society. Indeed, a new emphasis was given to the determinative influence of culture on society, in what came to be called the cultural turn. This, it might be noted, marked a return to the perspective of Boasian anthropology, characterized by a pre-occupation with cultural meaning and a sense of relativism that rejected social and political evolution.

Much of the theorizing that followed in this vein had real worth. On the other hand, the political implications of the cultural turn highlighted the difficulties in the way of pursuing a radical and democratic politics that could change society. If theorists referred to Marxism at all it was in a politically neutered form, or one without any political strategy that could help to emancipate humanity. Marxism was politically sterilized and represented as at best just another academic theory.[2] There continued to be Marxists—literary, analytical, so-called political, and feminist—but the resurgence of capitalism, the defeat of communism, and the preoccupation with identity and cultural studies, tended to marginalize their influence and discourage political engagement. Marxists tended to be seen as passé, grimly holding to an outmoded worldview. Indeed, the onslaught of new theory, seen as an end in itself in the midst of what amounted to a speed-up of academic research, only strengthened this view of a Marxism which had become old-fashioned.

At the other end of the spectrum from the emphasis on culture and relativism, there developed a powerful offensive by neoliberal economics that stressed the scientific power of rational economic thought. Rejecting the Keynesianism that had dominated the post-war period, neoliberal economics was at furthest remove from the skepticism and indecision that paralyzed other disciplines under the sway of postmodernism and the cultural turn. As an academic discipline it reinforced its intimate intellectual and even financial ties to capitalism and made itself incontestably the leading social science, using a scientistic approach based on positivism and methodological individualism, the presumption of rational choice, and quantitative analysis. Indeed, in what has been referred to as economics imperialism, it began to claim that its approach could revolutionize the study of history and anthropology, to say nothing of political science and sociology. While traditional exponents of these disciplines wallowed in self-doubt and withdrew from political engagement, the supporters of neoliberal thought advanced an agenda for dramatic social transformation based on the assumptions of rationality, universalism, and individualism which amounted to a parody of Enlightenment ideals. Neoliberalism pursued an instrumental rationality—so criticized by the Frankfurt School—to extremes.

As different as they are from each other, postmodernism and neoliberal economics had in common the goal of revoking history by insisting that it was possible to return to the past willy-nilly. Neoliberalism affected to believe that a return to the unfettered markets of the nineteenth century was possible. Postmodernism sought to deny the weight of history on the present, converting it into a theatrical backdrop on the present moment. By rejecting any possible alternative to capitalism, neoliberal economics and postmodernism both celebrated the human benefits of markets and the reign of commodities. Both were made more plausible by the flight of much productive capital from the capitalist heartlands to the Global South and the consequent disappearance from consciousness of collective productive activity in favor of individualized consumerism and a largely intangible finance capital. Only in such a context could one pretend to believe that markets operate as entities which can exist independently of the state and productive labor. The economic conditions that favored the postmodern are those described by Harvey as "based on a fetish world of fantasy and imagination built on pyramiding fictions that cannot last."[3] The postmodern condition as defined by Jameson arises directly out of this sensibility.

The discussion in this chapter is set within the institutional and political economic developments in academic life during the period of neoliberal consolidation and their corresponding intellectual/ideological reflection in the development of the disciplines, seen most significantly in the rise of postmodernism and neoliberal economics. Once again it is the attempt to deny history and especially the history of capitalism that is central in this evolution.

Postmodernism

The ebbing of the spirit of revolt and the apparent failure of Marxist politics, the fragmentation of radicalism into identity politics, growing economic uncertainty, and a capitalist counter-offensive fostered a mood of intellectual disenchantment which invaded American university campuses in the form of so-called French theory. The failure of the May 1968 revolution had created a sense of political vacuum in France and it was from there that postmodernism made its way into American academe. Certain intellectuals like Jean Baudrillard, Jacques Derrida, Michel Foucault, and Jean-François Lyotard shared a disabused and skeptical viewpoint with regard to Marxism, the Communist Party, and the Soviet Union. Moreover, it should be underlined that their rejection of left-wing politics reflected a certain embourgeoisment of the French intelligentsia as a whole, which became more and more evident from the 1970s onward, distancing them from street politics and popular causes.

While enjoying a passing celebrity in France, the teachings of these key postmodern writers were acclaimed in French, English, and comparative literature departments in the United States as the basis of a new postmodernist orientation which challenged the certainties of modernist ideology and aesthetics especially as reflected in Marxism. While largely unheard of outside the academy, the precepts of postmodernism fed off and at the same time infiltrated the world of advertising, fashion, architectural styles, and the frantic and seemingly meaningless consumerism that marked the 1980s. Indeed, postmodernist academics celebrated the supposedly democratic pleasures of mass consumption, while denigrating the snobberies of modernism and its established intellectual and aesthetic canons. The obliteration of the distinction between high and low or popular culture which had already characterized the 1960s was confirmed by postmodernism. Indeed, according to some postmodern theorists, fetishized commodities and media spectacles could provide the symbolic and aesthetic resources answering the need for a new form of spiritual satisfaction and entertainment to the masses in a way that echoed the *trompe l'oeil* of Baroque religious ritual and art.[4] At the same time, an unmistakable eagerness to make literature, art, and ideas marketable took hold in the face of creeping economic austerity and insecurity. At the very least, new theory became academically highly marketable. The postmodern embodied a capitulation to the seemingly overwhelming power of the capitalist status quo and on the part of some postmodern critics reflected a new found enthusiasm and celebration of it. At the same time, its mocking and sometimes humorous treatment of the traditional helped to endow it with a certain subversive quality that harmlessly echoed the rebelliousness of the 1960s, attracting the fashionably minded while continuing to repel conservatives.

There can be no question that postmodernism caught on because it fit with a certain post-revolutionary if not counter-revolutionary mood among some academics, particularly disabused Marxists, intellectually orphaned counter-culture intellectuals, and protagonists of identity politics. They were on the look-out for a new perch without falling back into the academic traditionalism they despised. Moreover, the new phase of commodified capitalist culture that gradually took form in the 1970s foreclosed such a regression. What the times demanded was an intellectual position that appeared to be an advance but which concealed a retreat or defeat. In this respect postmodernism reminds one of nineteenth-century romanticism, which was marked by a rejection of reason and politics in favor of intense subjectivity and irrationalism. Indeed, its superficial attachment to a mythical Gothic past, amnesia with regard to the French Revolution, and fetishistic attachment to the glitter of the new commodity culture suggests something deeper than a coincidence. On the other hand, romanticism did transcend the somewhat brittle and at times superficial rationality of Enlightenment thought. Postmodernism likewise put into question a perhaps too schematic and dogmatic Marxism while reflecting in the cultural sphere a new economic stage. Indeed, Fredric Jameson, who became one of postmodernism's most perceptive critics and may be said to have actually identified it as a new zeitgeist, characterized it as a social and political condition from which there was no easy exit. In other words, postmodernism represented a distinctive new cultural period in which even those who were critical had to try to understand it and find the critical means of overcoming it.

It is important to try to pinpoint the social and economic location of those who especially promoted or favored this ideology in academe. It should be recalled that academics and especially tenured academics in the 1960s still enjoyed the status of establishment intellectuals in the Gramscian sense. While some criticized the war in Vietnam mainly from a liberal position, they were after all employed by private or public institutions of higher learning in order to defend rather than overthrow the existing liberal and capitalist order. As pointed out by David Harvey, furthermore, postmodernism particularly resonated with some humanities and social science professors who were part of a broader milieu which included engineers, legal experts, scientists, managers, consultants, and other mind-workers who made up roughly 20 percent of the U.S. workforce. Members of this privileged group needed to be well-educated in analytical and symbolical skills, a training based on home environments in which children experienced an affluent and culturally enriched environment. This group constituted the core of an upper-middle stratum within capitalism which increasingly tended to segregate itself and its children in privileged enclaves insulated against the rest of society—traditional production workers, service workers, and the poor and unemployed who had little future. Beholden to capital for their privileged position, they were largely oblivious to the increasingly harsh social and economic experience of most workers under the thrall of neoliberalism.[5]

This cloistered and privileged group found postmodernism particularly plausible and reassuring in the wake of the tumult of the 1960s and 1970s. This against the reality that from the 1980s onward workers overall began to experience wage stagnation and job precariousness, and this was as true in universities as it was in the automobile industry. It was in these years that tenure track employment was becoming increasingly hard to get and that contract work within universities became more and more the norm. A kind of academic speed-up developed whereby unprecedented demands on the part of administrators for constant publication, cutting-edge research, and teaching excellence pervaded the universities and were internalized by faculty. Automobile workers easily understood the tightening of screws and production speed-ups by management. Academics, however, innocent in their understanding of their place in the mode of production, had difficulty comprehending what was happening to their working conditions. Meanwhile university tuition costs and student debt soared as students, increasingly chastened, clung to their aspirations for economic security and social mobility. The academic demands on students increased in order to secure access to professional schools and employment. These new and harsh realities were rendered more poignant by the fact that an air of normality continued to pervade life in the universities, with undergraduate and graduate enrollments still expanding as increasing fractions of the population saw higher education as indispensable to their economic and social future. Competitive individualism engulfed students as well as faculty.

Under such conditions postmodernism took hold in the elite academic institutions and spread through the universities. An intense competition developed among top universities to attract the stars of the movement to conferences. Berkeley, Buffalo, and NYU prided themselves in showcasing Foucault, while Yale, Cornell, and Irvine featured Derrida. The publicity surrounding the annual meetings of the Modern Languages Association relayed the concepts of deconstruction, post-Marxism, feminism, queer studies, black and Chicano studies to a confused wider public.[6] Postmodernists raised eyebrows and attracted attention by audaciously contending that the arbitrary assumption or illusion of an original irreducible real object conditioned the logocentrism of philosophy, that history was based on arbitrary and invented narratives and questionable facts, that social science was guilty of reductionism and cultural imperialism, and that even the exact sciences supposedly suffered from autism or a lack of external legitimatization. One could not speak of the truth of such sciences but only of their social construction—the one excluding the other.[7]

Postmodernism was in part an attempt to critique the thought of the European Enlightenment, which it viewed as a projection of power over the rest of the world. Above all it questioned its fundamental premise of human progress. Like the Enlightenment, postmodernism based itself on the individual but reached pessimistic rather than optimistic conclusions about human capacity. It cast doubt on the assumption that human beings are autonomous stable subjects capable of objective and rational analysis by means of which it is possible to discover generalizable truths that exhaustively explain the past or present world. Enlightenment ideas that were regarded as foundational wrongly presumed that it is possible to know the world based on looking at it from an objective reference point.[8] Postmodernism rejected the idea that there is a timeless, contextually free knowledge, and having made that point denied the possibility of knowledge altogether. Attempts to theorize the foundations of human existence and to use such theory to explain the present or past were acts of power that falsely pretended to be objective and politically neutral. More often than not such theorizations or meta-narratives turned out to be the lucubrations of white middle-class, culturally moribund intellectuals who wanted permanently to inflict their systems of thought on everyone else. Such meta-narratives were in fact merely attempts to retain power.[9]

The knowability of reality itself and the truth of representations of it are problematic and are only accessible through language and texts, according to postmodernists. Indeed, all phenomena can only be approached through literary and cultural analysis. But the ability of language to represent reality is questionable. A text has no stable reference or identification because words essentially only refer to other words and therefore a reader must approach a text by deconstruction, or eliminating any metaphysical or ethnocentric assumptions through an active role in defining meaning. Generalization based on a sense of totality and the capacity to abstract from singularities being impossible, heterogeneity, multiplicity, and difference are the substance of the knowledge that we have.

Postmodernism amounted to an across-the-board skeptical revolt against all received intellectual authority.[10] An immediate and obvious rejoinder to such skepticism is to point to the fact that in order to voice such skepticism the skeptic must herself take up an authoritative position, the basis of which is as uncertain as are all other statements. In other words, postmodernism, in putting itself forward as a counter-narrative, constitutes itself as a narrative. Moreover, the singularities that postmoderns insist upon are themselves only comprehensible as part of larger ordered structures, whether of language, society, or nature. And the postmodern position assumes that rational truth has to be absolute, whereas it need only be the best truth based on the evidence and argument available at the moment, or in other words a tentative and contingent knowledge better than existing alternatives. Perry Anderson, a brilliant champion of Marxism, characterizes postmodern thought as marked by three elements: the completely disproportionate importance given to language, the attenuation of what constitutes truth, and the randomization of history. While some scholars, he continues, view language as a screen through which one can gain an insight into the society or natural realm which lies behind it, postmodernists extend the jurisdiction of language to both encompass and occlude the perception of all major aspects of society or nature. Derrida, one of postmodernism's leading lights, even claimed that nothing exists outside of texts. Some take this so far as to mean that discourse (rather than cooperative social labor necessarily involving communication through language) actually constructs all aspects of society. Concomitant with the inflation of the power of linguistic signifiers is the weakening of the referents toward which they point, fostering skepticism about the possibility of determining truth and the consequent elimination of the very grounds of rational knowledge. History was accordingly scattered into a purely chance phenomena in which adjacency eclipsed any notion of a chain of temporal cause and effect. Postmodernism, concluded Anderson, "strafed meaning, overran truth, outflanked ethics and politics and wiped out history."[11]

The political implications of postmodernism need to be stressed. By downgrading the critical function of reason and undermining a historical perspective postmodernism gave up on criticizing capitalism and instead became complicit with it. As we have seen the number of critical thinkers within academe in the United States was limited to begin with, especially in the wake of McCarthyism. But as we have noted, at the height of the Cold War there still existed within its ranks a Herbert Marcuse, C. Wright Mills, Leslie White, or Walter LaFeber, who provided a critical and historical perspective on American society and opened the way toward the protests of the 1960s. Postmodernism, likewise, tried to disarm whatever critical capacity existed in the humanities and social sciences, paving the way for the academic capitalism of the new millennium and putting into question the future of these disciplines and thereby the existence of the university. But there were a sufficient number of so-called tenured radicals who clung to their Marxism. The most important of these was Fredric Jameson.

Enter Jameson

Jameson's analysis of postmodernism in his magisterial work, *Post-modernism, or, the Cultural Logic of Late Capitalism* (1991), is the most comprehensive and deepest examination of the postmodern condition.[12] Jameson views postmodernism as the reflection of fundamental changes in the nature of capitalism toward the close of the twentieth century. The term "late capitalism" stems from Ernest Mandel, head of the Fourth International and an authoritative Marxist economist, who coined the phrase in the 1970s.[13] Mandel viewed late capitalism as a third stage in capitalist history following the periods of national capitalism (1789–1880) and monopoly capitalism/imperialism (1880–1945). Assuming that capitalism was reaching some kind of endpoint or crisis, Mandel saw the period after 1945 as dominated by the multinational corporation, globalized markets, mass consumption, increasing commodification, and the worldwide dominance of finance capital. Mandel's view still holds water, but it does not fully capture the evolution of the system in its current phase, which is appropriately called neoliberalism. As its name suggests, this phase is marked by the characteristics of late capitalism, but now post-1980 also the full deregulation of international and national markets, the dismantling of the welfare state, the total commodification of society, as well as the decline of manufacturing in the West and the development of the information economy and the mass media based on corporate-controlled internet technology. This latest phase is the context of postmodernism.

As we have remarked, Jameson views postmodernism as less an ideology than a condition—a condition which he as well as everyone else is a part of and which he characterizes as both catastrophic and progressive at one and the same time. By linking his analysis with the narrative of historical materialism he has penetrated into the core aspects of postmodernism in a way that surpasses those who champion it. His analysis is premised on the view that narrative is a fundamental human characteristic, something postmodernists doubt or deny outright. The Marxist grand narrative, rooted in dialectical reason and the course of history, remains the key which opens the door to an understanding of subsidiary narratives. Indeed, in positioning himself this way, Jameson became at one and the same time the foremost expositor of postmodernism and its most incisive critic.[14]

According to Jameson, postmodernism lives in an eternal present the experience of which is that of an inchoate world of commodified things. Indeed, postmodernism is based on a new stage of capitalism in which the globe has more or less been fully commodified. Modernism in contrast reflected a period in which capitalism advanced in a world in which many social formations and the hinterlands of nature still continued to stand outside of its embrace. Postmodernism emerged at the point when this process came to complete itself, or when capitalism has completed its conquest of the planet. Under these circumstances the entire globe is subject to capitalism and accordingly becomes commodified or subject to culture of a capitalist kind.[15]

Parenthetically we should specify what such a commodity culture entails. According to Marx the cultural aspect of the commodity arises from its powerfully fetishistic character based not on its function as a useful object made by human beings, but on its status as an object of exchange which is experienced as having literally a superhuman power, or a power beyond human creation to which men and women feel compelled to submit themselves. The masking of the commodity in this way leads to the experience of it as something that has an innate force the acquisition of which becomes the object of desire. Commodities fill the contemporary world and as such are experienced as powerful and desirable entities that are produced and circulate magically. The contemporary commodified world is accordingly as much an enchanted world as was that of the Middle Ages dominated by the heavenly pantheon of the saints who hovered over and controlled humankind. Capitalist commodities are as much charged with meaning as was the pantheon of Catholic demigods or angels and saints. Such a realm is the cultural aspect of late capitalism. The fetishism of commodities means that capitalism has a powerful psychological attraction on humanity which cuts against a consciousness of socially and politically based class interests.

Jameson is highly critical of this current situation, which he associates with the suppression and loss of a sense of connection to real history tied to the evolution of the capitalist mode of production. A critical analysis committed to making sense of the present in terms of historical context and ideological critique is rejected by postmodernists. According to Jameson, insofar as it deals with history, postmodernist culture has transformed the past into a series of emptied-out stylizations (pastiches) or superficial cardboard mimickings that are so many interchangeable simulacrums, imitations of the real past emptied of context and made available as commodities for current consumption. What we are left with is a fascination with the present and the apparent triumph of capitalist commodity culture and its cultural forms.[16] But despite the hegemony of postmodernist consciousness the sense of history cannot be eliminated, but remains repressed and hidden in the collective subconscious which it troubles.

Jameson viewed postmodern skepticism of meta-narratives as undoubtedly a political and ideological position, but also as a genuine mode of experience stemming from the conditions of intellectual labor imposed by the late capitalist mode of production. Such skepticism arises from the fragmentation of experience, the invasion and commodification of the cultural realm by capitalism, and the resultant penetration of other spheres of society by this commodified sense of culture. Moreover, under the conditions of postmodernism there is a collapse of the distinction between the economic and social and the political and the cultural superstructure. In the face of these developments postmodernists claim that the complex differentiation between different spheres has been overcome by the crisis of foundationalism and the consequent relativization of truth claims. Jameson rejects this view, arguing instead that this perception is itself a subjective response to late capitalist commodification in which the base generates its superstructures with a new kind of dynamic.

The Cultural Turn

It was in this new commodified cultural environment that a cultural approach to the analysis of society gained purchase, becoming known as the cultural turn. An important source of the cultural turn was the work of Richard Hoggart and Stuart Hall at the Birmingham Centre for Contemporary Cultural Studies in England. The two in turn were inspired by the Marxist literary critic Raymond Williams and the historian Edward Thompson. Hoggart and Hall had sought to apply Marxist categories and especially the thought of Gramsci to the analysis of the past and present lives and the consciousness of the British working class. The concept of hegemony and the problem of class agency played an important role in this approach.[17]

Cultural studies as it developed in the United States, especially through the creation of scores of cultural studies departments, often tended to downplay the significance of class altogether and to lose its relationship to Marxist economic categories. Rather it was inclined toward falling back on the study of race and gender based on French theory and in particular the work of Foucault. The sometimes frivolous and uncritical analysis of American pop culture was one of its embarrassing strong points, dwelling on such matters as the meaning of Disney cartoons, Star Trek, Madonna, and various soap operas.[18] At one level this was justified as a rejection of the pretentiousness of high culture. On the other hand, it reflects a continuing American academic evasion, a reluctance to probe too deeply into the roots of commodity culture. But however frivolous some aspects of cultural studies might have become, the fact is that cultural theory saw an explosion of interest in the 1980s and 1990s though a range of disciplines including English, comparative literature, romance languages, film studies, anthropology, sociology, and philosophy, leading to a welcome dedifferentiation of the social sciences and humanities and a partial overcoming of departmental specialization in which, despite everything, a renewed Marxism found an increasingly important place.[19] On the other hand, insofar as Marxism came to exercise influence, it had little connection with mass politics or a real strategy of liberation.

Feminism and Post-Feminism

The academic employment of women dramatically increased during this period. Yet women continued to be under-represented especially in professional programs at universities. Their salaries were on average lower than those of men. On the other hand, feminist scholars began to produce powerful new scholarship both in terms of feminist theory and at the level of practical struggle for women's rights. Moreover, despite the prevalence of postmodernism, there continued to be feminist scholars who were preoccupied by the political and social struggle for equality for women. Particularly urgent was the need to mount a defense of women's rights in the face of the conservative reaction that marked the 1980s and 1990s. A key element of neoconservatism included an anti-feminism which insisted on, among other things, the otherness of women and the need to continue to keep them subjugated and dependent on men economically but also sexually.[20]

Catherine Mackinnon zeroed in on the importance of sexual objectification of women and its links with oppression. She has been concerned with the sexual harassment and exploitation of women which she links with the ongoing inequality of social power between men and women. Mackinnon, a professor of law at the University of Michigan, held that sexual objectification is the primary process of the subjection of women. Female sexuality is alienated when it is defined by men as something that exists for their pleasure. Pointing to rape, incest, sexual harassment, pornography, and prostitution, she emphasized sexual coercion as a means of enforcing patriarchy.[21]

Joan Wallach Scott, a distinguished historian of France, has chosen in her historical work and theorizing to de-emphasize the question of defining sexual and gender difference, instead placing the emphasis on the struggle for equality based on a respect for difference. France and especially the French Revolution and the Republican tradition have always been at the forefront of the interests of American historians, and Scott has become a leading practitioner in this field. She has used feminist theory to enrich her investigation of French history while her historical research has deepened our understanding of theoretical issues like the relationship between racism and gender.[22] Particularly outstanding has been her study on the politics of the veil, in which she exposes the colonial roots of the racism and exclusion directed against Muslim women and men in the name of French liberal republicanism and secularism.[23]

Meanwhile feminism itself came under criticism by women of color for its lack of attention to questions of race and ethnicity. It is alleged that feminism marginalizes or represses discussion of differences among women based on differences of power. From this perspective there is no such thing as a single universal identity among women.[24] Out of these concerns there developed the concept of intersectionality. This notion first emerged in the 1970s from the practice and theorizing of revolutionary black feminists and was further developed by women of color feminist theorists. The critical legal theorist Kimberlé Crenshaw is credited with actually coining the term in her writings on black women's experience of employment discrimination and domestic violence.[25] Here gender is just one axis of power among others including race, class, sexuality, citizenship status, ability, and so forth. Most intersectional analysis draws on the concept of social location, a "place" defined by these intersecting axes of domination, and asks how a social location shapes experience and identity. Intersectionality seeks to make visible the systems of oppression that maintain hierarchies of power and organize society, while also providing a means to theorize experience at the personal level.[26] Although "intersectionality" is, unfortunately, more often invoked than actually practiced, fully incorporating all of the axes of power/privilege, political analysis and action remains feminism's central task.[27] Such a task opens the possibility of obtaining a deeper sense of the way that class oppression is experienced by the individual subject, woman or man.

Intersectionality as well as feminist legal theory and history reflected an ongoing commitment to politics. But the 1990s also saw a rift develop between the activist feminism of the 1960s and what came to be called third-wave feminism which was less political and more individualistic. In the context of a third wave the feminism of the 1960s was referred to as second-wave feminism or a feminism that stressed the struggle for gender equality based on political activism. First-wave feminism had striven for voting or political and legal rights, which were regarded as superficial by second-wave feminists. Now third-wave feminism embraced voices that were overlooked in the second wave, focusing on diversity within the women's movement. Its theoretical roots lay in the poststructural literary criticism that emerged in academia during the 1980s. It drew on diverse rhetorical traditions like ecofeminism, women-of-color consciousness, queer theory, and postcolonial theory to break down bifurcations that second-wave feminism had long assumed: male/female, black/white, bondage/liberation. Like second-wave feminism the third wave decried sexual harassment, domestic abuse, and the wage gap, but added to them issues of more recent, global concern: HIV/AIDS and sexually transmitted diseases awareness, child sexual abuse, and equal access to technology. It sought to go beyond the constraints of second-wave politics.[28] Indeed, the third wave in its diversity represented a retreat from organized politics in conformity with neoliberalism.

Sociology

More significant still, and reflecting the cultural turn, was the work of French sociologist Pierre Bourdieu, whose influence in the United States began to rise in the 1980s. Bourdieu was born in 1931 in the extreme southwest of France, the son of a small farmer and postman. His intellectual brilliance led to his entry into the École normale supérieure in 1951. Among those who influenced him were Jean-Paul Sartre, but also the philosophers of science Georges Canguilhem and Gaston Bachelard, as well as Ludwig Wittgenstein. As a result of his army service in Algeria he became interested in sociology, and upon his return to France he was appointed assistant to the liberal sociologist Raymond Aron at the Sorbonne. An assistant professor at Lille he joined the École pratique des hautes études in 1964, breaking with Aron over the uprising of May 1968. In 1975 he joined the École des hautes études en sciences *sociales* (EHESS) and ten years later was inducted into the Collège de France. His later years were marked by an increasing political and intellectual resistance to neoliberalism.

Bourdieu's work represents a continuation of the main line of sociological thought, including Marx, Émile Durkheim, and Weber not to speak of structuralists like Claude Lévi-Strauss. Bourdieu's career as a great academic represents among other things a lifelong resistance to the French Communist Party and Marxism, paradoxically combining a certain anti-Marxist individualism and populism (*poujadisme*) with his mandarin intellectual status. But central to his thought is his attempt to expand Marx's notion of capital to include other kinds of advantage, most importantly so-called cultural capital. Cultural capital refers to non-financial social assets that promote social mobility beyond economic means, including education, intellect, style of speech, dress, or physical appearance.

Another key concept of Bourdieu's is the notion of *habitus*. *Habitus* consists of the ingrained perceptions, dispositions, and patterns of behavior that are internalized by individuals in the course of their socialization and which are strongly conditioned by social class. According to Bourdieu, society is made up of imbricated social fields: economic, political, cultural, religious, and so on. Each field organizes itself on the basis of a specific logic which is determined by its own presuppositions, functions, rules, and objectives. In each field individuals act according to the cultural, economic, social, and symbolical capital available to them. Within a field there are specific rules, but in each there is generally a struggle between those who are established and the newcomers. Still, all participants have an interest in the preservation of the field. Within the field in which they act participants are subject to what Bourdieu terms symbolic violence, based on their position in the field and more generally within society. Those who have the greatest amount of capital, especially cultural capital, within a field are in a position to dominate those with less. This domination is a form of symbolic violence because it is unstated and unconscious, and is experienced by those who are subject to it as a sense of inferiority or insignificance.

Though hostile to the schematic and reductive nature of Marxism, Bourdieu's notions of cultural capital, *habitus*, and symbolic violence nonetheless represent important additions to an understanding of capitalist class hegemony. On the other hand, much of what Bourdieu asserts about the basis of class hegemony had also been articulated by Gramsci, a connection which Bourdieu airily overlooked. Moreover, Gramsci associates his notion of hegemony with bourgeois control of the state, which he is interested in directly challenging—a task that Bourdieu largely dismisses. Bourdieu's ideas and especially the notion of cultural capital have proved increasingly popular in American sociology, perhaps in part because they stress the fundamental difficulties in the way of democratic change.[29] Indeed, the face of U.S. sociology has been altered fundamentally by Bourdieu's influence, spearheading the remarkable growth of cultural sociology, its influence spreading across a range of specialties. Economic sociology, the sociology of organizations, the sociology of education, the sociology of social movements, comparative historical sociology, urban sociology, poverty, race, immigration, network analysis and gender studies can be said to have taken or to be in the process of taking a cultural turn, and of incorporating Bourdieu's works and vocabulary into their literatures at the same time.[30] Beyond sociology, Bourdieu's thought has had an influence across the spectrum of American social science and humanities. The positive reception of Bourdieu alongside the rest of French theory of course also reflects the increasing cosmopolitanism of American scholarship.

Anthropology

While Jameson is the leading figure in the turn to culture within a historical materialist framework, the anthropologist Clifford Geertz is the leading exponent of an idealist approach known as symbolic anthropology. In contrast to Jameson, who points to the sameness of late capitalist commodity culture, Geertz stresses the indefinitely large diversity of cultural forms inherited from the past, which cannot be understood in terms of any underlying unity. The study of culture reduces itself to an appreciation of human difference rather than an underlying unity. Indeed, Geertz asserts not merely the autonomy of culture but its determinative character, and in that sense his work represents a return to the Boasian tradition. Geertz was born in 1926 in San Francisco. His parents divorced when he was three and he was raised by a distant relative in rural California. In 1943, at the age of seventeen, he volunteered for the U.S. Navy in which he served for two years (1943–5). After the war he attended college with funding from the GI Bill. English was his first major at Antioch College, but he found it too limiting and switched to philosophy, and then became attracted to anthropology. Under Talcott Parsons and Clyde Kluckhorn at Harvard he received his Ph.D. with a thesis on a village community in Java. He then assumed positions at the University of Chicago and the Institute for Advanced Studies at Princeton.

At Chicago Geertz became a champion of symbolic anthropology, which gives prime attention to the role of symbols in constructing public meaning. In his seminal work *The Interpretation of Culture* (1973), he outlined a view of culture as "a system of inherited conceptions expressed in symbolic forms by means of which men communicate, perpetuate, and develop their knowledge about and attitudes toward life."[31] His fundamental assumption was that study of culture leads to the conclusion that there are no universal human essences but only infinite variety. Culture cannot be defined by classifying its traits, but rather by understanding it as a system of programs or controls.[32] It is the duty of the ethnographer to describe this variety as best he can. According to Geertz, an ethnographer must present a thick description which is composed not only of facts, but also of commentary and interpretation, and once more interpretations of those comments and interpretations. His task is to extract meaning structures that make up a culture, and for this Geertz believes that a factual account will not suffice, for these meaning structures are layered on top of and into each other in a complex manner. As a result each fact may be subjected to intercrossing interpretations, which ethnography should study and unravel: "believing, with Max Weber, that man is an animal suspended in webs of significance he himself has spun, I take culture to be those webs, and the analysis of it to be therefore not an experimental science in search of law but an interpretative one in search of meaning."[33] Thick ethnographic description ultimately enables the ethnographer to sort out the structures of signification on which a culture bases itself.[34] Stress should be placed on this interpretation of society as text rather than on seeking for underlying causes: "as interworked systems of construable signs (what, ignoring provincial usages, I would call symbols), culture is not a power, something to which social events, behaviors, institutions, or processes can be causally attributed: it is a context, something within which they can be intelligibly—that is, thickly—described."[35] Geertz's anthropology amounts to an application of literary New Criticism to society, and represents a return to and deepening of the idealist approach pioneered by Boas and his school. Moreover, it is an approach which eschews both science and grand theories (Marxism), and as such has influenced the study of history among other disciplines in an idealist direction.

Taken to its limits, Geertz's insistence on diversity has contributed to an epistemological crisis in the discipline. Given the stress on the local, diversity, and interpretation, the intellectual authority of the anthropologist who is supposedly providing an objective account can easily be doubted. Some critics have asked whether anthropology and notably field anthropology really amounts to little more than a sophisticated form of travel writing. The anthropological fieldworker is unable to develop a really scientific description of another culture because of her own biases, memories, and convictions. At the same time, the inner dynamic of the culture under investigation can never be understood by the outside observer. Furthermore, even Geertz's notion of thick description can be criticized as part of a process of objectification of other peoples by Westerners. By the mid-1980s the critique of how anthropologists interpreted and explained the Other, essentially how they engaged in "writing culture," had become a full-blown epistemic crisis that is referred to as the postmodern turn. The driving force behind the postmodern turn was a deep skepticism about whether the investigator could adequately, effectively, or honestly integrate the context of investigation into the context of explanation and, as a result, arrive at true social knowledge. Anthropological representations are not neutral but embedded in power relations as between the imperialist countries and those of the underdeveloped world. A veritable crisis of representation resulted. One response by progressive anthropologists has been to turn the tools of anthropological investigation around in order to study colonialism and capitalist institutions, including universities and business organizations.[36] More significantly it has opened the door to the development of indigenous anthropology, pursued by and from the perspective of indigenous people. This has the potential of turning the table on the whole subject of anthropology, studying indigenous peoples, but also the history of anthropology as an imperialist project.[37]

Postcolonialism

As we have seen, a central feature of postmodernist thought was its distrust of the Enlightenment, whose influence was understood as being more the result of the power of the West than of objective truth. It was this view that opened the way to the emergence of postcolonial theory. The canonical text for this form of thought was Edward Said's *Orientalism* (1978).[38] Part of the Palestinian Diaspora, Said was educated at exclusive private schools in Egypt and the United States. He obtained a B.A. degree from Princeton (1957), and then an M.A. (1960) and a Ph.D. (1964) in English Literature from Harvard. In 1963 he joined Columbia University as a member of the departments of English and comparative literature where he taught until 2003. During his career Said emerged as a powerful and articulate spokesman for the cause of the Palestinians.

In *Orientalism* Said puts Western knowledge of non-Western peoples on trial. A central idea is that Western knowledge about the East is not generated from facts or reality, but from preconceived archetypes that envision all Eastern societies as fundamentally similar to one another and fundamentally dissimilar to the West. Such knowledge of the East is constructed with literary texts and public records that are often limited in their understanding of the facts of life in the Middle East. Following the ideas of Foucault, Said emphasized the relationship between power and knowledge in scholarly and popular thinking, in particular with regard to European views of the Islamic Arab world. He argued that Orient and Occident worked as oppositional terms, so that the "Orient" was constructed as a negative inversion of Western culture. The work of Gramsci was also important in shaping Said's analysis, especially the notion of hegemony, which Said employed to explain the pervasiveness of Orientalist constructs and representations in Western scholarship and their relation to the exercise of power over the "Orient."

Orientalism concluded that Western writing about the Orient depicts it as an irrational, weak, and feminized "Other," an existential condition contrasted with the rational, strong, and masculine West. This binary relation derives from the European psychological need to create a sense of cultural inequality between West and East; cultural difference is attributed to immutable cultural "essences" inherent to Oriental peoples and things. Said's articulation of orientalism had immense influence on the study of the relationship between European and non-European people across the globe. Said himself became the foremost spokesman for the cause of the Palestinian people and Arab and Islamic peoples in the West. But *Orientalism* itself has itself been criticized in that it tended to view the Arab subject as passive in the face of the overwhelming power of the cultural dominance of the West.[39] Moreover, the reception of his work came in the midst of a renewed offensive on the part of Western imperialism against the underdeveloped world in the 1980s and '90s. To Said's immense frustration, the influence of his work was largely limited to an increasingly cloistered world of theory confined to the universities.[40] Although obviously influenced by Marxism, it has to be said that he kept his distance from the latter as a result of the ongoing influence upon him of a certain American academic fastidiousness. As E. San Martin puts it "the anti-Marxism of postcolonial theory may be attributed partly to Said's eclecticism, his belief that American left criticism is marginal, and his distorted if not wholly false understanding of Marxism based on doctrinaire anticommunism and the model of 'actually existing socialism' during the Cold War."[41]

Said's work nonetheless proved seminal to the development of post-colonialism—a school which above all criticized assumptions of Western civilizational superiority, challenging European canons, and developing its own independent critical readings of Western and non-Western literature. Its origins were two-fold. On the one hand, at its most idealistic, its objective was to critique both the cultural legacy of past Western political, cultural, and economic imperialism and to mount an intellectual defense of the legacy of the post-1945 independence movements in the postcolonial states. It championed resistance to the ongoing influence of the West in the postcolonial situation, and the development of national literatures and cultures which could contest lingering dominance by the West.[42] Its aim was the noble one of helping to make what had hitherto been invisible visible.[43] On the other hand, there was something fundamentally ersatz about this movement. It purported to defend *culturally* national liberation movements at a time when such movements were in reality in retreat, hammered by military repression and the structural adjustment programs imposed by the West. In this context of retreat, such merely cultural protests rang hollow. All the more so as many of the intellectuals who took up the cudgels of postcolonialism did so while leaving their homelands in the underdeveloped world and making careers in the West and in the United States in particular. Indeed, the co-option of these intellectuals into the American academic system demonstrated once again the growing cosmopolitan reach of the United States and its universities. But the impotence and insignificance of postcolonialist theory in face of the renewed onslaught of Western imperialism seemed evident.[44]

Among the most prominent of postcolonial thinkers were Indian intellectuals like Dipesh Chakrabarty, Gayatri Chakravorty Spivak, Homi Baba, and Ranajit Guha. They were united in their rejection of Enlightenment universalism and its claims for the validity of certain social and economic categories independent of local culture and places. Their principal target was a Marxism which held that categories like class and exploitation are valid in all societies, European and non-European alike. Postcolonial thinkers asserted that the application of these concepts leads to practical and theoretical roadblocks, for these Marxist categories imprisoned the particularities of non-European cultures within the limits of European conceptions, misrepresenting them and suppressing their originality and strength. The assumption of universalism, according to these postcolonial intellectuals, is one of the foundations of colonial power which deliberately links all of humanity to its categories of analysis. It helps to consolidate Western dominance by imposing European categories on the rest of humanity. Those cultures which actually do not fit these categories are condemned to an inferior status, putting them in a state of implicit tutelage and preventing them from taking their own path of development. The imposition of these Western categories of thought is another strategy of imperialism, which blocks the development of alternative and indigenous ideologies and conceptions.[45]

The term *subaltern*, which has become central to postcolonial studies, entered the field through the works of the Subaltern Studies Group, a group of South Asian historians who included or were close to the above noted scholars. The group explored the political-actor role of the men and women who make up the mass of the population—rather than the political roles of the social and economic élites—in the history of South Asia. In the 1970s, the term *subaltern* began to be used to denote the colonized peoples of the South Asian Subcontinent, and described a new perspective on the history of an imperial colony, told from the point of view of the colonized man and woman, rather than from the point of view of the colonizers. Subaltern scholars mostly began as conventional Marxists under the influence of Gramsci, but as a group they evolved toward the position that subalterns on the Indian Subcontinent, because of their distinctive religious, ethnic, and communal traditions, have not evolved in ways parallel to the individualism and class differences that characterize the West. In the Indian countryside the great majority remain farmers, stubbornly upholding traditional Indian rather than Western values. Because of that, capitalism in India has not been able to conquer the countryside and really establish itself. Curiously, the subaltern school has ended up celebrating the otherness of India, representing another version of the myth of the superiority of agrarian society so familiar in the history of the West as well as the East.⁴⁶

History

The major postmodern historical thinker in American academe was Hayden White. White studied at Wayne State University and the University of Michigan, where he received his Ph.D. in 1956. Having taught at various universities, he was until his retirement a professor in the History of Consciousness Program at the University of California at Santa Cruz. He is best known for applying the concepts of literary theory to history, claiming that historical works are by their very nature simply narratives. Historians select and arrange data in order to make it available to readers using the modes of explanation, emplotment, formal argument, and ideological implication. Each of these modes breaks down into an emplotment according to the genres of romance, tragedy, comedy, and satire, and ideology whether anarchist, conservative, radical, or liberal. The mix depends on the proclivities of the historian. White rejects the scientific and objective pretensions of professional historians, stressing the creative and constructive character not simply of historical writing but also of historical knowledge. For White, the only grounds for preferring a given history over another are moral or aesthetic.⁴⁷

White argues that the formal aspects of historical writing entirely overshadow its content. This tends to reduce historiography to an individual and subjective matter little different from that of novelists each of whose works tell a unique story. On the contrary, we know that historians practice their craft as part of a community of scholarship in which the state of historical research in a given field and the canons of knowledge are understood and accepted by other scholars—and usually for good reason. In this context, the facts and the arguments on which historical knowledge is based play a central role. The formal aspects of a given narrative are not without importance, but they are secondary. Nonetheless, insofar as postmodernism or poststructuralism gained ground, it tended to erode belief in the idea of an underlying social and economic foundation to history or a community of research. Even the credibility of interesting conservative approaches to history—such as the New Economic History promoted by American economic historians Robert Fogel and Stanley Engermann, and the *Annales* School developed by the Frenchmen Fernand Braudel and

Emmanuel Leroy Ladurie, which aspired to make history into a science—suffered as a result.[48]

Few historians influenced by postmodernism or poststructuralism took things as far as White. Some advanced their idealist assumptions by proposing a culturalist approach that minimized the influence of material factors in favor of cultural or political cultural determinants of class consciousness. E.P. Thompson's assertion of the centrality of working-class self-activity was important in reintroducing the importance of culture and agency into Marxism. But it also proved very controversial in the hands of some of Thompson's epigones. Thompson admitted that the development of capitalist industry had something to do with the emergence of the working class. But he put the emphasis on the notion that the working class emerged through a history of its own making. It was above all the development of its collective consciousness that made it into a class. On the face of it, such a view merely tends to underscore Marx's conception of class-for-itself as against class-in-itself, or the objective conditions of wage labor making for the formation of class consciousness. Marx himself judiciously stresses both class-for-itself and class-in-itself as necessary conditions for the development of class consciousness.

Thompson's stress on the importance of the cultural determinants of class subsequently led some poststructuralist thinkers to a questioning of the notion of class altogether. British scholars like Patrick Joyce and Gareth Stedman Jones took Thompson's emphasis on the cultural aspect of class to the point of rejecting the Marxist notion of class-in-itself (the notion that the existence of a class must reflect its common relations to the means of production) as well as that of class-for-itself (the consciousness of this common condition, the political aims and projects and cultural trends that develop out of it). For these poststructuralists, to tie economic and social location to consciousness is to be economically determinist. Class has meaning only insofar as its members recognize themselves to be a member of such a grouping, irrespective of any "objective" or "economic" determination. According to them, English workers demonstrably did not recognize themselves as such. In their eyes, those who insist on the existence of class-in-itself are guilty of class essentialism. In contrast, they stress the importance of culture or political culture in the development of class consciousness. On this basis these poststructuralists have questioned whether English workers during the Industrial Revolution can be considered to have belonged either to a class-in-itself or a class-for-itself. Such a view found a certain resonance among American historians, some of whom were always uncomfortable with a Marxist view of class. In England this debate arose not because the existence of the working class could be doubted, as in America, but because of the failure of the extremely class-conscious English workers to become revolutionary, especially given the ravages of Thatcherist conservatism with its attacks on the left and the working class during the 1980s. Thompson himself disavowed such a culturalist view, which suggested that he had rejected the emphasis on economic and material factors characteristic of his fellow British Marxist historians, particularly Maurice Dobb:

> I find actively unhelpful recent attempts to suggest a rupture in British Marxist historiography between the work of Maurice Dobb and the historiography of the 1960s (including the work of myself...). I see on *both* sides of this supposed "break" a *common* tradition of Marxist historiography submitted to an empirical discourse (albeit with differing emphases); and "culturalism" is a term which I refuse.[49]

Rather, Thompson showed that Marxist history could fully confute the charge of reductionism. And as far as the issue of the existence or non-existence of a nineteenth-century working class goes, it is clear that insisting that class can be understood only by the existence of a class-for-itself is a relapse into idealism.

Neoliberal Economics

At one level neoliberalism is an ideology. Literally "neoliberalism" means "new liberalism," and "liberalism" in its continental European (as opposed to North American) sense means "free market economics." As such it is a resurrection of the orthodox "laissez-faire" economic ideology that prevailed until the great slump of the 1930s.[50] In that sense it shares with postmodernism the impulse to question the idea of historical progress. It also shares with postmodernism a benign attitude toward the commodification of everything. Indeed, its ambition is to theorize this process in a way that would include the cost of everything including health, marriage, and children. Both celebrate the notion of everything solid melting into air, the one the triumph of words over things, the other the dominance of finance over productive capital. No doubt both neoliberalism and postmodernism are also committed to individualism, methodological and otherwise, but they part company on the issue of rationality. While postmodernists were fundamentally pessimistic about the power of human reason, neoliberals took it as axiomatic and universal. For them the rational choices of individuals were the ground of all human behavior, economic but also political and cultural. Other disciplines like history or anthropology assume a reasonable human subject who deploys rationality in different cultural and historical contexts. On the other hand, these disciplines also take for granted the existence of non-rational factors. Capitalism, for example, developed out of rational market behavior but also out of impulsions toward unlimited accumulation (greed, hoarding) and commodity fetishism. Neoliberalism, on the other hand, holds that the rational, calculating, wealth-maximizing individual is a universal type common to all societies present and past. Based on this premise, the goal is to understand the past and present constraints on the behavior of the rational individual, whether institutional, political, customary, or social—and to eliminate them. This ideology contends that, freed of restraints, market economies will run smoothly of themselves steadily producing more wealth. Any problems that arise are supposedly a result of "unnatural monopolies" (especially in the labor market), which prevent the free movement of prices and wages successfully adjusting supply and demand. State intervention is seen as distorting the economy and has to be restricted to defending private property, national defense, and, in the monetarist version of neoliberalism, overseeing the money supply. This ideology is backed by a supposedly rigorous "neoclassical" economic theory, which purports to show mathematically that free markets always "clear"—that is, all labor will be employed producing goods that are all sold.

Such was the cloistered nature of university departments that the ultra-rational approach of neoliberal economics could be taught in one classroom while next door an English professor could be extolling the anti-rational views of the postmodernists, and never did the twain meet. Actual intellectual engagement and debate was rare. A notable exception was the challenge mounted by the University of Chicago cultural anthropologist Marshall Sahlins to the notion of capitalist "homo economicus" as a universal type. Basing his account on the ideas of Marx, Karl Polanyi, and Alexander Chayanov, Sahlins insisted on the importance of diverse modes of production and cultural values in shaping the economic goals of individuals in diverse societies.[51]

But Sahlins's objections to the conception of an economically rational human nature, important though they were to the basic assumptions of the humanist and social science disciplines, have been largely ignored by academic economists under the thrall of neoliberalism. The reemergence of neoliberal economics represents an attempt to revive a once-discredited approach to economics that would reinforce laissez-faire public policy. The principles of laissez-faire had been largely discredited in the wake of the Depression and World War II. Keynesianism, especially in the form given to it by Samuelson, came to dominate both policy-making and university teaching in the United States during the Golden Age of the 1950s and '60s. This reflected a compromise between a working class whose bargaining power had increased and a capitalist class which concluded that profitability was enhanced rather than diminished by some state interference. During these prosperous decades, the national economy was increasingly dominated by near-monopolies that worked with the state to ensure global dominance. But Keynesianism proved unable to deal with the outbreak of stagflation that marked the mid-1970s, which was reflected in declining profit margins. Additionally, the social and labor unrest of the 1960s and '70s in the United States and elsewhere deeply worried the American ruling class. As a result, policy-makers and economics departments increasingly looked to neoliberalism for answers to both the economic malaise and social and political upheaval. The University of Chicago became the intellectual focal point of the neoliberal revival in the United States.

Postmodernism and the cultural turn do not seem to have attracted much outside financial support. Indeed, in conservative quarters, such approaches are sometimes denounced as "cultural Marxism," no doubt because of their anti-traditionalist or vaguely subversive connotations. But the reverse has been the case for neoliberalism, and for obvious reasons. From its inception neoliberalism has benefited from substantial private funding. In 1946 Harold Luhnow, a wealthy Midwestern businessman, endowed the Free Market Project at the University of Chicago Law School, from which the powerful Chicago school of economics developed. Backed by funds from corporations and their heads, and channeled through a proliferation of foundations and think-tanks, neoliberal ideas were repackaged and retailed to the general public. The teachings of neoliberalism were based on so-called research and transformed into teaching materials, news stories, policy agendas, and legislative programs.[52] While their influence within universities was at first limited, and suspect, conservative foundations have lately been able to supply significant funding to universities in the form of grants and endowments designed to promote neoliberal ideas. For example, the Koch Family Foundation went from funding only seven universities to funding over 300 schools by 2013.[53]

Neoliberal economics claimed that the economy would resolve its own problems if it were freed from distortions to the market—whether these came from state intervention or from trade union interference with the flexibility of the labor market. Free trade would prevent national monopolies distorting prices, and unemployment would settle at the "natural rate" necessary to prevent wages eating into profits. At the same time the market would force discipline on the population.

Unlike liberalism, and despite its anti-state posture, neoliberalism does not in practice believe that the implementation of its program is the result of the lifting of social and governmental constraints. Rather it is a question of active political and ideological intervention, in which the state plays a key role.[54] The goal of neoliberals is not to destroy the state but to control and redefine it in the service of the market.[55] The market is nonetheless represented as an autonomous machine or device that is the most powerful imaginable processer of information. The idea that the market might selectively favor the creation of some information while suppressing other information is not acknowledged. Indeed, for the purposes of propaganda it is agreed that the market be represented as neutral and inevitable.[56] The question of popular legitimacy is addressed by viewing the state as much as possible as itself part of the market, assimilating political institutions to the model of private institutions and regarding citizens as consumers.[57] Freedom is not the positing of a human or political and social ideal but rather the production of autonomous self-governing individuals equipped with a neoclassical sense of rationality and motives of deep self-interest striving to improve their lot by engaging in market exchange.[58] Free markets for capital are essential both nationally and internationally. Corporations can do no wrong and are the bedrock of wealth creation. If there are anomalies, the market corrects itself.[59] Inequality is essential and promotes progress.[60]

Milton Friedman became the most famous member of the Chicago School, helping to establish the economics department at Chicago as the premier neoliberal economics department, while promoting neoliberalism in policy circles and through the media. Born in 1912 in New York City, he graduated at Rutgers University in 1932 and completed his M.A. at Chicago in the following year. During the New Deal and the war he worked for the government as a statistician and statistical theorist. In 1946 he began teaching and received his Ph.D. at the University of Chicago. Friedman developed challenging economic analyses in several fields, including an extremely clever critique of Keynes's conception of the role of economic demand based on long- rather than short-term expectations. Contrary to what he regarded as Keynes's flawed view, he argued that the economy could be regulated not by government interference, income redistribution, and state expenditure, but by controlling the money supply.[61] While not without utility in managing a thriving capitalist economy, the recent economic crisis has demonstrated that such a policy can perhaps prevent a complete economic meltdown but cannot reignite growth.

The two main beliefs of the Chicago School are that neoclassical price theory can explain observed economic behavior, and that free markets efficiently allocate resources and distribute income, implying a minimal role for the state in economic activity. Chicagoans subscribe to the efficient-markets hypothesis, which claims that market prices fully reflect all available information. Robert Lucas's "Expectations and Neutrality of Money," published in 1972 in the *Journal of Economic Theory*, was the first paper to incorporate the idea of rational expectations into a dynamic general equilibrium model. The notion of rational expectations is an equilibrium concept that attributes a common model to nature and to all agents in the model. The agents in Lucas's models are fully rational, based on the available information, they form expectations about future prices and quantities, and based on these expectations, they act to maximize their expected lifetime utility.[62] Ronald Coase, another member of the Chicago School, postulated that firms are created as a means of reducing costs when the transaction costs in the market become excessive. He also argued that the dangers of monopoly are exaggerated, as monopoly durable-goods producers do not have market power so that they cannot commit to not lowering prices faced with market pressures.[63] Eugene Fama, a younger member of the School, sought to apply the efficient-markets hypothesis to the behavior of financial markets. Beyond the normal utility-maximizing agents, the efficient-market hypothesis requires that agents have rational expectations; that on average the choices of the market agents are correct (even if no one person is); and that whenever new relevant information appears, the agents update their expectations appropriately. It should be underscored that it is not required that the agents be rational. The efficient-markets hypothesis allows that when faced with new information, some investors may overreact and some may underreact. All that is required by the hypothesis is that investors' reactions be random and follow a normal distribution pattern, so that the net effect on market prices cannot be reliably exploited to make an abnormal profit, especially when considering transaction costs. Prices fully reflect the amount of information available.

Economics Imperialism

Garry Becker and Richard Posner were instrumental in the development of economics imperialism, which refers to the economic analysis of seemingly non-economic aspects of life. Becker extended the reach of neoclassical economics to the study of discrimination, crime, the development of human capital, and the family.[64] Posner sought to extend the reach of neoclassical economics to the law. Their "disciplinary imperialism" led them frequently to challenge conventional wisdom by applying price theory to seemingly non-economic topics. Indeed, economics imperialism was not accidental. It formed part of an ambitious goal to create a new academic culture that would invade and cannibalize the established disciplines like political science, law, history, anthropology, etc., by applying neoclassical theory to them. Insofar as history goes, the reinterpretation of the past by the economic imperialists entails viewing the past anachronistically, that is, strictly within the context of the present with little understanding of different modes of production and cultural influences.[65] The emergence of such analysis has been attributed to a method that, like that of the physical sciences, permits refutable implications testable by standard statistical techniques. Central to the approach are the combined assumptions of maximizing behavior, stable preferences, and market equilibrium, applied with as much rigor as possible. The original assumption of economics imperialism was one that perceived all social and economic life as if maximizing behavior in perfectly rational markets actually existed. A second phase still draws on market rationality but accounts for non-market behavior as the rational response to market imperfections.[66] The anachronistic and ahistorical view of market rationality, which is itself a product of capitalist ideology, is ignored. Indeed, it seems evident that the deep and profound influence of neoclassical economics is a product of, and reinforced, the global triumph of capitalism. Its imperialism reflects the goal of creating full neoliberal cultural hegemony.

The influence of neoclassical economics is especially apparent in political science, notably in the sub-specialty known as public choice, in which the state and the public sector are dissolved into the economic. George Stigler, a close colleague of Friedman, elaborated on the neoclassical theory of price and sought to apply rational choice theory to the political order.[67] Public choice, or public choice theory, has been described as "the use of economic tools to deal with traditional problems of political science." Public choice employed microeconomic theory and geared it toward extending economic assumptions of self-interest and rationality to the political arena, with the idea of treating political and economic actors symmetrically. It is the subset of positive political theory, which models voters, politicians, and bureaucrats as mainly self-interested. Where public choice applied micro-economic theory, as in, "the supply of and demand for collective action," political economy made use of game theory, as in, "greed, rationality, equilibrium." The result was a higher standard of defining the rationality of political actors, including their informational states, and of making sure that all of their strategies and beliefs were consistent with each other so that they constitute an equilibrium. Instead of emerging as the completely dominant approach, however, rational choice has been forced to co-exist with one of three complementary approaches in political science: the rationalist approach, which focuses on individual agency; the culturalist approach, which centers on collective identities; and the structuralist approach, which emphasizes historical institutionalism.[68] Breaking from its recent ahistorical approach, there has been some attempt to study the past of the discipline based on the contradictions between its scientific pretensions, commitment to liberal democratic values, and proximity to the state.[69]

Philosophy

The conservative bent of neoliberal economics was reinforced at Chicago by the presence of the political philosopher Leo Strauss. Arriving in the United States as a political refugee in 1937, Strauss taught at the New School and Hamilton College prior to his appointment at Chicago in 1949. He was deeply affected by the thinking of conservative thinkers like Nietzsche, Schmidt, and Heidegger, and was a proponent of the ideas of the natural inequality of human beings as understood by the ancient philosophers Plato and Aristotle. Deeply hostile to liberalism and Marxism, he rejected any notion of human progress as illusory and dangerous. Strauss attacked the notion of government intervention in society. According to him, a good society is one composed of good and virtuous citizens. Efforts by the state to politically implement equality or freedom undermined the virtue of citizens by relieving them of the responsibility for their own individual actions. The unstated conclusion to this view is that individuals must look to themselves for a livelihood. Strauss further believed that religion and nationalism, however counterfeit, promoted the morality of the individual citizen, while liberalism and secularism undermined it. He called for a moral and intellectual elite to promote these traditional ideals instrumentally. Behind this seemingly high-minded and contradictory rhetoric lay the demand for the liquidation of the interventionist state and the restoration of the free market as the basis for restoring profitability and imposing social discipline.[70] Defenders of Strauss claim that he was not interested in contemporary politics. In fact, he was a staunch and uncompromising Cold Warrior. His ideas became the inspiration for the many influential neoconservative intellectuals, journalists, and policy-makers who were his students.[71]

In contrast to Strauss, Richard Rorty championed a revivified American liberalism. Whereas the conservative Strauss fell back on Aristotelian realism and Platonist idealism, largely ignoring modern history and thought, Rorty based himself on a form of neo-pragmatism and postmodernism. Raised in a family of anti-communist New York socialists, Rorty enrolled at the University of Chicago shortly before turning 15. At Chicago he studied philosophy in a department which at that time included Rudolph Carnap, Charles Hartshorne, and Richard McKeon, analytical philosophers who were Rorty's teachers. He received his Ph.D. at Yale in 1956 and thereafter pursued a highly successful career at Yale, Wellesley, Princeton, the University of Virginia, and ultimately Stanford. At some point along the way he reverted to pragmatism while coming under the influence of post-modernism. On Rorty's account the development of modern epistemology, including that of analytical philosophy, is not only an attempt to legitimate our claim to knowledge of what is real, but also an effort to legitimate phil-osophical reflection itself. Epistemology, in Rorty's account, is wedded to a picture of the mind's structure working on empirical content to produce in itself items—thoughts, representations—which, when things go well, correctly mirror reality. To loosen the grip of this picture on our thinking is to challenge the idea that epistemology—whether traditional Cartesian or twentieth-century linguistic—is the essence of philosophy. On the contrary, knowledge is a matter of conversation and social practice rather than an attempt to mirror nature. Explaining rationality and epistemic authority by reference to what society lets us say constituted the essence of what Rorty called epistemological behaviorism, an attitude common to Dewey and Wittgenstein.

Epistemological behaviorism leaves no room for the kind of practice-transcending legitimation that Rorty identifies as the defining aspiration of modern epistemology. He objects to the quest for objectivity as representing an unwillingness to settle for the best beliefs and most reasonable explanations that fallible human beings can muster.[72] Indeed, his philosophical position represents a fundamental break from the regnant analytical philosophy.[73] The provocative and counter-intuitive force of Rorty's treatment of rationality and science in terms of conversational ethics is undeniably powerful and convincing. It is important to realize, though, that Rorty is not denying that there is any bona fide use for notions like truth, knowledge, or objectivity. Rather his point is that our ordinary uses of these notions always depend for their content and rationale on particular features of their varying contexts of application. His further point is that when we abstract away from these different contexts and practices, in search of general notions, we are left with pure abstract hypostatizations incapable of providing us with any guide to action at all.

At the same time as he attacked traditional philosophy Rorty sought to salvage a political project of liberal social and economic justice in an era of neoconservative ascendancy. In sharp contrast to the onslaught of neoliberal economics and conservative political theory, Rorty was a staunch defender of liberalism, including the civil rights movement and the legislative achievements of L.B.J's "Great Society." In Rorty's view, these movements and individuals represent a rich and enviable political legacy for the United States, one that needs to be resuscitated and reclaimed in order to counter the rise of a conservative, anti-statist hegemony. This represented a brave attempt to defend the democratic social and political gains of New Deal liberalism in the face of the neoliberal assault. It buttresses itself against postmodern skepticism and political apathy by rooting itself in the American pragmatic tradition. On the other hand, Rorty used this pragmatism and liberalism to launch an attack on New Left radicalism, which he pictures as being essentially nihilistic. Rorty argues that the political culture of the anti-war movement, of black power, and of certain groups within the New Left and counter-culture did lethal damage to the long tradition of left/liberal reform in the United States. More precisely, the critiques of the United States developed by key figures in these movements mistakenly went beyond the boundary of traditional left/ liberal critiques. In Rorty's view, the reformers of the past had advocated social and political change from a patriotic position, one that celebrated the history of the United States and embraced the legacy of Jefferson, Lincoln, Whitman, John Dewey, and many others. These people, he argues, shared the conviction that the United States was a great experiment in political change full of social promise. The rupture in this genealogy comes with intellectuals, activists, and protestors who exhibit no love of country and who see the United States as a malevolent power in the world rather than as a model.[74] But Rorty should be faulted for not resolutely facing the consequences of the upheavals of the 1960s, and especially the developing crisis of capitalism and the threat to the rest of the world from American imperialism. Nothing reveals his affinity to postmodernism more than his lack of a sense of historical depth and his anachronistic nationalist parochialism.

The Sokal Affair

The rejoinder to postmodernist skepticism on the part of analytical philosophers and scientists has been to concede that scientific knowledge is socially contingent, but to insist nonetheless that it is based on the best evidence and reasoning available and therefore relatively truer than other accounts. It is repeatedly pointed out that complete skepticism, which is the view of some postmodernists, is self-contradictory in that its own skeptical assertions must be treated skeptically. But the conflict between scientific positivists and postmodernists did not remain at this polite level, giving rise as it did to the famous Sokal Hoax, which helped bring the neoliberal decades of the second millennium to a conclusion.[75] The affair was a publishing hoax perpetrated by Alan Sokal, a professor of physics at NYU. In 1996 Sokal submitted a piece to *Social Text*, an academic journal of postmodern cultural studies. The submission was an experiment to test the journal's intellectual seriousness and, specifically, to determine whether a distinguished journal whose editors included Jameson, among other celebrities of cultural studies, would publish an article filled with scientific nonsense if it sounded plausible to those holding postmodern preconceptions. The article, entitled "Transgressing the Boundaries: Towards a Transformative Hermeneutics of Quantum Gravity," was published in the spring/summer 1996 "Science Wars" issue of *Social Text*. It proposed that quantum gravity is a social and linguistic construct. At that time, the journal did not practice academic peer review and it did not submit the article for outside expert review by a physicist. On its publication Sokal revealed that the article was a hoax, noting that "the fundamental silliness of my article lies, however, not in its numerous solecisms but in the dubiousness of its central thesis and of the reasoning adduced to support it. Basically, I claim that quantum gravity ... has profound political implications."[76] The resultant academic and public furor concerned the scholarly merit of humanistic commentary about the physical sciences; the influence of postmodern philosophy on social disciplines in general; academic ethics, including whether Sokal was wrong to deceive the editors and readers of *Social Text*; and whether the journal had exercised appropriate intellectual rigor before publishing the pseudoscientific article.

Sokal himself was a Marxist. The Marxist view of epistemology is historical and materialist, rejecting both skepticism and the static and idealist quality of analytic philosophy. Scientific knowledge is directly related to the development of the productive forces of society. It is itself the product of techniques and institutions which themselves are subject to change and in turn affect the kind of scientific knowledge that can be produced. As such, scientific concepts are rational and objectively true but not autonomous of society nor immobile. They change or become subject to contradiction and negation in relation to the further intellectual and economic development of society as well as their own internal logic. Analytical philosophy, like Marxism, takes its cue from science, developing its discussion of things philosophical from the premises of scientific knowledge which it takes to be true. But, unlike Marxism, analytical philosophy has been reluctant to view its philosophical discussions from the perspective of social development. Rather it prefers to view its subject as self-enclosed or based only on scientific ideas and the endogenous logic which is internal to the scientific disciplines. This claim makes it an easy target for postmodernists like Rorty, especially insofar as it holds on to claims for the unchanging and law-like nature of science or of the philosophical truths it purports to deduce from such principles. Postmodernism thus represented a negation of such claims and as such did a real service. On the other hand, insofar as postmodernism continues to represent scientific knowledge as absolute knowledge, and refuses to see its ongoing negation as part of a historical process which leads to an acceptance of new and partial knowledge, it becomes nihilistic.

Sokal's piece had the initial merit of exposing the hollow arguments of those who have facilely challenged the existence of objective truth based on a critical investigation of nature and society. Moreover, it exposed the hothouse and sterile quality of much of the theory that had developed within academe in the age of neoliberalism. Indeed, the Sokal affair suggests the futility of academic theorizing, especially about society in the absence of progressive social and political movements. In the wake of the crisis of 2008, there are signs that such movements are beginning to develop. In the meantime, we can only reassert with Jameson that scientific knowledge needs to be understood within the context of the grand narrative of Marxism. Such a historical narrative sees the progress of scientific learning as part of a dialectical and historical development of the forces of production. Scientific ideas not only prove themselves in terms of their congruence with existing experiential knowledge and theory, enhancing human control over the world, they also potentially advance humanity's ability to live in harmony with nature. But meanwhile, from the 1980s onward, the universities themselves were being transformed. Reflecting the increasingly neoliberal times, public funding of higher education was reduced and tuition fees and student debt were rising. Access to tenure track employment was increasingly unavailable and employment was becoming increasingly precarious and unremunerative. Private funding of changes in programs and curriculums grew so as to favor business. Faculty and student interest in, and influence on, university governance waned as the hand of university administration grew heavier. Indeed, deferring to the power of business, administrators increasingly resorted insofar as possible to the methods of governance of private corporations.

5

The Neoliberal University

After 1945 universities enjoyed a golden age. With the help of government they transformed themselves into institutions open to millions of students and actively pursued research in many disciplines. Universities during the Cold War produced a cornucopia of new positive knowledge in the sciences, engineering, and agriculture, but also in the social sciences and humanities, useful to business and government. In the case of the humanities and social sciences such knowledge, however real, was largely instrumental in character or tainted by ideological rationalizations. It was not sufficiently grounded in history and tended to conceal or rationalize the question of class conflict and the drive of American imperialism overseas. Too much of it was used to control and manipulate ordinary people within and without the United States in behalf of the American state and the maintenance of the capitalist order. In the Gramscian sense it was part of the ideological state apparatus. There were scholars who continued to search for critical truth even at the height of the Cold War, but they largely labored in isolation. This state of affairs was disrupted in the 1960s with the sudden burgeoning of Marxist scholarship made possible by the upsurge of campus radicalism attendant on the anti-war, civil rights, and black liberation struggles. But the decline of radicalism in the 1970s saw the onset of postmodernism, neo-liberalism, and the cultural turn.

Postmodernism, we can admit, served as a corrective to a perhaps too schematic Marxism. But in the end it was an untenable skepticism. We can even suggest that the mathematical models of neoliberal economics might be of use in a society which was not riddled with class conflict and economic crises. But as practiced in the United States it constituted a crude and overstated scientism. Both postmodernism and neoliberal economics deliberately turned their back on history. The cultural turn deserves more respect, but whatever intellectual interest there might be in it there is little doubt that the net effect of all three was to delink the humanities and social sciences from the revolutionary politics that marked the 1960s. But the ongoing presence in many universities of radicals who took refuge in academe under neoliberalism made possible the survival of Marxist ideas, if only in an academic guise.

As the new millennium drew closer the humanities and social sciences entered a serious crisis. They retreated into skepticism, had difficulty finding their intellectual footing, skirted politics and became preoccupied with enrollments and funding. University bachelor degrees in the humanities reached a peak in the late 1960s and early 1970s but have declined since. In the 1960s they numbered 18 percent of all undergraduate degrees while they were only 8 percent by 2004. The figures for Masters and Ph.D. degrees were similar.[1] In contrast to this decline, neoliberal economics thrived both within and without the universities. Meanwhile higher learning overall seemed more than ever a growth industry. As we have noted, enrollment by 2000 in the more than 4,000 academic institutions in the United States rose to 16 million. In 2007 1.6 million B.A. degrees were awarded. Close to 50 percent of young adults were enrolled in some form of university or higher educational institution. More Latino and black students than ever before were attending universities and colleges, and in four-year co-educational institutions women were in the majority. Meanwhile American universities were extending their reach overseas as an integral part of U.S. capital's internationalization or imperialism. American universities overwhelmingly topped the ranks of the world's top universities and continued to attract a disproportionately large number of foreign students, whose tuition fees bolstered university budgets.[2] The attraction of foreign students majoring in science and technology was proving important to the manufacturing economy in the United States, where they provided an important source of trained labor. Research and development activities were being internationalized, spurred by globalized American corporations. Universities in other countries were being restructured in conformity with the U.S. model and American universities were opening campuses in other countries. The growing international reach of American academe is paralleled by the increasing influence of American media, advertising, and entertainment, and must be understood as just as much an aspect of U.S. imperialism as its military, financial, and economic power overseas.

While this extension of the influence of American universities abroad was part of the extensive spread of capitalism more generally, the neoliberal period also saw the intensification of American capitalism. While the former refers to the geographical expansion of American capitalism around the world, the intensification of capitalism refers to the commodification and marketization of those spheres of social life that were previously outside the logic of profit making. The development of academic capitalism was part of this process of intensification. Academic capitalism refers to the variety of ways in which markets, states, and higher education are increasingly inter-related and the implications of the blurring of the lines between these spheres. The building blocks of academic capitalism were the broad set of new circuits of knowledge, organizations, networks, and related modes of action that link institutions as well as faculty, administrators, academic professionals, and students to what is described as cognitive or knowledge capitalism.[3] In other words, whereas in an earlier phase universities were mainly involved in non-productive or not immediately profitable research, from the 1980s onward they increasingly sought to move as far as possible toward productive activity, i.e., labor that directly leads to profits. Such a transformation has fostered the creation of new forms of knowledge based on new linkages between academia, government, and private business which might foster profitability. The downside of course is that such a transformation is likely to lead to an erosion of the capacity of academic institutions to generate positive knowledge, let alone critical thought.

As the new millennium dawned, American universities increasingly assumed a corporate character. NYU, Northwestern, Carnegie-Mellon, and Texas A&M were busy establishing campuses in the Persian Gulf oil states, while Cornell, MIT, and the University of Chicago had all created branches in Singapore. This was the tip of an iceberg which has seen the establishment of scores of branches of American universities and colleges overseas as part of an effort to export and profit from the success of the American model of higher education.[4] Meanwhile, within the United States, many less than front-rank institutions remained committed to the idea of catching up to the elite institutions by building a prestigious research component and raising their ranking among universities. Star faculty and students were recruited. Large amounts of money were spent on infrastructure and services in the fruitless quest to attract federal dollars.[5] But, continuing a long-established pattern, the overwhelming bulk of federal money—the largest source of funding—went to a relatively small number of well-established institutions.[6] The problem was compounded by the steady decline in public funding of universities since the late 1970s. Among the initial responses to the new circumstances were sharp increases in tuition. It was under these conditions that the transition to the neoliberal university began.[7]

In 2005 an article in *Philanthropy News Digest* explained that:

less than 14 percent of the University of Oregon's total revenue came from state funds in 2003–04, compared to 32 percent in 1985–86, while tuition fees accounted for more than 33 percent of the university's budget, compared to 22 percent 20 years ago. Meanwhile, the University of Michigan has lost 12 percent of its state funding, or $43 million, over the past two years. According to UM spokeswoman Julie Peterson, state money now only accounts for 8 percent of the university's budget. "We can't rely on state funding alone," said Peterson. "It simply isn't enough."[8]

Public institutions raised tuition fees and chased private funding to the point that the distinction between private and public institutions was increasingly lost. Meanwhile cutbacks in programs were increasingly determined by what is called the program prioritization process—an attempt to make cuts according to so-called rational and often quantifiable criteria. Less scientific but quite effective was the hiring of more and more non-tenured or contingent teachers with lower salaries and fewer benefits. It is estimated that up to 70 percent of teaching is now done by so-called adjunct or contingent faculty. In contrast, universities dramatically expanded the number of administrators while boosting administrative salaries, especially those of university presidents.[9]

The Business of Universities

As we have seen, the presidents and governing boards of institutions of higher learning had long fashioned themselves according to the model of business, operating like the governors of private corporations. Moreover, big business had an inordinate influence on university governance. But now university presidents explicitly presented themselves as corporate CEOs with almost unlimited discretionary powers. As a result, the relationship between university presidents and administrators and faculty post-1945, which was already arm's length, became yet more distant in the neoliberal age, fully approximating that between workers and management in private corporations. Increasingly large bureaucracies totally controlled decision-making in the universities. Whereas lip-service continued to be given to the indispensable role of faculty in university governance, their actual role in administrative decisions has long since been reduced to control of their classrooms, a restricted role in appointing new faculty members, and some say in determining the curriculum. All important business was now in the hands of administrators many of whom had little or no previous experience as faculty.[10]

From the 1970s onward the influence of large corporations in university governance has become overwhelming. Their influence over education policy at the national level is manifest through the activities of the Business Higher Education Forum, whose goal is to use the institutions of higher education to allow the United States to maintain and enhance its competitive edge globally.[11] Today there is evidence that the number of university trustees connected to science-based corporations significantly influences the amount of R&D funding a university receives from government. It seems that this is a result of the rise of an executive science network that plays an instrumental role in relations between universities, government, and industry, helping to shape the policies of universities in the direction of neoliberalism.[12] It is not merely that private business has infiltrated the universities. There has been an intellectual rapprochement between academic scientists involved in basic and applied research which has brought universities into closer collaboration with business.[13]

Beyond their increasing concern with endowment portfolios and investment in student debt, universities have become deeply enmeshed in the web of finance and real-estate development which reflects the overall financialization of the U.S. economy. As we have noted, this in itself is a symptom of an increasingly serious economic and political crisis in which the universities are implicated. Indeed, a growing number of academic institutions, such as, for example, Chicago State University, Howard University, and Louisiana State University, are effectively insolvent. It is especially smaller schools that are threatened.[14] In the meantime, given the shortfall in funding, maintaining and enhancing university endowments has become a crucial matter for private universities. University endowments total over 1 trillion dollars, with some 80 institutions with holdings of more than 1 billion dollars.[15] Harvard tops the list with over 32 billion dollars in investments. Harvard Management Company, Inc. (HMC) is an American investment management corporation, a wholly owned subsidiary of Harvard that manages the endowment funds.[16] The company employs financial professionals to manage the approximately 11,000 funds that constitute the endowment. The company directly manages about one third of the total endowment portfolio while working closely with the external companies that manage the rest. The HMC is headed by a professional, who holds the titles of president and chief executive officer. Jack Meyer managed HMC from 1990, when the endowment was worth $4.8 billion, to September 2005, when its value had reached $25.9 billion. During the last decade of his tenure, the endowment earned an annualized return of 15.9 percent. It is noteworthy that an important source of this endowment money is tax write-offs offered by the federal government for donations to private universities. In contrast, public universities have little or no access to such an income stream, which has become increasingly significant.

Given the crucial role of financial investments in funding universities they have become more deeply connected to and dependent on Wall St. than ever. Mounting student debt further ties universities to finance capital. While those institutions that could afford it tried to attract students through expensive sports programs and enhanced campus services including shopping malls, tuition fee increases at most universities imposed an increasingly heavy burden of debt. As a percentage of public college revenues, for example, revenue from tuition increased from 23 percent in 1987 to 47 percent in 2012. Payments of interest on debt from students enrolled in these institutions amounted to 28 billion dollars over the same decade. Net tuition revenue increased from 23 percent in 1987 to 30 percent in 2002 to 47 percent in 2012 as a share of all educational revenue for public colleges.[17]

Moreover, this debt load loomed all the larger as young people were faced with the urgent necessity of obtaining university degrees in an increasingly difficult job market, especially so in the wake of the financial crisis of 2008. A recent story in *Bloomberg Business Week* highlights the gravity of the situation:

> Tiffany Roberson works for the state of Texas as a parole officer, teaches part-time, and is living with her parents after having completed her master's degree. She's held off marrying her boyfriend of four years and starting a family because she owes more than $170,000 in federal and private student loans that she took out to pursue her education in criminal justice. "I've never gone into default," the 30-year-old says. "What really hurts is people say I'm a bum for living at home."

Stories like Roberson's are sadly common in the United States. Student loans today are one of the only deteriorating pockets of consumer credit, with balances and delinquency rates rising to record highs even as a strengthening economy allows Americans to reduce total borrowing. Outstanding student debt topped $1 trillion in the third quarter of 2013, and the share of loans delinquent for 90 days or more rose to 11.8 percent, according to the Federal Reserve Bank of New York. By contrast, delinquencies for mortgage, credit card, and auto debt all have declined from their peaks.

The New York Federal Reserve's move to measure the size of the student loan load says a lot about how concerned the central bank is about a possible threat to the economy. "Our job is to really understand what's happening in the financial system," and the "very rapid rise in student loan debt over the last few years" can "actually have some pretty significant consequences to the economic outlook," New York Fed President William Dudley told reporters in November 2013. "People can have trouble with the student loan debt burden—unable to buy cars, unable to buy homes—and so it can really delay the cycle."[18]

As the *Business Week* story makes clear, the crisis is not merely personal but threatens the economy as a whole, in a way that is comparable to the crisis in housing debt. Defaults on loans by students unable to find work are rising, despite claims that the economy is improving. In fact, both housing and student debt have played a part in stymying the recovery of the U.S. economy from what amounts to a depression that shows every sign of being structural and indeterminably if not indefinitely long. So much so that some students and parents are beginning to question the value of a university degree as a long-term economic investment. A downturn in enrollment could prove catastrophic to the finances of many universities. Moreover, the accumulation of debt by students in lower income groups undoubtedly exacerbates the problem of already existing class inequality within the United States. Indeed, the mounting costs of higher education combined with downward mobility risks the loss altogether of access to higher education for the majority of citizens, thereby threating to undermine what remains of one of the achievements of post-1945 society.[19]

The problem of student debt has become a major economic and political issue. Indeed, as the issue gained saliency following the crisis of 2008 it became clear that some university officials were involved in steering students to preferred lenders who charged higher rates of interest to the benefit of universities and some of their officials. Increasingly in their practices universities resemble big businesses. This new reality was addressed in a *Time Magazine* article on the complicity of universities in student debt entitled "How American Universities Turned into Corporations."[20] Another increasingly important aspect of university business activity is real estate. As we have seen in the case of Berkeley and Columbia in the 1960s, the encroachment of universities into urban neighborhoods, real-estate speculation, and displacement of local populations has become a major issue. Its ongoing importance can be seen from the fact that in 2013 the University of California, Berkeley, appointed its first vice-chancellor for real estate, Robert Lalanne of the Lalanne Group, a Bay Area development company.[21]

President Obama attempted to address the issue of student debt by announcing a college rating system in August 2013.[22] It would rate colleges as high-, low- or middle-performing, based on data from the Integrated Postsecondary Education Data System (IPEDS), the National Student Loan Data System (NSLDS), and earnings information. Federal financial aid currently totaling $167 billion would largely be given to "high-performing" colleges, with those deemed "low-performing" seeing a gradual reduction in aid. Relatively low student debt is one of the important metrics on the basis of which federal funds are to be dispensed. It is entirely characteristic of the current neoliberal order that pressure from certain universities forced Obama to abandon this program of debt relief. On the other hand, many other factors included in the rating system, which were designed to foster the redesign of higher education to produce graduates who meet the needs of business, have been retained. At the beginning of 2015 Obama took things further by proposing to ensure the upgrading of the workforce by making tuition free at community colleges.

Some universities across the United States have been involved in urban revitalization projects with varying degrees of success. In 1992, for example, 100 of the more than 4,000 colleges and universities nationwide applied for grants whose aim was to revitalize poor urban neighborhoods. But most refrain from doing so because success rates are not high.[23] In fact such endeavors, whose objective is to mitigate poverty and urban blight, seem to run into difficulty because they conflict with the primary research and educational missions of the universities, but also on account of the essentially business outlook of university administrators. In short, despite the great intellectual expertise within universities, the present context of capitalism arguably makes them more part of the problem of poverty than the solution. Universities are more and more geared to help the process of capitalist accumulation, which stands at 180 degrees opposed to addressing the problems of urban blight. Moreover, the idea that somehow expertise or education by themselves can resolve problems of poverty and inequality is a persistent illusion of liberal ideology.

On the upside there can be no question that the graduates of universities have better and more secure jobs than those lacking such degrees, especially in an increasingly unstable economic environment. Indeed, it has been shown that the greater the concentration of university graduates in cities the higher the wages for both university graduates and non-graduates. Some businesses are actually being created as spin-offs of academic research. In this respect the development of science and technology parks at universities is particularly important. Decline in public funding from the 1970s led to the spread of research parks, of which today there are some 170 nationwide, employing close to 400,000 people. Some important start-up businesses, including Google at Stanford, emerged from these facilities. Firms associated with universities and university research have pioneered new drugs, new medical technology, optical devices, and electronics, expanding local employment while providing good salaries. Particularly beneficial to local economies have been the development of medical-hospital complexes which generate large amounts of employment and economic activity. But the presence of universities alone is no guarantee of entrepreneurial dynamism. According to the standard university rating systems, Washington University in St. Louis, for example, ranks higher as an institution than the University of Washington in Seattle. Yet well-paid employment and other economic benefits have lagged in the one city while expanding dramatically in the other. Arizona State University and the University of Florida are among the largest universities, but Phoenix and Gainsville are far from being hubs of innovation. Yale and Cornell are top universities but New Haven and Ithaca are backwaters when it comes to economic activity.

Having a research university in a city is a key factor in creating economic opportunity but only as part of a cluster of other innovative enterprises. Universities are most effective in shaping a local economy when they are part of a wider complex of economic activity including a thick market of specialized labor and intermediate activities.[24] There is no conclusive evidence, it should be underlined, that the number of world-class universities (as defined by rankings such as the Shanghai Index of Universities) in a nation directly increases productivity. Professor Clifford Tan Kuan Lu of the School of Economics of the Malaysian Campus of the University of Nottingham has produced a global quantitative analysis of the relationship between the two factors. The author does not contest that higher education has a positive impact on the economy. What is at issue is the importance of having universities that are among the elite as defined in the global university ranking tables. To be sure the results show that there is a strong and significant relationship between having a large number of elite universities per capita and GDP per capita. But having such top universities has little to do with actual growth. What counts in terms of growth is rather to have a large number of good rather than top institutions. This suggests that, beyond a certain point, elite higher education may in fact be more of an investment in status and prestige than an investment to increase growth.[25] These findings tend to confirm the view noted above that universities contribute to productivity and growth as part of a wider complex of economic activity.

The Case of NYU

The role of NYU in Manhattan provides a key illustration of the nexus between a university, real estate, and financial interests and city government. These relationships have been perceptively explored by Andrew Ross.[26] As is well known, NYU has been relentlessly committed to expansion for decades. But it would seem that unbridled growth is opposed to its parallel quest for academic prestige. The latter, after all, is supposed to be a scarce commodity, available only to the select few, and not to a place like NYU with its ever expanding student body, ever denser real-estate presence in Manhattan, and far-flung international branch campuses. One of the answers is that it is responding to the open invitation of New York urban managers to help diversify the economy of a city that relies too heavily on its FIRE (finance, insurance, and real estate) industries. Not long after he came into office, John Sexton, NYU's president, spoke publicly about how the intellectual, cultural, and educational industries now formed an ICE sector, large enough in its own right to stand alongside the city's anchoring FIRE sector. Statistics were generated to show that ICE may be more resilient and profitable in the long run than FIRE. FIRE + ICE became the promotional banner under which the NYU administration pushed its interests through the city bureaucracy.

These are not altogether distinct sectors, and least of all in the case of NYU, which has a massive real-estate presence and whose basic revenue depends on the student loan business—one of the most lucrative sectors of the finance industry. For evidence of the interlocking of FIRE and ICE interests, one need look no further than NYU's own board of trustees, which includes Catherine Reynolds, who owns a company—Educap—that makes high-interest, predatory loans to students. On the same board are some of city's biggest land developers, Wall Street's wealthy financiers, and a bevy of corporate tycoons. Collectively speaking, they are members of the city's "permanent government" which calls the shots especially on shaping land use, and no elected politician can afford to alienate a body with that kind of clout. Practically speaking, they are the governors of the city's growth machine, and they now see urban universities as essential drivers of urban growth. NYU has an extraordinarily large board of trustees made up of some 65 members, many of whom are, in typical fashion these days at colleges and universities, billionaires. No faculty members of any stripe are on the board.

Growth does not pay for itself since taxpayers pay, though it is a relatively efficient way of transferring public monies into private pockets. There are many streams of public funds that flow into this private university. Government grants from multiple federal agencies are a basic source of funding for its research operations ($337 million in grants and contracts from federal, state, and city sources). The New York State Dormitory Authority heavily subsidized the dormitory buildings NYU erected as it made the transition from local commuter college to residential national university. And the university collects tens of million a year from New York State in grants.

A much larger revenue stream comes from federal student loans— $108,641,000 in 2011. In 2010, NYU had $659 million in total student debt. It is a national leader in the debt carried by its graduates, at 40 percent more than the national average. According to a recent *Newsweek* ranking, NYU is now the fourth least affordable university in the United States. And in the latest *Princeton Review* college rankings, its financial aid and administration ranked first—for being the worst. The projected $5 billion expansion plan is certain to increase the student debt burden. Most of the current student loans are federal money, so we can add these on to the public inputs received by this private university at a time when public universities are being put to the sword.

But how does this public cash find its way into private pockets? Any analysis of payroll distribution would show a clear skewing of compensation toward two employee classes: senior administrators whose salaries have skyrocketed over the last 15 years, and key faculty who are conduits for top grant funding or who generate lucrative intellectual property for the university (NYU also tops the list of universities that extract revenue from intellectual property licensing—another way in which public monies in the form of research grants gets propertized as an excludable private good). Like many other universities NYU has on its board leaders in high-tech industries who push forward the neoliberal and corporate transformation of the university. But the most pervasive community rumor about NYU lies in its ties to real-estate interests. Several graduates have described their alma mater as "a real-estate company which also issues degrees." As one of the city's two or three largest landowners, the university has an extensive real-estate portfolio, and it is perpetually buying, selling, and leasing buildings, or land-banking properties for future uses and returns. It's fair to conclude then that NYU is a non-profit institution that generates profits for others. Because its books are closed—and there is no pretense of fiscal transparency—not much can be said about the private profit structure, though there is little that would surprise long-serving employees. Nor is it a leap to observe that $5 billion worth of construction in the heart of downtown is a huge boost in general to the business climate of downtown development, and that it will enrich builders and contractors, amplify area rents, and add nothing to the city's affordable housing stock. Yet the result is assumed to be in the public interest. Why? Because it is cloaked in the public goodness that is the stock-in-trade of any educational institution.

Perhaps the most important, and least understood, aspect of NYU's expansion rests upon its debt financing. The absence of a business plan on the administration's part has attracted a good deal of disbelief, and rightfully so. What kind of entity is able to raise $5 billion in the current economic landscape? More telling yet was the response of one administrator to queries about the proposed funding of the plan: "NYU is not afraid of debt," she assured her audience, in a tone reminiscent of the freewheeling credit culture of the early 2000s. This kind of comment evokes an intimacy with debt and bond ratings that is essential to the capital funding of modern universities. In fact, the overhang of debt and the threat of insolvency among institutions of higher learning both public and private is increasingly serious.[27]

The ability of universities to raise tuition fees at will is the basic collateral requirement for securing a good credit rating, which makes it much cheaper to borrow money to service existing debts and finance large-scale construction. In turn, this capital-intensive construction generates more space per capita, which is a key metric in the *U.S. News and World Report*'s college rankings. Indeed, the need for NYU to improve on this metric is the only rationale offered by President Sexton for new expansion. NYU, according to him, falls too far behind Harvard on this rating. Invariably, however, universities need to increase enrollment, as NYU intends to do in order to secure the tuition-backed bond issues, and so the rationale behind the enterprise falls apart. But the outcome, for the bond financiers, hedge funds, and institutional investors, not to mention the construction industry in general, is an ongoing bonanza. With mortgage and other credit markets still in the doldrums, universities have become a very attractive option for investors looking for high returns on debt-financed growth. Money capital has poured into construction bonds, student loans, and other financial instruments spun out of the tuition bubble.

Universities in the Image of Neoliberalism

Neoliberal economics, which now dictates how universities operate, was itself the intellectual spawn of academic economists. Its ostensibly scientific and mathematical approach and laissez-faire bias gave neoliberal professors formidable power as proponents of an alternative to Keynesianism. By the time of Reagan, their access to money, closeness to capital and policy-makers, and apparent scientific rigor made economics in its neoliberal form the leading discipline within humanities and social science faculties. In the 1990s those economics professors who were stars in the field were paid as much as $500,000 per annum, and $300,000 was not uncommon—well above the scale for academics in most universities.[28] This was true even of newly minted Ph.D.s without significant publications. Moreover, the teaching loads of most professors of economists were lower than in other fields. These favorable conditions partly reflected the market as economists were in great demand not only in academe but also in business and government.

As we have noted in the previous chapter, economics imperialism sought to remake other disciplines—political science, history, anthropology, law—in its image in an effort to create a comprehensive neoliberal culture ensuring ideological hegemony. But its ambitions went beyond these disciplines toward the refashioning of the universities themselves in the image of the market. Neoliberal policies toward universities have to be seen as part of an attempt to recast the institutions of the public sector, including not only education but also health, transportation, housing, and welfare, according to the discipline of the market. Backing up such policies were not only university administrators but business leaders and governments aggressively trying to increase productivity in an increasingly competitive global market. As it became more and more difficult to realize profits they were accordingly determined to reduce their tax burden while curbing public institutions that operated on non-market principles.

The policy recommendations of neoliberals therefore had the force not merely of administrative fiat since they were backed by government bodies and business leaders who controlled the purse strings and who were determined to bring universities more closely under their control. Growing public debt and reduction of expenditure on public services including higher education put weapons in their hands. Price tickets were put on the cost of such public services and the insistent demand for self-financing grew increasingly loud. The Gramscian model of the post-war period, in which universities were absorbed into the state apparatus, did not disappear. But the emphasis shifted from the pursuit by universities of the public good, which always included the business community, toward more or less exclusively serving business and themselves becoming business-like. While overall public funding declined, it remains the case that the major part of the money for this approach favoring business was siphoned from the public sector. Moreover, the losses that accrued were socialized at the expense of the taxpayers.

According to neoliberals, then, most public institutions were wasteful and unproductive and represented a drag on the market while sapping the self-reliance of individuals. All public sector institutions needed to be restructured to bring them more into line with the market and to make them serve the needs of the latter as much as possible. As the major centers of knowledge production, universities especially needed to be more closely aligned with business. The quest for disinterested knowledge or knowledge for knowledge's sake, including focusing on basic or theoretical science as against immediately useful or profitable knowledge, was deemed to be out of date. Universities had to be reformed to direct their teaching and research according to the dictates of the private sector.

In order to carry out such a reformation a new approach to university administration was required which, oddly enough, would impose as much as possible market rationality and consumer choice. Such measures would force students and faculty to take responsibility, moving them in the direction of becoming self-reliant and entrepreneurial actors in the market. Education was less a public right or a direct government respon-sibility and more a private investment made by knowledge consumers in order to eventually improve their prospects in the market. Students should be subject to a users' pay system that would inculcate responsibility by forcing them to use their own or borrowed funds to purchase the best product available. Once neoliberalism established itself as the dominant ideology with respect to university governance its proponents could use its rhetoric of freedom and deregulation to justify efforts to free universities or their research components from state regulation of tenure, employee salaries, and public disclosure in the name of increased efficiency and com-petitiveness, as happened at the University of Wisconsin, for example.[29] Meanwhile, in the same state, the populist governor Scott Walker has taken matters into his own hands by forcing through legislation that sharply curtails the terms of tenure in institutions of higher learning in Wisconsin. This has been met with howls of protest from tenured Wisconsin faculty but also from the American Association of University Professors and a myriad of other academic bodies. But Walker has succeeded so far because his assault on tenure is part of an attack on the rights and benefits of public employees in a state where there has been a massive decline in private sector employment. Walker has been able to play off the resentment that has developed against public employees on the part of private sector employees and the unemployed.

Proponents of this neoliberal approach to higher learning believed that the success of their educational reforms required the institution of a new relationship between administrators and professors. It was this administrative layer that imposed new types of management theories and practices like Total Quality Management, otherwise known as New Public Management or Human Resource Management, which were deliberately designed to submit faculty to the disciplinary control of administrators and increase the distance between the two groups as between management and labor. Professors were to follow new "rational" performance standards imposed from above rather than professionally controlling and monitoring their own performance. They were also increasingly required to demonstrate to auditors through regular and frequent formal assessments that their performance met standards of delivery and productivity. Such assessments had the advantage of ensuring control over the labor of academics. This approach deployed a combination of free market rhetoric and an unprecedented degree of managerial discipline. In order to approximate to market standards it was claimed that the strictest possible administrative control from above was necessary.[30] The contradictions between market and bureaucratic management were somehow overlooked. And despite efforts to objectively measure overall institutional quality, faculty performance and productivity, or student satisfaction and outcomes, the categories chosen to do so have been found to reflect a high degree of arbitrariness and subjectivity.[31] On the other hand, it is remarkable the degree to which academics have accepted and internalized neoliberal norms, especially that of relentless competition against colleagues.[32]

The Knowledge Economy

The goal of such educational policies at the national level was to move toward what by the 1990s was referred to as the knowledge economy, a concept endorsed by neoliberal economists at the OECD, the World Bank, the EU, and even UNESCO. It was claimed that a shift was taking place from the production of physical goods to that of immaterial services. Partly in consequence, production was becoming more "knowledge-intensive," in other words, products were likely to sell more thanks to both the increasingly sophisticated techniques used to make them and the ideas that they embody and that are used to market them, all of which rely on research by skilled and educated workers. The success of companies and national economies alike is therefore increasingly dependent, not on the physical plant and equipment that they have built up over years and decades, but on their "human capital" – that is, on the skills, knowledge, and imagination of their workforces. It is by successfully using these skills to supply what the world market wants that individuals, firms, and whole countries can make profits and prosper.

There is undoubtedly some truth to this view, which stresses human rather than fixed capital, but the shift from the one to the other is exaggerated. Undoubtedly skilled or educated labor has become more important, but no sharp distinction should be drawn between fixed and variable capital. As Alex Callinicos has pointed out, the most successful economies, namely Germany and China, are enjoying success because they are not focused on services making use of labor alone, but are producing, investing in, and exporting machine goods.[33] Moreover, the continued successful production of fundamental material goods is indispensable to the foundations of national economies. Such reservations hardly concern those who dwell on educated human capital and who falsely believe that services and finance can provide a base for the economic life of society. These same people ignore the shift of most production of material goods to low-wage under-developed countries.

Indeed, the purveying of half-truths is an essential feature of the neoliberal approach to the reform of the universities. Whatever credibility it has depends on the forgetting of history, to say nothing of ignoring the actual workings of the market. The claim, for example, that universities were unproductive and a barrier to the private sector that sapped self-reliance comes close to being an outright lie. Public sector spending, including that on universities, made it possible to undergird the market after its failure in the 1930s. Recalling the history of American universities since 1945 it seems clear that the universities along with other elements of the public sector, including military spending and profitable war-making overseas, saved American capitalism and enabled it to reach unprecedented heights. Spending on human services—health, education, and welfare—not only stimulated the economy but also upgraded the workforce. If there was waste in the system it came mainly in the form of military production or the production of commodities that were essentially useless except for the purposes of generating profits or pursuing imperialism. Be that as it may, billions of dollars of government money were poured into the universities to finance research and programs designed to serve the military. Indeed, it was from this source that the resources came which helped build the extraordinary research capacity of American universities. Undoubtedly the consequence of this, as we have seen, was to make American universities worldwide leaders in the production of new knowledge while at the same time inflicting grievous harm on the ideological and institutional framework of the universities by restricting freedom of thought. The new knowledge and trained workers produced by universities represented an essentially free good which was immensely helpful in raising the productivity and the bottom lines of American businesses. Moreover, as everyone knows, academia traditionally has been based on self-policing, intensive competitiveness, and professional standards whose existence had little or nothing to do with markets and immediate profitability. In this light to accuse the professors of that time of a lack of responsibility, as if the only kind of responsibility is that produced by the marketplace, is ironic to say the least.

As we have seen, serving the interests of business was always a major goal of post-1945 universities largely funded by governments and guided by business-backed foundations. The pursuit of theoretical knowledge for its own sake—a hallmark of university science and humanities decried by neoliberals—is an example of long-term investment which the private sector cannot and will not make. Such investment is of course a goal worthy in itself. But can it seriously be argued that it did not pay off in the capitalist sense of ultimately enhancing profitability while affording American universities enormous international influence and power? Indeed, as we know, the goals of government in that period were even larger. In the wake of the New Deal, government assumed the responsibility of making university education much more broadly available as part of its liberal-democratic vision, which included the idea of an educated citizenry and the pursuit of the public good as a foundation of the state. At the same time, the democratic goal that inspired the creation of the mass university was designed to produce a better-educated workforce, which again served the purposes of business. Neoliberalism is uninterested in developing the virtue of citizens, Leo Strauss's belief in the market notwithstanding. Its view of political morality holds that individual virtue is a product of the discipline of the market rather than the product of civic institutions like public universities. Education for the neoliberals is by no means a public right but rather a potentially profitable private investment which produces rational consumers and disciplined workers. Such ideas can only lead to the undermining of the bourgeois form of the democratic state, moving society back toward nineteenth-century levels of poverty and political disenfranchisement while undermining the ideological and institutional foundations of capitalism.

Whatever neoliberals may think of their reform program, its real purpose with respect to the universities is to strengthen the stranglehold of business and to use this power to parasitize or cannibalize the public goods universities produce while imposing ideological control over higher education and suppressing critical thought—a goal completely at odds with democracy, innovation, and the production of serious knowledge. At the same time, it needs to be underscored that the bulk of funding to both public and private institutions of higher learning continues to come from the public sector. It is a case of siphoning these financial resources to favor private enterprise and refashioning the university in order to do this. Neoliberals may in the long term succeed in achieving this goal, which may become a case of killing off the goose that lays the golden eggs. Destroying the public character of the universities as well as other institutions may help eventually to undermine and delegitimize capitalism itself. Or, putting it another way, the free market as conceived by neoliberalism is parasitizing public institutions like universities to the point that the framework of capitalism itself is imperiled. At the least, the undermining of the role of the humanities and social sciences would represent an attack on the heart of the concept of the university, which from first to last was based on the arts curriculum. But so driven are the powers that be to sustain a crisis-ridden capitalism that they drive forward heedless of longer-term consequences.

In *The Last Professors* Frank Donoghue forecasts the transformation of most universities into businesses or trade schools. The transformation will be driven by student impatience with the restrictions of the traditional liberal arts education, with its expensive four-year time commitment and its abstract curriculum. The transformation will also be driven by the decline in public funding of universities. The bachelor of arts or science degree will be superseded by a certificate certifying the student's qualifications for his or her future occupation. Likely the two-year college, perhaps run for profit, will replace the traditional university. At the same time Donoghue believes that the well-funded top universities will be reserved for the rich and upper-middle class and will continue to offer a liberal arts education as a mark of prestige and class status.[34] Donoghue's chilling scenario reflects the growing class polarization in the United States. It entails the demise for the most part of the public university which in the post-1945 period represented an important aspect of liberal democracy. Christopher Newfield's forecast is more nuanced than Donoghue's. He doesn't envision a complete disappearance of the humanities and social science departments. Rather he foresees a collapse of their research function and their reduction to mere teaching and service functions as part of amalgamated units.[35] Of course, such predictions presume that there will be no class-based resistance, which reflects the pessimism and apathy of academics and other citizens in the neoliberal period.

Ranking the Universities

The business and government elites in the United States are at the heart of the neoliberal project. Through the practices of neoliberalism American universities have extended their reach internationally. As Richard Munch points out, the administrative aspect of Human Resources Management or New Public Management (NPM) has become a universal model for the rational targeted management of universities as well as other public agencies and organizations. Governments that do not apply NPM risk being considered irresponsible or even irrational.[36] Fundamental to the objectives of NPM as applied to universities is the drive to transform them as much as possible in the direction of the market. The main move in this direction has been the reduction of block grants and the growth of financing based on external funding on a competitive basis. But while market rhetoric is applied to this change it is not a competition in a market with a large number of suppliers and demanders but rather the petitioning of a great number of demanders from a nearly monopolistic supplier, namely, the science, social science, or humanities foundations funded by governments. The consequence of this monopolistic structure is a strong tendency toward uniformity and conformity to centrally established parameters of research. Such parameters tend to foster intellectual conformity.[37]

Reinforcing this change is the full emergence of the so-called entrepreneurial university. The institutional accumulation of capital—economic as well as social and cultural, to use Bourdieu's terms—by universities worldwide piggy-backs on or colonizes the struggle for recognition and honors on the part of individual researchers and scholars. The production, distribution, and use of knowledge is organized by the increasingly entrepreneurial universities striving for the accumulation of capital. The university itself acts like a strategically managed entrepreneur eager to achieve success in the competition for funds, scholars, and students, replacing the scientific community as a basic institution of collaborative knowledge production. Under the auspices of the entrepreneurial university knowledge is increasingly privatized and patented in the quest to earn monopoly rents or cultural capital in the global competition for economic innovation.[38]

The process of globalization of universities has been facilitated by the emergence of global ranking tables which above all favor the projection of the academic influence of American institutions of higher learning. The three most important such surveys are the literature databases of the Thompson Institute for Scientific Information in Philadelphia, the Shanghai ranking of the 500 most visible universities, and the rankings of the *Times Higher*

Education Supplement. The U.S. occupies a hegemonic position on all these lists. In the Shanghai ranking 17 of the top 20 universities are American as are 36 of the top 50. Critics allege that these lists privilege past rather than current performance and are biased in favor of English-language publications and citation indicators. They do not effectively mirror academic reality but rather construct it in a new way. Not only are they tilted in favor of American institutions but they create for themselves a stratification of the academic field into top, medium, and low-ranking universities involved in struggles for maintaining or improving their position in the rankings. The competition among academics for recognition within the scholarly communities is colonized by this new struggle between entrepreneurial universities.[39] The EU has recently responded to this pro-American bias by supporting the emergence of a European-based ranking system known as U-Multirank. Indeed, a recent OECD study called the Program for the International Assessment of Adult Competencies in 2011 and 2012 tested 166,000 adults ages 16 to 65 in the OECD countries for literacy and math skills. On this measure, the United States battles for last place with Italy and Spain. Countries that traditionally trounce America on the testing of 15 year olds, such as Japan and Finland, also have much higher levels of proficiency and skill among adults.[40] Meanwhile within the United States it is the annual rankings of universities by the magazine *U.S. News and World Report* that holds the greatest sway among the general public. Its influence is illustrated by the reaction of Peter Cohl, a Cornell alumnus who, on hearing the news of Cornell's decline in the ratings, claimed that "my value as a human being feels like it's dropping."[41]

Knowledge and Property

Driven by the need for revenue and for reasons of prestige universities have become deeply enmeshed in seeking intellectual property rights or monopolistic control of patents, inventions, copyrights, and even trademarks. The number of patents applied for by universities has multiplied from a few score in the 1970s to over 5,000 at the turn of the millennium. Much of this activity is driven by the quest for revenue.[42] In an early phase of capitalism such rights undoubtedly helped innovation; generally, rights were relatively specialized and the litigation that arose from such claims did not pose inordinate costs. Today claims of intellectual property rights covers just about everything and the system is riddled by conflicting claims. The dominant economic view is that protection of such intellectual property rights is key to economic innovation. Indeed, the contention is that the privatization of new knowledge in this way is creating new links on a national and global level with private industry.[43] On the contrary, the economic progress of the recent past was due not to intellectual property rights but was the fruit of earlier public investment in science and technology. Rather than facilitating the spread and application of knowledge such claims are creating an atmosphere of exclusivity and secrecy. Litigation is becoming more important than creativity. Indeed, the spread of intellectual property rights that are being actively pursued by universities will actually obstruct future progress by promoting fragmentation of information, unnecessary duplication of effort, secrecy, and lawsuits. This is all the more threatening to the American economic future as intellectual property already constitutes an increasingly large share of property in the U.S. and elsewhere. Activities surrounding intellectual property are fast becoming the core of economic activity in the U.S. and other advanced capitalist countries.[44] The ascendancy of intellectual property rights represents a grave threat to the vigor of the scientific process. Historically science has been a collaborative process in which large numbers of individuals contribute a part to a cumulative and collective process. This ethos is at antipodes to a system of intellectual property which depends on a single agent claiming credit for an entire process built on the aggregation of previous endeavors.[45]

As we have seen, military orientated or business funding has played an important role in the funding of research in science and technology in American universities. Nonetheless a certain space existed for pure research. With the decline of government funding of universities their dependency on private funding—or the influence of corporate funding aimed at new profitable innovations, or the demand for research directed at producing income from intellectual property rights—has sharply increased and the amount available for pure research has declined.[46] Corporations achieve several advantages from university-based rather than in-house research. It is cheaper, more efficient, and more effective than corporate research and is shielded from public criticism by the prestige of universities. Funding for research in the humanities and social sciences meanwhile is withering, as is overall support for these branches of learning. While there might be an immediate benefit to those involved, including the researchers, the scientific process as a whole more than likely suffers as a blanket of secrecy envelops scientific and technological research.[47] In an environment in which the sharing of knowledge predominates the sharing of information is likely to spark further innovation, whereas a closed environment fragments and unnecessarily duplicates activities, inhibits the flow of new ideas, and reduces the likelihood of spin-offs.[48] Moreover, business is interested in projects that have the potential to yield short-term profits rather than investing in long-term investigations that will potentially lead to important scientific breakthroughs paying major economic and social dividends. Overall innovation is likely to be inhibited.[49]

Privatizing Learning

Traditional universities both public and private are becoming increasingly entrepreneurial. But kicking neoliberal aspirations up a notch they are being challenged by universities run explicitly as for-profit businesses. By 2000 there were hundreds of thousands of students being taught at 200 for-profit postsecondary facilities, with approximately 6 percent of students nationally enrolled at such institutions. Foremost among these schools is the University of Phoenix, which, according to its proponents, is considered the model of future higher education that someday will eclipse the traditional university.

Phoenix University has 112 campuses worldwide and confers degrees in over 100 degree programs up to the doctoral level. It previously had over 200 campuses, but closed 115 of them in 2013. The university attained a peak enrollment of almost 600,000 students in 2010, but its numbers have declined precipitously since then. The enrollment drop has been attributed to operational changes amid criticism of high debt loads and low job prospects for university students. In October 2013 it was reported that the University of Phoenix's total degree enrollment was 269,000, an 18 percent decline from 2012. New degree enrollment fell 22 percent to 41,000. Attendant on these difficulties are charges of peculation.

Phoenix University is enmeshed in a larger corporate structure closely tied to finance capital. It is a wholly owned subsidiary of Apollo Group, Inc., a publicly traded Phoenix-based corporation that owns several for-profit educational institutions. The company owns and operates five higher-learning institutions: the University of Phoenix, Western International University, Axia College, the College for Financial Planning, and the Institute for Professional Development. It also owns Insight Schools (online public high schools for Washington, Wisconsin, and other locations). Additionally, Apollo Education Group, Inc. is the owner of BPP Holdings in the United Kingdom. It joined forces with the Carlyle Group for tactical investments in education to expand its student base. Apollo also purchased UNIACC college in Santiago, Chile, and ULA College in Mexico. The Carlyle Group is an American-based global asset management firm, specializing in private equity. It operates in four business areas:

private equity, real assets, market strategies, and fund of funds, through its AlpInvest subsidiary. Carlyle's private equity business has been one of the largest investors in leveraged buyout transactions over the last decade, while its real-estate business has actively acquired commercial real estate. Since its inception, Carlyle has completed investments in such notable companies as Booz Allen Hamilton, Dex Media, Dunkin' Brands, Freescale Semiconductor, Getty Images, HCR Manor Care, Hertz, Kinder Morgan, Nielsen, and United Defense. As of December 31, 2012, Carlyle had $170 billion in assets under management across 113 funds and 67 fund of funds vehicles. The educational practices of the Apollo Group overall have come under increased judicial scrutiny while enrollments at its universities has plunged. As a result, its stock valuation has precipitously declined

Very recently, yet another alternative to the traditional university has emerged in the form of massive open online courses (MOOCs). Internet technology spurred this move by providing access to higher education in response to, on the one hand, the mounting costs of tuition and, on the other, the demand for higher education in the underdeveloped world. The first MOOCs emerged from the open educational resources (OER) movement. The term MOOC was coined in 2008 by Dave Cormier of the University of Prince Edward Island and Bryan Alexander of the National Institute for Technology in Liberal Education, in response to a course called "Connectivism and Connective Knowledge."[50] It was led by George Siemens of Athabasca University and Stephen Downes of the National Research Council, and consisted of 25 fee-paying students in extended education at the University of Manitoba, as well as over 2,200 online students from the general public who paid nothing.

Online education provider ALISON is often cited as the first MOOC, pioneering the systematic aggregation of online interactive learning resources made available worldwide with a free tuition model. Its stated objective is to enable people to gain a basic education and workplace skills. Contrary to other MOOC providers with close links to American institutions such as MIT and Stanford University, the majority of ALISON's learners are located in the developing world, with the fastest growing number of users in India. Other MOOCs soon emerged. Jim Groom from the University of Mary Washington and Michael Branson Smith of York College, City University of New York hosted MOOCs through several American universities.

Business interests rapidly intruded, seeing in MOOCs a vast profit-making opportunity. Venture capital poured into the field. According to the *New York Times*, 2012 became "the year of the MOOC" as several well-financed providers, associated with top universities, emerged, including Coursera, Udacity, and edX. In the fall of 2011 Stanford University launched three courses, the first of which was "Introduction Into AI," launched by Sebastian Thrun and Peter Norvig. Enrollment quickly reached 160,000 students. The announcement was followed within weeks by the launch of two more MOOCs, by Andrew Ng and Jennifer Widom. Following the publicity and high enrollment numbers on these courses, Thrun started a company he named Udacity and Daphne Koller and Andrew Ng launched Coursera. Coursera subsequently announced university partnerships with the University of Pennsylvania, Princeton, Stanford, and the University of Michigan.[51] Concerned about the commercialization of online education, MIT created the not-for-profit MITx. The inaugural course, 6.002x, launched in March 2012. Harvard joined the group, renamed edX, that spring, and the University of California, Berkeley, joined in the summer. The initiative then added the University of Texas System, Wellesley College, and Georgetown University.

Completion rates in these courses are typically lower than 10 percent, with a steep participation drop starting in the first week. Perhaps the most important experiment in using MOOCs came at the University of California campuses between 2012 and 2015, a period of massive retrenchment. Seven million dollars were invested, which allowed students to enroll in courses throughout the system. Non-enrolled students were also allowed to register for credit primarily in order to raise revenue. While the on-campus use of MOOCs has been reasonably successful, very few non-enrolled students have completed the course.[52] One online survey published a "top ten" list of reasons for students dropping out. These included courses requiring too much time, or being too difficult or too basic; poor course design leading to "lecture fatigue" from courses that were just lecture videos; lack of a proper introduction to course technology and format; clunky technology and trolling on discussion boards. Hidden costs were also cited, including required readings from expensive textbooks written by the instructor that also significantly limited students' access to learning material. Other non-completers were "just shopping around" when they registered, or were participating for knowledge rather than a qualification. Providers are exploring multiple strategies for increasing the often single-digit completion rates in many MOOCs, which represent a step beyond the system of massive lecture sections which have been a characteristic of campus-based learning for many years. The latter were already problematic from the perspective of facilitating critical learning and generating a sense of emotional and intellectual engagement on the part of students. The low completion rates in MOOCs indicate that the problem of student disaffection is only compounded by them.

MOOCs are widely seen as a major part of a larger potentially disruptive innovation taking place in higher education. In particular, the many services offered under traditional university business models are predicted to become unbundled and sold to students individually or in newly formed bundles. These services include research, curriculum design, content generation (such as textbooks), teaching, assessment and certification (such as granting degrees), and student placement. MOOCs threaten existing business models by potentially selling teaching, assessment, and/or placement separately from the current package of services. In the free-tuition business model, the basic product—the course content—is given away free. "Charging for content would be a tragedy," said Andrew Ng. But "premium" services such as certification or placement would be charged a fee.

The larger non-profit organizations involved in the MOOCs movement include the Bill & Melinda Gates Foundation, the MacArthur Foundation, the National Science Foundation, and the American Council on Education. University pioneers include Stanford, Harvard, MIT, the University of Pennsylvania, CalTech, the University of Texas at Austin, the University of California at Berkeley, San Jose State University, and the Indian Institute of Technology, Bombay. Related companies include Google and the educational publisher Pearson plc. Venture capitalist firms involved include Kleiner Perkins Caufield & Byers, New Enterprise Associates, and Andreessen Horowitz. Starbucks recently announced a partnership with Arizona State University to offer the remission of tuition fees to students who enroll in the university's online degree programs. An elitist variation on MOOCs is the Minerva Project, backed by venture capital and offering seminar-like internet instruction based on a university with no real campus or tenured faculty but a more personalized and innovative curriculum. The changes predicted from MOOCs and other internet-based schemes generate objections in some academic quarters who fear for the future of tenured faculty, teaching, and scholarship and the integrity of traditional universities.

Should one-size-fits-all vendor-designed courses become the norm, it is feared that two classes of universities will be created: one consisting of well-funded colleges and universities in which privileged students get their own real professor, the other of financially stressed private and public universities in which students watch a bunch of video-taped lectures. More fundamental is the threat of massively undercutting the costs of faculty labor and of fixed capital in maintaining traditional universities. There can be no doubt that MOOCs as well as private for-profit institutions threaten the traditional university and its faculty.

Resistance

Tenured faculty can resist these trends by fighting for more control over the accreditation process. They can also resist by unionization. Unionization of faculty has recently made progress at primarily teaching rather than research institutions. But it has progressed even at top schools which are part of the SUNY system and at the University of Illinois at Chicago. The evidence suggests that unionization helps to bolster the flagging salaries of academics.[53] On the other hand, tenured faculty at research-orientated institutions continue to resist unionization. Traditional resistance to unionization based on petty bourgeois illusions about professionalism inhibits such a movement on a large scale. This resistance is reinforced further by the overall decline in rates of unionization in American society. But it is also a reflection of the conservatism of tenured faculty, who are desperately clinging to their privileged positions in an increasingly insecure profession.[54] Nonetheless it is significant that the newly formed union at the University of Illinois includes both tenured and non-tenured faculty, and that the unions at Temple University and Pitt University are moving in the same direction.

Unionization of tenured faculty is difficult, despite the fact that what remains of their autonomy is being undermined by administrators in a long-term process of proletarianization. Indeed, this process is likely to force unionization. More immediately promising is the possibility of unionization of non-tenured or contingent faculty including graduate students, who together make up the bulk of teaching personnel. A report by the American Association of University Professors published in April 2014 showed that adjuncts now constitute 76.4 percent of U.S. faculty across all institutional types, from liberal arts colleges to research universities to community colleges. A study released by the U.S. House of Representatives in January of the same year revealed that the majority of these adjuncts live below the poverty line.

But organizing part-timers is even more difficult than organizing tenured faculty, as they are a transient element on their way elsewhere or having other employment off campus. On the other hand, the execrable situation of contractual employees with few or no benefits and low pay may impel unionization. The situation of graduate students is particularly deplorable.

With limited funding enabling them to finish their degrees, accumulated debt, and dim prospects for employment, unionization would seem to be an important option. Drives to unionize non-tenured university teachers are growing. The rise of new social movements seems to be connected to the growing interest in unionization. Self-identification as an activist is tied to an interest in joining a union, as well to the decline of a sense of community within the university.[55]

Already in 2006, 6,000 post-docs in the University of California system had created a UAW-affiliated union. As of the same date 40,000 graduate students were already members of a union across the United States. The Service Employees International Union has been especially active in organizing. In Washington D.C., the Service Employees have unionized American University, Georgetown, George Washington and Montgomery College. In the Los Angeles area, adjuncts at Whittier College and the University of La Verne recently filed with the National Labor Relations Board for a union election. In Boston, Tufts University's part-time faculty voted to join the Service Employees' Union in September 2006, and an October vote at Bentley University failed by two votes. Campaigns are underway at Northeastern and Lesley.[56] In a major breakthrough, all of the campus branches of Pitt University are in the midst of a unionization drive which would include both the adjunct and tenured faculty in a single union.[57] The Northeast, California, and the Chicago region seem particular hotbeds of unionization drives and labor unrest. *Labor Notes* in 2013 reported that organizing efforts by the Service Employees are currently underway at 22 college campuses. Given the part-time nature of contractual employment, a metropolitan strategy is being pursued attempting to unionize all academic institutions in a city at the same time.[58] On February 25, 2015 a National Adjuncts Walkout Day was declared a partial success. Graduate students at some of the United States' most prestigious universities launched a national day of action in October 2015 as part of a years-long campaign to unionize teaching assistants and other student workers. Graduate students at Harvard and Yale are also trying to organize.

Bringing tenured and non-tenured faculty together is truly a key link. A more concrete barrier to the unionization of tenured faculty is the continued force of the 1979 Supreme Court decision that blocked the unionization of the tenured faculty at Yeshiva University by deciding that they were "managerial employees". A recent decision of the National Labor Relations Board has questioned this ruling, arguing that the corporatization of the university has vitiated the supposed managerial prerogatives of tenured faculty.

Students on the whole have been passive in the neoliberal years. They have been inhibited from protesting as a result of the difficulties of finding work and paying off debts. Furthermore, surveys indicate that most students throughout the neoliberal era have been apolitical, self-absorbed, and individualistic. Insofar as they have protested in recent decades they have mobilized over specific concerns like gender inequality, environmental issues, or minority rights. But in 2011 the Occupy Movement that swept the United States, and which was largely consisted of university students, demonstrated widespread concern over economic crisis and social inequality. Indeed, many who participated questioned the viability of capitalism. While these movements petered out or were actively put down by the state, they dramatically increased class consciousness and awareness of social inequality throughout society and are likely portentous of the future. Brief as it was, with its incipient recognition of the issue of class Occupy set the ideological context within which other emerging issues began to be seen. The Boycott, Divestment and Sanctions Movement on campus, which has struggled to maintain itself in the face of opposition from wealthy Zionists in complicity with university administrators, took on new life in the wake of the massive Israeli assault on Gaza in the summer of 2014. In November 2015 at the University of Missouri—the state in which the notorious Ferguson riots occurred in reaction to the police shooting of Michael Brown—student and faculty strikes erupted. The race issue was to the fore but the ensuing controversy helped to reveal the intersection— partial to be sure—of the class and racial questions in American life. The president of the university was forced from office and sympathy demonstrations and sit-ins broke out in other universities across the United States. In a key development, on 15 November students walked out of classrooms across the United States to protest ballooning student loan debt and to rally for tuition-free public colleges and a minimum wage hike for campus workers. At this point there appeared to be a growing convergence of the movement against racism with those demanding economic justice in the universities as well as in society at large. The Bernie Sanders presidential campaign finally served to politicize the social and economic issues of racism, inequality, and sexism under the mantle of class, and in so doing reawakened student interest in politics across the United States. Sanders' democratic socialist message resonated both within the ranks of students but also with the working population at large. Rising class consciousness is changing the overall political context in favor of democratic change both within and without the universities.

In which direction can resistance to the corporate university lead? In our treatment of the Berkeley Free Speech Movement of the 1960s we pictured university researchers, teachers, and students as initially being in the thrall of capitalism. They either trained or were being trained as managerial cadres. On the other hand, however temporarily, that control was threatened by the student-led movement. Capitalism's control of these managerial cadres is today once again powerful. Under neoliberalism society is dominated by financial capitalists who implement their rule by employing and rewarding the educated managerial class who are more vital than ever to the system. Academics and researchers in universities, as well as the highly skilled and educated who work in government or high-tech industries, are constituents of this elite group, as are students who hope to find employment as part of it. On the other hand, the alliance between this managerial academic group and financial capitalists is by no means a solid one. At many levels—ecological, political, economic—capitalism seems beleaguered. There is the possibility that in an ongoing and deepening capitalist crisis this stratum could cut its ties to financial capital and form an alliance with a populist majority whose aim would be the socialist reorganization of society. That would be particularly the case if this stratum felt its status imperiled or felt that the system itself was foundering. There is now the potential for growth in political and class consciousness and organization, including increasing links between university campuses and popular struggles in society at large.

In response to this rising discontent among students, researchers, and teachers across America there has also been a buildup of security and police presence on campus. The CIA and the Pentagon are once more actively engaged in funding and recruiting students and faculty on campus. What with simmering racial and economic angst and the further extension of direct U.S. imperialist intervention in the Middle East and Eastern Europe, the likelihood of campus unrest is growing.[59]

The abrupt firing of pro-Palestinian Professor Stephen Salaita at the Champaign campus of the University of Illinois has become a focal point of the struggle against the stifling of dissent on university campuses. Of Palestinian descent, Salaita was a professor of English at Virginia Tech when he was offered a contract at the University of Illinois at Champaign to teach indigenous studies. He accepted the offer, but then in response to the massive attacks on Gaza in 2014 he vehemently criticized Israel in successive Twitter messages. The University of Illinois chancellor, Phyllis Wise, along with the board of governors, abruptly cancelled the job offer, complaining of Salaita's incivility and claiming that no actual contract had been concluded. Salaita sued, charging breach of contract, suppression of free speech and academic freedom, and political collusion. In August 2015 a federal judge ruled that Salaita's case had standing, except on the question of collusion. In the immediate aftermath Chancellor Wise offered her resignation amid the surfacing of evidence proving that messages pertinent to the case had been destroyed by Wise and others, and that political collusion with wealthy Zionist donors and senior politicians had indeed been involved. The judge then reinstated the charge of political collusion. The case as it stands had already given the University of Illinois an enormous black eye and had focused national attention on the suppression of free speech and academic freedom by administrators, politicians, and wealthy donors, not only at Illinois but throughout the system of higher education. The attempt to stifle debate on the Palestinian question on university campuses by Zionist individuals and organizations was a focal point of the scandal. In November 2015 Salaita dropped his claims against the university in return for a damages payment of $875,000. Overall the Salaita case has given an enormous boost to the fight for free speech both on and off university campuses.

Meanwhile, the growing use of MOOCs, while threatening the interests of some faculty, also reflects the fact that the aspiration to self-improvement on the part of people all over the world is increasing rather than diminishing. Moreover, it is notable that while enrollment, funding, and graduate work in arts faculties are in trouble, there is evidence that the thirst for the humanities has not diminished. Despite economic insecurity, undergraduate enrollment on humanities courses has continued to sustain itself over recent decades, which brings us back to the fundamental questions raised by the students in the Free Speech Movement at Berkeley 50 years ago. While university administrators, politicians, businessmen, and neoliberal economists seek to turn knowledge into an exchange value it is proving difficult to do so. Indeed, the creation and dissemination of knowledge is being held captive by the fetters of academic capitalism. The incredible accumulation of academic knowledge begs to be set free as a use value to contribute to a general intellect which issues from mass democratic consciousness.

No fundamental shake-up of the academic disciplines in this direction has so far occurred. But, since the onset of the 2008 crisis, we have witnessed the rapid decline of postmodernism and the deepening crisis of neoliberal economics, which is now under siege. The tremendous popularity of Thomas Piketty's *Capital in the Twenty-First Century* reflects this crisis, while the work itself tries to save the methodology of neoclassical economics. On the other hand, the increasing recognition of the importance of a Marxist approach to ecology, spearheaded by the editor of *Monthly Review* John Bellamy Foster, is especially noteworthy. Likewise, the arrival in the United States of the theoretically orientated conferences organized by the journal *Historical Materialism*, taking their place alongside the annual meetings of Left Forum and Socialism, augurs well for the future of Marxist theory and practice in the United States. Indeed, the worldwide prestige of the *Historical Materialism* journal and the affiliated Chicago-based book publisher Haymarket Press is of great significance, joining the ongoing influence of *Monthly Review* and *Science & Society*. Especially notable is the fact that these journals have an impact both inside the academy and also beyond it. This is also true of new Marxist journals like *Jacobin*, the online *Viewpoint Magazine*, and *Red Wedge*, which are attracting the attention of students. The popularity of David Harvey's reading of Marx's *Capital* in both book format and on the internet is also a heartening sign of the revival of interest in Marx in the United States. Indeed, Marx's classic work has re-emerged as a focal point of current academic debate about the causes and likely outcome of the contemporary crisis of capitalism.[60] The influence of Marxism within universities can only increase as the movement for democratic socialism in American society at large continues to grow.

The current revival of Marxism is important because its powerful and sophisticated theory makes possible a reintegration of the humanities and social sciences while offering a comprehensive critique of the problems facing American society. Furthermore, Marxism bases itself on class struggle and revolution—the only effective means of assuming control of the state, thereby transforming society from capitalism to socialism and releasing the majority of the population from wage slavery, commodity fetishism, and the political tyranny of plutocratic democracy. As this analysis of the American university suggests, Marxism does so by offering a comprehensive and critical understanding of the evolution of society, including the history of its universities. As our analysis shows, what we are witnessing today is a form of class struggle from above in which the capitalist class is attempting to restructure American society and indeed the whole world in order to aggregate wealth to itself and to strengthen its economic and political power in the face of an ongoing capitalist crisis. As part of this offensive it is trying to dramatically reduce public spending which benefits the majority of the population and to weaken public sector institutions or force them to serve the interests of capital. Serving the interests of capital involves the transformation of the state into an instrument of surveillance and outright coercion deployed against the population, as well as milking its resources in the service of business. The ascendancy of academic capitalism is an integral part of this program.

At present the neoliberal agenda remains ascendant in academe. A key principle in any fightback will be to assert that higher education is a right not a privilege. Of equal importance is the defense of the principle that universities should educate citizens rather than satisfy consumers, and serve the public and collective good rather than capitalism and private interests. In pursuit of these ends, insisting on the right to pursue critical inquiry is fundamental. Undergirding such goals should be the demand for the restoration of public funding to universities.[61] Basic to these goals is the provision of job security and benefits to non-tenured faculty. As to the students, it should be recalled that the provision of free public education through high school was the result of both popular demand and the need of the capitalist economy for literate and numerate workers. Today a bachelor's degree or equivalent is required for most decently paid jobs and the economy requires educated workers generally. It is absurd that students should have to assume enormous debts to pay for an education whose costs should be borne by society as a whole, and especially by capital. Moreover, students have the right to assume that following graduation they can look forward to decently paid jobs rather than joining the reserve army of unemployed labor.

According to the neoliberal agenda the restructuring of the universities is part of an overall process of economic restructuring to enhance profitability and productivity while instilling social discipline. As key sites of training, research, and economic development, universities have become central locations within the structure of contemporary capitalism for which knowledge industries, some based in the universities, are increasingly the leading edge. The labor force within academic institutions, including most teachers and researchers, are of course already made up of wage workers. One of the most important trends of the neoliberal period is the growing proletarianization of the tenured faculty. In the face of these currents imposed from above the obvious rejoinder is the organization of an effective class struggle from below based on increasing class consciousness and unified trade unions which would include tenured and non-tenured teachers as well as students and non-academic workers. Knowledge workers—who by definition have high levels of skill, work at strategic locations, and need to cooperate with one another in an increasingly interdependent work process—are at one level ideal subjects for a new stage of struggle against capitalism. Such a struggle would see the transformation of universities into important public and democratic institutions whose workers would produce knowledge as a use value, thereby helping to improve the economic, cultural, and ecological condition of the mass of humanity. Under socialist conditions such knowledge would be free to be as rational, critical, and self-aware as possible. In the meantime, democratization of the governance of universities ought to be the central objective of resistance.

Notes

Introduction

1. Paul Fain, "'Nearing the Bottom': Inside Higher Education," *Inside Higher Education*, May 15, 2014.
2. Raymond A. Morrow, "Critical Theory and Higher Education: Political Economy and the Cul-de-Sac of the Postmodernist Turn," in *The University, State and Market: The Political Economy of Globalization in the Americas*, ed. Robert A. Rhoads and Carlos Alberto Torres, Stanford: Stanford University Press, 2006, pp. xvii–xxxiii.
3. Perry Anderson, "Components of the National Culture," *New Left Review*, No. 50, July–August, 1968, pp. 3–4.
4. Pierre Bourdieu, *The Field of Cultural Production: Essays on Art and Literature*, New York: Columbia University Press, 1993, pp. 86–7.
5. Karl Marx, Letter to Arnold Ruge, Kreuznach, September 1843, *Letters from the Deutsch-Französische Jahrbücher*, at https://www.marxists.org/archive/marx/works/1843/letters/43_09.htm
6. Larry Ceplair, *Anti-Communism in Twentieth-Century America*, Santa Barbara: Clio, 2011, pp. 1–2, 12.
7. Carlo Vercellone, "From the Mass Worker to Cognitive Labor: Historical and Theoretical Considerations," in *Beyond Marx: Theorizing the Global Labor Relations of the Twenty-First Century*, ed. Marcel van der Linden and Karl Heinz Roth, Leiden, Boston: Brill, 2014, pp. 217–43.

1   The Birth of the Corporate University

1. Christopher Newfield, *Ivy and Industry: Business and the Making of the American University, 1880–1980*, Durham NC: Duke University Press, 2003, p. 78.
2. Thorstein Veblen, *The Higher Learning in America: A Memorandum on the Conduct of Universities by Business Men*, New York: A.M. Kelley, 1965, pp. 63–7; Clyde W. Barrow, *Universities and the Capitalist State: Corporate Liberalism and the Reconstruction of American Higher Education, 1894–1928*, Madison: University of Wisconsin Press, 1990, pp. 31–59; David Smith, *Who Rules the Universities? An Essay in Class Analysis*, New York: Monthly Review Press, 1974; Neil Smith, *American Empire: Roosevelt's Geographer and the Prelude to Globalization*, Berkeley: University of California Press, 2003, pp. 37–57.
3. Jonathan R. Cole, *The Great American University: Its Rise to Preeminence, Its Indispensable National Role, Why It Must Be Protected*, New York: Public Affairs, 2009, p. 38.

4. Newfield, *Ivy and Industry*, p. 27.

5. John R. Thelin, *A History of American Higher Education*, 2nd edn, Baltimore: Johns Hopkins University Press, 2011, p. 239.

6. David Nugent, "Knowledge and Empire: The Social Sciences and United States Imperial Expansion," *Identities*, Vol. 17, No. 1, 2010, pp. 9–10.

7. Thomas C. Patterson, *A Social History of Anthropology in the United States*, Oxford and New York: Berg, 2002, p. 73.

8. Parmar Inderjeet, *Foundations of the American Century: The Ford, Carnegie, and Rockefeller Foundations in the Rise of American Power*, New York: Columbia University Press, 2012, p. 40.

9. Nugent, "Knowledge and Empire," pp. 15–6; Donald Fisher, *Fundamental Development of the Social Sciences: Rockefeller Philanthropy and the United States Social Science Research Council*, Ann Arbor: University of Michigan Press, 1993.

10. Fisher, *Fundamental Development of the Social Sciences*, p. 238.

11. Timothy Reese Cain, *Establishing Academic Freedom: Politics, Principles, and the Development of Core Values*, Basingstoke: Palgrave Macmillan, 2012, p. 13.

12. Ibid., pp. 39–41.

13. Ibid., pp. 33–5; William G. Bowen and Eugene M. Tobin, *Locus of Authority: The Evolution of Faculty Roles in the Governance of Higher Education*, Princeton: Princeton University Press, 2015, p. 42.

14. Newfield, *Ivy and Industry*, p. 59.

15. Barrow, *Universities and the Capitalist State*, pp. 203–41; Cain, *Establishing Academic Freedom*, pp. 55–62.

16. Ellen Schrecker, *No Ivory Tower: McCarthyism and the Universities*, New York: Oxford University Press, 1986, pp. 19–21; Cain, *Establishing Academic Freedom*, p. 28.

17. Cain., pp. 18–23.

18. Ibid., pp. 76–7.

19. Ibid., p. 83.

20. Ibid., p. 126.

21. Ibid., p.129.

22. Ibid., pp. 123–4; Timothy Reese Cain, "Unionised Faculty and the Political Left: Communism and the American Federation of Teachers on the Eve of the Second World War," *History of Education: Journal of the History of Education Society*, Vol. 41, No. 4, 2012, pp. 515–35.

23. Schrecker, *No Ivory Tower*, pp. 65–6.

24. Cain, *Establishing Academic Freedom*, pp. 158–9.

25. Schrecker, *No Ivory Tower*, pp. 76–82.

26. Cain, *Establishing Academic Freedom*, p. 170.

27. Robert Cohen, *When the Old Left Was Young: Student Radicals and America's First Mass Student Movement, 1929–1941*, New York: Oxford University Press, 1993, pp. 43, 52.

28. Cohen, *When the Old Left Was Young*, pp. 130, 240.

29. Richard C. Lewontin, "The Cold War and the Transformation of the Academy," in *The Cold War and the University: Toward an Intellectual History of the Post-War Years*, ed. Noam Chomsky et al., New York: New Press, 1997, p. 12.

30. Rebecca S. Loewen, *Creating the Cold War University: The Transformation of Stanford*, Berkeley: University of California Press, 1997, pp. 88–9.

31. Thomas Bender, "Politics, Intellect and the American University 1945–95," in *American Academic Culture in Transition: Fifty Years, Four Disciplines*, ed. Bender and Carl E. Schorske, Princeton: Princeton University Press, 1997, p. 24.

32. Seymour Melman, *Pentagon Capitalism*, New York: McGraw-Hill, 1971, pp. 231–4.

33. Lewontin, "The Cold War and the Transformation of the Academy," pp. 2, 8, 18.

34. C. Wright Mills, *White Collar: The American Middle Classes*, New York: Oxford University Press, 1951, pp. 129–39.

35. Bender, "Politics, Intellect and the American University," p. 17.

36. Ibid., pp. 23–4.

37. Francis Stonor Saunders, *Who Paid the Piper? The CIA and the Cultural Cold War*, London: Granta Books, 1999, p. 134. See also Christopher Simpson, *Science of Coercion: Communication Research and Psychological Warfare, 1945–1960*, New York: Oxford University Press, 1994, p. 28.

38. Saunders, *Who Paid the Piper?*, pp. 134–45.

39. Loewen, *Creating the Cold War University*, pp. 196–7.

40. Ibid., pp. 197–202; Allan Needell, "Project Troy and the Cold War Annexation of the Social Sciences," in *Universities and Empire: Money and Politics in the Social Sciences During the Cold War*, ed. Christopher Simpson, New York: New Press, 1998, pp. 22–4.

41. Simpson, *Science of Coercion*, pp. 80–1.

42. Ibid., p. 61.

43. Stuart Ewen, *PR! A Social History of Spin*, New York: Basic Books, 1996; J. Michael Sproule, *Propaganda and Democracy: The American Experience of Media and Mass Persuasion*, Cambridge: Cambridge University Press, 1996, pp. 224–61.

44. Jack Hexter, "The Historian and His Day," *Political Science Quarterly*, Vol. 69, No. 2, 1954, pp. 219–33; Hexter, *Reappraisals in History*, New York: Longmans, 1961, pp. 6–9.

45. Kees van der Pijl, "Historicising the International: Modes of Foreign Relations and Political Economy," *Historical Materialism*, Vol. 18, No. 2, 2010, p. 5.

46. Anderson, "Components of the National Culture," p. 8.

47. Peter D. Thomas, *The Gramscian Moment: Philosophy, Hegemony, Marxism*, Leiden: Brill, 2009, pp. 70, 163, 172, 180.

48. David H. Price, "Uninvited Guests: A Short History of the CIA on Campus," in *The CIA on Campus: Essays on Academic Freedom and the National Security State*, ed. Philip Zwerling, Jefferson: McFarland, 2011, pp. 38–42; Kenneth J. Heineman, *Campus Wars: The Peace Movement at American State Universities in the Vietnam Era*, New York: New York University, 1993, pp. 20–6.

49. Giles Scott-Smith, *The Politics of Apolitical Culture: The Congress for Cultural Freedom and the Political Economy of American Hegemony 1945–1955*, New York: Routledge, 2002, p. 77.

50. Saunders, *Who Paid the Piper?*, pp. 89–91, 200–1, 342, 379.

51. Scott-Smith, *The Politics of Apolitical Culture*, p. 146.

52. Irene L. Gendzier, *Managing Political Change: Social Scientists and the Third World*, Boulder: Westview, 1985, pp. 87–104.

53. Paul Buhle and Dan Georgakas, "Communist Party, USA," in *Encyclopedia of the American Left*, ed. Paul Buhle, Dan Georgkas, and Mari Jo Buhle, New York: Garland, 1990, pp. 147–57.

54. Michael Denning, *The Cultural Front: The Laboring of American Culture in the Twentieth Century*, London and New York: Verso, 1998, p. 6.

55. Sanders, *Who Paid the Piper?*, p. 53.

56. Ibid., pp. 133–6.

57. Ibid., p. 86.

58. Ibid., pp. 89, 91, 92.

59. Ibid., pp. 161–6.

60. Jessica Wang, *American Science in an Age of Anxiety: Scientists, Anticommunism and the Cold War*, Chapel Hill: University of North Carolina Press, 1999, p. 272.

61. Wang, *Age of Anxiety*, pp. 274–9.

62. Schrecker, *Who Paid the Piper?*, p. 188.

63. Ibid., p. 94.

64. Ibid., pp. 105–12, 127.

65. Peter Novick, *That Noble Dream: The "Objectivity Question" and the American Historical Profession*, Cambridge: Cambridge University Press, 1988, p. 326.

66. Schrecker, *Who Paid the Piper?*, p. 116.

67. David Parker, *Ideology, Absolutism and the English Revolution: Debates of the British Communist Historians*, London: Lawrence & Wishart, 2008.

68. Quoted in Schrecker, *Who Paid the Piper?*, p. 216.

2 The Humanities and Social Sciences in the Cold War

1. Bourdieu, *The Field of Cultural Production*.

2. The young and astute legal scholar and political theorist Samuel Thompson pointed this out to me.

3. Thomas, *The Gramscian Moment*, pp. 416–20.

4. Carl Schorske, "The New Rigorism in the Human Sciences," *Daedalus*, Vol. 126, No. 1, 1997, p. 293.

5. Novick, *That Noble Dream*, pp. 310–14.

6. Jack Goody, *The Theft of History*, Cambridge: Cambridge University Press, 2007.

7. Novick, *That Noble Dream*, pp. 302–3.

8. Arthur S. Link, "Annual Address of the President of the American Historical Association, Delivered on December 28, 1984," *American Historical Review*, Vol. 90, No. 1, 1985, pp. 1–17.

9. Robert B. Townsend, *History's Babel: Scholarship, Professionalization, and the Historical Enterprise in the United States, 1880–1940*, Chicago: University of Chicago Press, 2013, pp. 181–3.

10. On Brinton's conservatism see Novick, *That Noble Dream*, pp. 243, 266.

11. Bailey Stone, *The Anatomy of Revolution Revisited: A Comparative Analysis of England, France and Russia*, Cambridge: Cambridge University Press, 2013.

12. Eric P. Kaufman, *The Rise and Fall of Anglo-America*, Cambridge MA: Harvard University Press, 2004, p. 219.

13. David S. Brown, *Richard Hofstadter: An Intellectual Biography*, Chicago: University of Chicago Press, pp. 53–4.

14. Eric Foner, *Who Owns History? Rethinking the Past*, New York: Hill and Wang, 2002, pp. 28–9, 39.

15. John Higham, "The Collapse of Consensus History," *Journal of American History*, Vol. 76, No. 2, 1989, pp. 460–6.

16. David Montgomery, *The Fall of the House of Labor: The Workplace, the State and American Labor Activism, 1865–1925*, New York: Cambridge University Press, 1987, p. xxviii.

17. Brown, *Richard Hofstadter*, pp. 165–6.

18. Ellen Schrecker, *Many Are the Crimes: McCarthyism in America*, Boston: Little, Brown, 1998, pp. 410–11.

19. Foner, *Who Owns History?*, pp. 121–2.

20. Michael Rogin, *The Intellectuals and McCarthy: The Radical Specter*, Cambridge MA: MIT Press, 1967, pp. 183–5, 264.

21. Herbert Shapiro, "The Impact of the Aptheker Thesis: A Retrospective View of 'American Negro Slave Revolts'," *Science & Society*, Vol. 48, No. 1, 1984, pp. 52–73; Joseph Cephas Carroll, *Slave Insurrections in the United States, 1800–65*, Newburyport: Dover, 2012.

22. Gary Murrell, "On Herbert Aptheker and his Side of History: An Interview with Eric Foner," *Radical History Review*, Vol. 78, No. 3, 2000, p. 14.

23. Novick, *That Noble Dream*, pp. 245, 49.

24. Ibid., p. 330.

25. Ibid.

26. James M. Cypher, "From Military Keynesianism to Global-Neoliberal Militarism," *Monthly Review*, Vol. 59, No. 2, 2007, pp. 37–55.

27. Henry Heller, *The Cold War and the New Imperialism: A Global History, 1945–2005*, New York: Monthly Review Press, 2006, pp. 31–3.

28. Frank A. Ninkovich, *The Diplomacy of Ideas: US Foreign Policy and Cultural Relations, 1938–1950*, Cambridge: Cambridge University Press, 1981, pp. 113–35, Sam Lebovic, "From War Junk to Educational Exchange: The World War II Origins of the Fulbright Program and the Foundations of

American Cultural Globalism, 1945–1950," *Diplomatic History*, Vol. 37, No. 2, 2013, pp. 280–312.

29. Liping Bu, *Making The World Like Us: Education, Cultural Expansion, and the American Century*, Westport: Praeger, 2003, p. 181.

30. Karen M. Paget, *Patriotic Betrayal: The Inside Story of the CIA's Secret Campaign to Enroll American Students in the Crusade Against Communism*, New Haven: Yale University Press, 2015, pp. 85, 87, 92.

31. David Colander and Harry Landreth, "Lorie Tarshis at Yale," in *Keynesianism and the Keynesian Revolution in America: A Memorial Volume in Honour of Lorie Tarshis*, ed. O.F. Hamouda and B.B. Price, Cheltenham: Edward Elgar, 1998, pp. 59–72.

32. Quoted in William J. Barber, "The Career of Alvin H. Hansen in the 1920s and 1930s: A Study of Intellectual Transformation," *History of Political Economy*, Vol. 19, No. 2, 1987, p. 191.

33. Schorske, "The New Rigorism in the Human Sciences," p. 296.

34. Barber, "The Career of Alvin H. Hansen," p. 108.

35. George Watson, "The Empire of Lionel Trilling," *Sewanee Review*, Vol. 115, No. 3, 2007, pp. 484–90.

36. Michael Kimmage, *The Conservative Turn: Lionel Trilling, Whittaker Chambers and the Lessons of Anti-Communism*, Cambridge: Harvard University Press, 2009, p. 64.

37. James A. Berlin, *Rhetorics, Poetics and Cultures: Refiguring College English Studies*, Urbana: National Council of Teachers of English, 1996, pp. 15–6.

38. Kimmage, *The Conservative Turn*, p. 99.

39. Ibid., p. 101.

40. Russell Reising, "Lionel Trilling, the Liberal Imagination, and the Emergence of the Cultural Discourse of Anti-Stalinism," *Boundary 2*, Vol. 20, No. 1, 1993, pp. 94–124.

41. Terry Eagleton, *Marxism and Literary Criticism*, Hoboken: Taylor and Francis, 2012, pp. 140–3.

42. Mark Walhout, "New Criticism and the Crisis of American Liberalism," *College English*, Vol. 49, No. 8, 1987, p. 863.

43. Christopher Phelps, "Why Wouldn't Sidney Hook Permit the Republication of His Best Book," *Historical Materialism*, Vol. 11, No. 4, 2003, p. 312.

44. Ibid., p. 306.

45. Ibid., pp. 307–8.

46. Saunders, *Who Paid the Piper?*, pp. 72, 74, 77–80.

47. John Capps, "Sidney Hook and Anti-Communism," *Transactions of the Charles S. Peirce Society*, Vol. 40, No. 4, 2004, pp. 803–16.

48. Alan M. Wald, *The New York Intellectuals: The Rise and Decline of the Anti-Stalinist Left from the 1930s to the 1980s*, Chapel Hill: University of North Carolina Press, 1987, p. 268.

49. Russell Jacoby, *The Last Intellectuals: American Culture in the Age of Academe*, New York: Basic Books, 1987, pp. 3–27.

50. George A. Reisch, *How the Cold War Transformed Philosophy of Science: To the Icy Slopes of Logic*, Cambridge: Cambridge University Press, 2005, p. 5.

51. Ibid.

52. Ibid., p. 3.

53. Ibid., p. 215.

54. Anselme Jappe, "Sohn-Rethal and the Origin of 'Real Abstraction': A Critique of Production or a Critique of Circulation," *Historical Materialism Journal*, Vol. 21, No. 1, 2013, pp. 3–14.

55. Thomas S. Kuhn, *The Structure of Scientific Revolutions*, Chicago: University of Chicago Press, 1962.

56. Reisch, *How the Cold War Transformed Philosophy of Science*, pp. 219, 221.

57. Ibid., p. 269.

58. Ibid., pp. 272–6.

59. Ibid., pp. 278–9, 310–12, 318.

60. Ibid., p.308.

61. Ibid., p. 353; Joel Isaac, *Working Knowledge: Making the Human Sciences from Parsons to Kuhn*, Cambridge MA: Harvard University Press, 2012.

62. Talal Assad, "Two European Images of Non-European Rule," in *Anthropology and the Colonial Encounter*, Ithaca, NY: Ithaca Press, 1975, p. 103.

63. Li-Chaun Tai, *L'anthropologie francais entre sciences coloniales et decolonisation*, Paris: Publications de la société française d'histoire d'outre-mer, 2010, pp. 12–14.

64. David Goddard, "Limits of British Anthropology," *New Left Review*, No. 58, 1969, pp. 69–79.

65. Patterson, *A Social History of Anthropology in the United States*, pp. 55–67.

66. Ibid., p. 79.

67. Gerard Colby, *Thy Will be Done: The Conquest of the Amazon. Nelson Rockefeller and Evangelism in the Age of Oil*, New York: HarperCollins, 1995, p. 130.

68. Patterson, *A Social History of Anthropology in the United States*, pp. 92–6.

69. David H. Price, *Threatening Anthropology: McCarthyism and the FBI's Surveillance of Activist Anthropologists*, Durham NC: Duke University Press, 2004, p. 112.

70. Marc Pinkoski, "American Colonialism at the Dawn of the Cold War," in *Anthropology at the Dawn of the Cold War: The Influence of Foundations, McCarthyism and the Cold War*, ed. Dustin Wax, London: Pluto Press, 2008, pp. 72–81.

71. William J. Peace, *Leslie A. White: Evolution and Revolution in Anthropology*, Lincoln: University of Nebraska Press, 2004, p. 179.

72. Ibid., p. 69.

73. Ibid., p. 91.

74. Ibid., p. 110.

75. Patterson, *A Social History of Anthropology in the United States*, pp. 162–3.

76. Peter Sandler, *Return from the Natives: How Margaret Mead Won the Second World War and Lost the Cold War*, New Haven: Yale University Press, 2013, pp. 223–53.

77. David H. Price, "Cold War Anthropology: Collaborators and Victims of the National Security State," *Identities: Global Studies in Culture and Power*, Vol. 4, No. 3–4, 1998, pp. 390–3.

78. Ibid., pp. 402–6.

79. Ron T. Robin, *The Making of the Cold War Enemy: Culture and Politics in the Military-Intellectual Complex*, Princeton: Princeton University Press, 2001, pp. 24, 62.

80. Loewen, *Creating the Cold War University*, pp. 196–7.

81. Martin Nicolaus, "The Professional Organization of Sociology: A View from Below," in *Ideology in Social Science: Readings in Critical Social Theory*, London: Fontana, 1972, pp. 47–9; Anderson, "Components of the National Culture," 1968, pp. 7, 10.

82. Ibid., pp. 8–9.

83. D. Sciolli, 2001, "Talcott Parsons," in *International Encyclopedia of the Social and Behavioural Sciences*, 26 vols, ed. Neil Smelser and Paul B. Balte, Amsterdam and Paris: Elsevier, 2001, pp. 11063–8.

84. Sigmund Diamond, *Compromised Campus: The Collaboration of Universities with the Intelligence Community, 1945–1955*, New York: Oxford University Press, 1992, pp. 37–9.

85. Erving Goffman, *The Presentation of Self in Everyday Life*, Garden City: Doubleday, 1959.

86. Michael Jacobsen, *The Contemporary Goffman*, London and New York: Routledge, 2010.

87. Josef K. Glowa, *Spielwelten: Performanz und Inszenierung in der Renaissance* by Klaus W. Hempfer, review by Helmut Pfeiffer, *Sixteenth Century Journal*, Vol. 35, No. 4, 2004, p. 1226.

88. Ellen Herman, *The Romance of American Psychology: Political Culture in the Age of Experts*, Berkeley: University of California Press, 1995, pp. 95–6.

89. Frank C.P. van der Horst, Helen A. LeRoy, and René van der Veer, "'When Strangers Meet': John Bowlby and Harry Harlow on Attachment Behavior," *Integrative Psychological and Behavioral Science*, Vol. 42, No. 4, 2008, pp. 370–88; Deborah Blum, *The Monkey Wars*, New York: Oxford University Press, 1994, pp. 79–104.

90. Joy Damousi and Mariano Ben Plotkin, *Psychoanalysis and Politics: Histories of Psychoanalysis Under Conditions of Restricted Political Freedom*, New York: Oxford University Press, 2012, pp. 210, 216.

91. Herman, *The Romance of American Psychology*, p. 128.

92. Harry Harlow, I. E. Farber, and Louis Jolyon West, "Brainwashing, Conditioning, and DDD (Debility, Dependency, and Dread)," *Sociometry*, Vol. 20, No. 4, 1957, pp. 271–85.

93. Herman, *The Romance of American Psychology*, p. 129; Alfred M. McCoy, *A Question of Torture: CIA Interrogation, From the Cold War to the War on Terror*, Metropolitan Books: Henry Holt, 2006; John Marks and Vincent Marchetti, *The CIA and the Cult of Intelligence*, New York: Knopf, 1975.

94. Bruce Cumings, *The Origins of the Korean War*, 2 vols, Princeton: Princeton University Press, 1981, 1990.

95. Shuibo Wang, "They Chose China" (2005), National Film Board of Canada, at www.nfb.ca/film/they_chose_china

96. Susan L. Carruthers, "'The Manchurian Candidate' (1962) and the Cold War Brainwashing Scare," *Historical Journal of Film, Radio and Television*, Vol. 18, No. 1, 1998, pp. 75–94.

97. Domenico Losurdo, "Toward a Critique of the Concept of Totalitarianism," *Historical Materialism*, Vol. 12, No. 2, 2004, pp. 25–55.

98. John G. Gunnell, "The Reconstitution of Political Theory: David Easton, Behavioralism and the Long Road to System," *Journal of the History of the Behavioral Sciences*, Vol. 49, No. 2, 2013, pp. 190–210.

99. Smith, *American Empire*, p. 21.

100. Ibid., p. 382.

101. Ibid., p. 383.

102. Van der Pijl, "Historicising the International," p. 13.

103. Nugent, "Knowledge and Empire," pp. 18–22.

104. Robin W. Winks, *Cloak & Gown: Scholars and the Secret War: 1939–61*, New York: Morrow, 1987, pp. 54–5, 114–5.

105. Immanuel Wallerstein, "Unintended Consequences," in *The Cold War and the University: Toward an Intellectual History of the Post-War Years*, ed. Noam Chomsky et al., New York: New Press, 1997, p. 198.

106. Mills, *The Power Elite*, New York and Oxford: Oxford University Press, 1956.

107. C. Wright Mills, *Letters and Autobiographical Writings*, Berkeley: University of California Press, 2001, pp. 311–41.

108. William Appleman Williams, *The Tragedy of American Diplomacy*, New York: Dell, 1959.

109. Raymond Williams, *Culture and Society, 1780–1950*, London: Chatto & Windus, 1958.

110. Harvey J. Kaye, *The British Marxist Historians: An Introductory Analysis*, Cambridge: Polity Press, 1984.

111. Keith Michael Baker and Joseph Zizek, "The American Historiography of the French Revolution," in *Imagined Histories: American Historians Interpret the Past*, ed. Anthony Molho and Gordon S. Wood, Princeton: Princeton University Press, 1998, p. 363.

112. Mark Poster, *Existential Marxism in Postwar France: From Sartre to Althusser*, Princeton: Princeton University Press, 1975, pp. 55–7, 61, William S. Lewis, *Louis Althusser and the Traditions of French Marxism*, New York: Lexington Books, 2005, pp. 101–2, 106–7.

113. Antonio Gramsci, *The Open Marxism of Antonio Gramsci*, ed. Carl Marzani, New York: Cameron Associates, 1957.

114. Gyorgy Lukács, *History and Class Consciousness*, London: New Left Books, 1971.

115. Russell Jacoby, *Social Amnesia: A Critique of Conformist Psychology from Adler to Laing*, Boston: Beacon Press, 1975, pp. 3–4.

116. Herbert Marcuse, *One-Dimensional Man: Studies in Ideology of Advanced Industrial Society*, Boston: Beacon Press, 1964, p. 2.

3 The Sixties

1. Vercellone 2014, "From the Mass Worker to Cognitive Labor," pp. 217–43.

2. Clark Kerr, *The Uses of the University*, Cambridge: Harvard University Press, 1963.

3. Ibid., p. 41.

4. M. Soo and C. Carson, "Managing the Research University: Clark Kerr and the University of California," *Minerva*, Vol. 42, No. 3, 2004, p. 221.

5. Kerr, *The Uses of the University*, pp. 114–5.

6. Ibid., pp. 87, 90.

7. Smith, *American Empire*, pp. 11–35.

8. Kerr, *The Uses of the University*, p. 42.

9. Ibid.

10. Ibid., pp. 103–4.

11. Hal Draper, *Berkeley: The New Student Revolt*, Introduction by Mario Savio, Alameda: Center for Socialist History, 1965.

12. Hal Draper, *The Mind of Clark Kerr* (October 1964), at http://www.marxists.org/archive/draper/1964/10/kerr.htm

13. Calvin Trillin, "Letter From Berkeley," *The New Yorker*, March 13, 1965.

14. Mario Savio, "Sit-In Address on the Steps of Sproul Hall," December 2, 1964, at http://www.americanrhetoric.com/speeches/mariosaviosproulhallsitin.htm

15. David Harvey, *Seventeen Contradictions and the End of Capitalism*, Oxford: Oxford University Press, 2014, pp. 238, 242.

16. Eric Hobsbawm, *The Age of Extremes*, New York: Vintage, 1996, p. 298.

17. Admittedly the process of proletarianization is historically uneven with new phases of capitalism throwing up new middle sectors while other sectors undergo full proletarianization or become redundant. Nonetheless, the trend today in academia is toward the proletarianization of faculty. See Hal Draper, *Karl Marx's Theory of Revolution*, 2 vols, New York: Monthly Review Press, 1977, Vol. 2, pp. 613–27.

18. On the notion of prefigurative politics see Christian Scholl, "Prefiguration," in *Key Words For Radicals: The Contested Vocabulary of Late Capitalist Struggles*, ed. Kelley Fritsch, Clare O'Connor, and A.K. Thompson, Chico: AK Press, 2016.

19. W.J. Rorabaugh, *Berkeley at War: The 1960s*, New York: Oxford University Press, 1990, pp. 87–90.

20. Robert Cohen, "The Many Meanings of the FSM," in *The Free Speech Movement: Reflections on Berkeley in the 1960s*, ed. Robert Cohen and Reginald E. Zelnick, Berkeley: University of California Press, 2002, p. 10.

21. Jessica Wang, *American Science in an Age of Anxiety: Scientists, Anticommunism, and the Cold War*, Chapel Hill: University of North Carolina Press, 1999, pp. 269–70.

22. Jo Freeman 2002, "From Freedom Now! to Free Speech: The FSM's Roots in the Bay Area Civil Rights Movement in The Free Speech Movement," in *The Free Speech Movement*, ed. Cohen and Zelnick, pp. 73–83.

23. Martin Waldo, "'Holding One Another': Mario Savio and the Freedom Struggle in Mississippi and Berkeley," in *The Free Speech Movement*, ed. Cohen and Zelnick, pp. 83–102.

24. Ibram H. Rodgers, *The Black Campus Movement: Black Students and the Racial Reconstitution of Higher Education, 1965–1972*, New York: Palgrave Macmillan, 2012, p. 36.

25. Ibid., pp. 49–65.

26. Ibid., p. 62.

27. Aldon Morris, "Black Southern Student Sit-in Movement: An Analysis of Internal Organization," *American Sociological Review*, Vol. 4, No. 6, 1981, p. 756.

28. Wesley C. Hogan, *Many Minds, One Heart: SNCC's Dream For A New America*, Chapel Hill: University of North Carolina Press, 2007, pp. 13–8.

29. Morris, "Black Southern Student Sit-in Movement," p. 755.

30. Rodgers, *The Black Campus Movement*, pp. 64–5.

31. Ibid., pp. 70–1.

32. Maurice Isserman and Michael Kazin, *America Divided: The Civil War of the 1960s*, New York: Oxford University Press, 2012, p. 162.

33. Port Huron Statement, 1962, at http://coursesa.matrix.msu.edu/~hst306/documents/huron.html

34. Isserman and Kazin, *America Divided*, p. 163.

35. Lucian W. Pye, *Guerilla Communism in Malaya: Its Social and Political Meaning*, Princeton: Princeton University Press, 1956.

36. Anne Marlowe, "The Picture Awaits: The Birth of Modern Counterinsurgency," *World Affairs*, summer 2009.

37. Nils Gilman, *Mandarins of the Future: Modernization Theory in Cold War America*, Baltimore: Johns Hopkins University Press, 2003, p. 73; David Marannis, *They Marched into Sunlight: War and Peace, Vietnam and America*, New York: Simon & Schuster, 2004; David Milne, *America's Rasputin: Walt Rostow and the Vietnam War*, New York: Hill and Wang, 2008, pp. 41–130.

38. Irene L. Gendzier, *Managing Political Change: Social Scientists and the Third World*, Boulder: Westview, 1985, pp. 6, 13–4.

39. Robin, *The Making of the Cold War Enemy*, pp. 31–3.

40. 40 Milne, *America's Rasputin*, pp. 41–130.

41. Walt Whitman Rostow, *The Stages of Economic Growth: A Non-Communist Manifesto*, Cambridge: Cambridge University Press, 1960.

42. Heineman, *Campus Wars*, p. 268.

43. David Barber, *Hard Rain Fell: SDS and Why It Failed*, Jackson: University of Mississippi Press, 2008.

44. Marannis, *They Marched into Sunlight*, pp. 348–99.

45. Max Elbaum, *Revolution in the Air: Sixties Radicals Turn to Lenin, Mao and Che*, London and New York: Verso, 2002, pp. 59–90.

46. Stefan M. Bradley, *Harlem vs. Columbia University: Black Student Power in the Late 1960s*, Urbana: University of Illinois Press, 2009, p. 28.

47. Blake Slonecker, "The Columbia Coalition: African Americans, New Leftist Counterculture at the Columbia University Protest of 1968," *Journal of Social History*, Vol. 41, No. 4, 2008, pp. 967–96.

48. Seth Rosenfeld, *Subversives: The FBI's War on Student Radicals and Reagan's Rise to Power*, New York: Farrar, Straus and Giroux, 2012, p. 470.

49. Kenneth J. Heineman, *Put Your Bodies on the Wheels: Student Revolt in the 1960s*, Chicago: Ivan R. Dee, 2001, p. 3.

50. Barber, *Hard Rain Fell*, pp. 146–60.

51. I.F. Stone, *The Killings at Kent State: How Murder Went Unpunished*, New York: Vintage Books, 1971.

52. Tim Spofford, *Lynch Street: The May 1970 Slayings at Jackson State College*, Kent: Kent State University Press, 1988, pp. 34–79.

53. Rodgers, *The Black Campus Movement*, pp. 78–9.

54. Martha Biondi, *The Black Revolution on Campus*, Berkeley: University of California Press, 2012, pp. 8, 23, 29–30.

55. Ibid., p. 38.

56. Noliwe M. Rooks, *Black Power/White Money: The Surprising History of African American Studies and the Crisis of Race in Higher Education*, Boston: Beacon Press, 2006.

57. Bobby Seale, "Seale Speech" (1967), San Francisco Bay Area Television Archive, at https://diva.sfsu.edu/collections/sfbatv/bundles/190420

58. Biondi, *The Black Revolution on Campus*, pp. 48–57.

59. Noam Chomsky "The Responsibility of the Intellectuals," *New York Review of Books*, February 23, 1967.

60. Noam Chomsky, *American Power and the New Mandarins*, New York: Pantheon, 1969, pp. 27–8.

61. Ibid., p. 28.

62. Ibid., p. 33.

63. Ibid., p. 58.

64. Elbaum, *Revolution in the Air*, p. 39.

65. Marilyn Jacoby Boxer, *When Women Ask the Questions: Creating Women's Studies in America*, Baltimore: Johns Hopkins University Press, 1998, p. 141.

66. A. Clay Schoenfeld, "The University-Environmental Marriage," *Journal of Higher Education*, Vol. 50, No. 3, 1979, pp. 289–309.

67. Paul Burkett, *Marxism and Ecological Economics: Toward a Red and Green Political Economy*, Leiden: Brill, 2006; John Bellamy Foster, *The Ecological Revolution: Making Peace With the Planet*, New York: Monthly Review Press, 2009.

68. Eugene D. Genovese, *Roll, Jordan, Roll: The World the Slaves Made*, New York: Vintage, 1976; *The Political Economy of Slavery: Studies in the Economy and the Society of the Slave South* , New York: Pantheon, 1965.

69. Robin Blackburn, *The Making of New World Slavery: From the Baroque to the Modern 1492–1800*, London: Verso, 1997, p. 554.

70. Dorothy Ansart and Judith Grier, Inventory to the Records of the Office of Public Information on the Vietnam War Teach-Ins, 1965–1966, Special Collections and University Archives, Rutgers University Libraries, AnsartRG 07/A2/01.

71. Novick, *That Noble Dream*, p. 435.

72. James R. Barrett, "Class Act: An Interview with David Montgomery," *Labor: Studies in Working-Class History of the Americas*, Vol. 1, No. 1, 2004, pp. 23–54.

73. Robert Brenner, *Merchants and Revolution: Commercial Change, Political Conflict and London's Overseas Traders, 1550–1663*, Princeton: Princeton University Press, 1993.

74. Robert Brenner, "Agrarian Class Structure and Economic Development in Pre-Industrial Europe," *Past & Present*, Vol. 70, No. 170, 1976, pp. 30–75; "The Origins of Capitalist Development: A Critique of Neo-Smithian Marxism," *New Left Review*, Vol. 104, 1977, pp. 25–93; "Dobb on the Transition from Feudalism to Capitalism," *Cambridge Journal of Economics*, Vol. 2, No. 2, 1978, pp. 121–40.

75. Rodney Howard Hilton et al., *The Transition from Feudalism to Capitalism*, London: New Left Books, 1976.

76. C. Wright Mills, *The Sociological Imagination*, New York and Oxford: Oxford University Press, 1959, p. 42.

77. Alvin Ward Gouldner, *The Coming Crisis in Western Sociology*, New York: Basic Books, 1970.

78. William G. Domhoff, *Who Rules America?*, Englewood Cliffs: Prentice-Hall, 1967.

79. Immanuel Wallerstein, *The Modern World System*, New York: Academic Press, 1974.

80. Eric R. Wolf, *Europe and the People Without History*, Berkeley: University of California Press, 1982.

81. Eleanor Leacock, "Anthropology," in *The Left Academy: Marxist Scholarship on American Campuses*, ed. Bertell Ollman and Edward Vernoff, New York: McGraw-Hill, 1982, pp. 242–76.

82. Mark Solovey, "Project Camelot and the 1960s Epistemological Revolution: Rethinking the Politics-Patronage-Social Science Nexus," *Social Studies of Science*, Vol. 31, No. 2, 2001, pp. 171–206.

83. Kathleen Gough, "Anthropology: Child of Imperialism," *Monthly Review*, Vol. 19, No. 11, 1967.

84. Friedrich Engels, *The Origin of the Family, Private Property and the State in the Light of the Researches of Lewis H. Morgan*, London: Lawrence & Wishart, 1972.

85. Maurice Godelier, *Rationality and Irrationality in Economics*, London: New Left Books, 1972.

86. Emmanuel Terray, *Marxism and Primitive Societies: Two Studies*, New York: Monthly Review Press, 1972.

87. Sam Tanenhouse, "Fear and Loathing: How Leslie Fiedler Turned American Criticism on its Head," *Slate*, February 4, 2003.

88. Marshall McLuhan, "Mussolini is the Message," *Manitoban*, December 1, 1933, republished in *Canadian Dimension*, Vol. 32, Issue 3, May/June 1998.

89. Grant Havers, "The Right-Wing Postmodernism of Marshall McLuhan," *Media Culture Society*, Vol. 25, No. 4, 2003, pp. 511–27.

90. Richard Ohmann, *English in America: A Radical View of the Profession*, New York: Oxford University Press, 1976, pp. 27–50.

91. S.I. Homer, *A Short History of the Marxist Literary Group*, at http://mlg.eserver. org/about/a-short-history-of-the-mlg

92. Christopher Pawling, "The American Lukács? Fredric Jameson and Dialectical Thought," in *Fredric Jameson: A Critical Reader*, ed. Sean Homer and Douglas Kellner, Basingstoke: Palgrave MacMillan, 2004, pp. 22–41.

93. Robert T. Tally, *Fredric Jameson: The Project of Dialectical Criticism*, London: Pluto, 2014, p. 41.

4   The Retreat from History

1. This is relative to the past since as late as 2015 there was still ample evidence of continued American intellectual and academic isolationism. See Charles Kurzman, "The Stubborn Parochialism of American Social Sciences," *The Chronicle of Higher Education*, January 19, 2015.

2. Perry Anderson, *In the Tracks of Historical Materialism*, London: Verso, 1981, p. 28.

3. Harvey, *Seventeen Contradictions*, p. 243.

4. Perry Anderson, *The Origins of Postmodernity*, London: Verso, 1998, p. 23.

5. Harvey, *Seventeen Contradictions*, p. 188; S.F. Reardon and Karen Bischoff, "The Continuing Increase in Income Segregation, 2007–2012," *American Journal of Sociology*, Vol. 116, No. 4, 2011, pp. 1092–153; Thomas E. Edsall, "How the Other Fifth Lives," *New York Times*, April 27, 2016.

6. François Cusset, *French Theory: How Foucault, Derrida, Deleuze & Co. Transformed the Intellectual Life of the United States*, Minneapolis: University of Minnesota Press, 2008, p. 77.

7. Ibid.

8. Stuart Sim, "Postmodernism and Philosophy," in *The Routledge Companion to Postmodernism*, London: Taylor & Francis, 2005, p. 3.

9. Anderson, *The Origins of Postmodernity*, p. 25.

10. Sim, "Postmodernism and Philosophy," p. 3.

11. Anderson, *In the Tracks of Historical Materialism*, p. 64.

12. Fredric Jameson, *Postmodernism, or, The Cultural Logic of Late Capitalism*, Durham NC: Duke University Press, 1991.

13. Tally, *Fredric Jameson*, p. 92.

14. Anderson, *The Origins of Postmodernity*, p. 54.
15. Ibid., p. 55.
16. Ibid., p. 56.
17. Robin Blackburn, "Remembering Stuart Hall," *New Left Review*, No. 86, 2014, pp. 81–3.
18. Cusset, *French Theory*, pp. 136–8.
19. Jameson, *Postmodernism*, p. 85.
20. Andrew Hartman, *A War for the Soul of America: A History of the Culture Wars*, Chicago: University of Chicago Press, 2015, pp. 134–43.
21. Estelle Freedman, *No Turning Back: The History of Feminism and the Future of Women*, New York: Ballantine, 2007, p. 270.
22. Chris Beasley, *What is Feminism? An Introduction to Feminist Theory*, Thousand Oaks and London: Sage, 1999, p. 17.
23. Joan Wallach Scott, *The Politics of the Veil*, Princeton: Princeton University Press, 2007.
24. Beasley, *What is Feminism?*, p. 104.
25. Sharzad Mojab Mojab, *Marxism and Feminism*, London: Zed Books, 2015, pp. 203–15.
26. Wendy G. Smooth, "Intersectionality from Theoretical Framework to Policy Intervention," in *Situating Intersectionality: Politics, Policy, and Power*, ed. Angelia R. Wilson, Basingstoke: Palgrave Macmillan, 2013, p. 11.
27. Johanna Brenner, "21st Century Socialist-Feminism: Part I," *International Viewpoint*, August 24, 2014.
28. Jed Woodworth, "Feminism, Third-wave," in *Culture Wars in America: An Encyclopedia of Issues, Viewpoints, and Voices*, ed. Roger Chapman and James Ciment, London: Routledge, 2013.
29. J. Sallaz and J. Zavisca, "Pierre Bourdieu in American Sociology, 1980–2005," *Annual Review of Sociology*, Vol. 33, 2007, pp. 21–41.
30. Michèle Lamont, "How Has Bourdieu Been Good to Think With? The Case of the United States," *Sociological Forum*, Vol. 27, No.1, 2012, pp. 228–37.
31. Clifford Geertz, *The Interpretation of Culture*, New York: Basic Books, 1973, p. 5.
32. Ibid., p. 8.
33. Ibid., p. 5.
34. Ibid., p. 9.
35. Ibid., p. 14.
36. Katy Gardner and David Lewis, *Anthropology, Development, and the Post-Modern Challenge*, London: Pluto Press, 1996, pp. 23–4; Marilyn Strathern, *Audit Cultures: Anthropological Studies in Accountability, Ethics, and the Academy*, New York: Routledge, 2000.
37. Joy Hendry and Laara Fitznor, *Anthropologists, Indigenous Scholars and the Research Endeavour: Seeking Bridges Towards Mutual Respect*, London: Routledge, 2012.
38. Edward W. Said, *Orientalism*, New York: Vintage, 1978.

39. Hosam Aboul-Ela, "Is There an Arab (Yet) in This Field? Postcolonialism, Comparative Literature, and the Middle Eastern Horizon of Said's Discourse Analysis," *Modern Fiction Studies*, Vol. 56, No. 4, 2010, p. 732.

40. Timothy Brennan, "Edward Said as a Lukácsian Critic: Modernism and Empire," *College Literature*, Vol. 40, No. 4, 2013, pp. 14–32.

41. E. San Juan Jr., "Post-colonialism and the Problematic of Uneven Development," in *Marxism, Modernity and Post-Colonial Studies*, ed. Crystal Bartolovich, Cambridge: Cambridge University Press, 2002, pp. 221–39.

42. Alfred J. López and Robert P. Marzec, "Postcolonial Studies at the Twenty-Five Year Mark," *Modern Fiction Studies*, Vol. 56, No. 4, 2010, pp. 677–88.

43. Robert Young, "Postcolonial Remains," *New Literary History*, Vol. 43, No. 1, 2012, p. 23.

44. San Juan Jr., "Post-colonialism and the Problematic of Uneven Development," p. 222.

45. Vivek Chibber, *Postcolonial Theory and the Specter of Capital*, London: Verso, 2013.

46. Tom Brass, *Peasants, Populism and Postmodernism: The Return of the Agrarian Myth*, New York: Frank Cass, 2000.

47. John Bellamy Foster, "Afterword," in *In Defense of History: Marxism and the Postmodern Agenda*, ed. John Bellamy Foster and Ellen Meiskins Wood, New York: Monthly Review Press, 1997, p. 188.

48. Jan de Vries, "Great Expectations: Early Modern History and the Social Sciences," *Review*, Vol. 22, No. 1, 1999, pp. 121–49.

49. Heller Henry, *The Birth of Capitalism*, London: Pluto, 2011, p. 194.

50. Chris Harman, "Theorising Neoliberalism," *International Socialism*, Vol. 117, 2007.

51. Marshall Sahlins, *Culture and Practical Reason*, Chicago: University of Chicago Press, 1976, pp. 53–5; *Stone Age Economics*, London: Routledge, 2003.

52. Dieter Plewhe, "Introduction," in *The Road From Mont Pèlerin*, ed. Philip Mirowski and Dieter Plewhe, Cambridge MA: Harvard University Press, 2009, p. 29; Stephen J. Ball, *Global Education Inc.: New Policy Networks and the Neo-Liberal Imaginary*, London and New York: Routledge, 2012.

53. "Koch Family Foundations," *The Center for Media and Democracy*, at http://www.sourcewatch.org/index.php/Koch_Family_Foundations#Koch_University_Funding_-_Koch_and_Academic_Freedom

54. Mirowski and Plewhe, *The Road from Mont Pèlerin*, p. 434; Leo Panitch and Martijn Konings, "Myths of Neoliberal Deregulation," *New Left Review*, Vol. 57, 2009, pp. 67–83.

55. Mirowski and Plewhe, *The Road from Mont Pèlerin*, p. 434; Greg Albo, "Neoliberalism, the State and the Left: A Canadian Perspective," *Monthly Review*, Vol. 53, No. 12, 2002, pp. 46–55.

56. Mirowski and Plewhe, *The Road from Mont Pèlerin*, p. 435.

57. Ibid., p. 437.

58. Natalie Delia Deckard and Alison Heslin, "After Postnational Citizenship: Constructing the Boundaries of Inclusion in Neoliberal Contexts," *Sociology Compass*, Vol. 10, No. 4, 2016, pp. 294–305.

59. Mirowski and Plewhe, *The Road from Mont Pèlerin*, p. 437.

60. Ibid., p. 440.

61. David Laidler, "Chicago Monetary Traditions," in *The Elgar Companion to the Chicago School of Economics*, ed. Ross B. Emmett, Cheltenham: Elgar, 2010, pp. 75–6.

62. Levon Barseghyan, "Lucas, Robert," in *The New Palgrave Dictionary of Economics*, 2nd edn, ed. Steven N. Durlauf and Lawrence E. Blume, Basingstoke: Palgrave Macmillan, 2008.

63. Steven G. Medema, "Ronald Harry Coase," in *The Elgar Companion to the Chicago School of Economics*, pp. 258–64.

64. Pedro Nuno Teixera, "Gary S. Becker," in *The Elgar Companion to the Chicago School of Economics*, pp. 253–8.

65. Amiya Kumar Bagchi, "Contextual Political Economy, Not Whig Economics," *Cambridge Journal of Economics*, Vol. 38, No. 2, 2014, pp. 545–62.

66. Ben Fine, "The General Impossibility of Neo-Classical Economics," *Ensayos Revista de Economia*, Vol. 20, No. 1, 2011, p. 5.

67. Edward NikKhah, "George J. Stigler," in *The Elgar Companion to the Chicago School of Economics*, pp. 337–441.

68. Susanne Lohmann, "Rational Choice and Political Science," in *The New Palgrave Dictionary of Economics*.

69. John G. Gunnell, "The Historiography of American Political Science," in *The Development of Political Science: A Comparative Survey*, ed. John G. Gunnell, David Easton, and Luigi Graziano, London and New York: Routledge, 2002, pp. 13–33.

70. Shadia B. Drury, *The Political Ideas of Leo Strauss*, New York: Palgrave Macmillan, 2005.

71. Adi Armon, "Leo Strauss: Reading Karl Marx During the Cold War," in *Against the Grain: Jewish Intellectuals in Hard Times*, ed. Ezra Mendelson, Stafani Hoffman, and Richard I. Cohen, New York: Berghahn Books, 2014, pp. 32–50.

72. Charles Guignon and David R. Hiley, *Richard Rorty: Contemporary Philosophy in Focus*, Cambridge: Cambridge University Press, 2003.

73. Neil Gross, *Richard Rorty: The Making of an American Philosopher*, Chicago: University of Chicago Press, 2008, p. 4.

74. David S. Churchill, "Spectres of Anti-communism: Richard Rorty and Leftist Thought in Twentieth-Century America," *Canadian Review of American Studies*, Vol. 38, No. 2, 2008, pp. 275–91.

75. Lingua Franca editors, *The Sokal Hoax: The Sham That Shook the Academy*, Lincoln: University of Nebraska, 2000.

76. Ibid., pp. 50–1.

5   The Neoliberal University

1. Cole, *The Great American University*, p. 156.

2. Thelin, *A History of American Higher Education*, pp. 369–74.

3. Ilka Kauppinen, "Academic Capitalism and the Informational Fraction of the Transnational Capitalist Class," *Globalisation, Societies and Education*, Vol. 11, No. 1, 2013, pp. 1–22.

4. List of American Colleges and Universities Abroad 2014, *Wikipedia*, September 2014.

5. Thelin, *A History of American Higher Education*, pp. 377–8.

6. Donna Fossum, Lawrence S. Painter, Elisa Eiseman et al., *Federal Investment in Research and Development at the Nation's Universities and Colleges*, Santa Monica: Rand Corporation, 2004, pp. xii, 11–12.

7. Wesley Shumar, *College for Sale: A Critique of the Commodification of Higher Education*, London: Falmer Press, 1997; Stanley Aronowitz, *The Knowledge Factory: Dismantling the Corporate University and Creating True Higher Learning*, Boston: Beacon Press, 2000, pp. 80–1; Henry Steck, "Corporatization of the University: Seeking Conceptual Clarity," *Annals of the American Academy of Political and Social Science*, Vol. 585, No. 1, 2003, p. 69.

8. Quoted in Juan Cole, "State Universities Versus State Prisons: And Marijuana Legalization as a Solution," *Informed Comment*, December 2008, at http://www.juancole.com.

9. Thelin, *A History of American Higher Education*, pp. 387–8.

10. Benjamin Ginsberg, *The Fall of the Faculty: The Rise of the All-Administrative University and Why it Matters*, New York: Oxford University Press, 2011, pp. 5–7.

11. Sheila Slaughter, *The Higher Learning and High Technology: Dynamics of Higher Education Policy Formation*, Albany: State University of New York Press, 1990, p. 221.

12. Charles Mathies and Sheila Slaughter, "University Trustees As Channels Between Academe and Industry: Toward An Understanding of the Executive Science Network," *Research Policy*, Vol. 29, No. 1, 2013, pp. 1–21.

13. Newfield, *Ivy and Industry*, pp. 174–6.

14. Tom Lindsay, "More U.S. Colleges Poised to Go Bankrupt, According to Three Studies," *Forbes Magazine*, November 18, 2015, www.forbes.com.

15. National Association of College and Universities Business Officers, Common Fund Study of Endowments 2015, at http://www.nacubo.org/Research/NACUBO-Commonfund_Study_of_Endowments.html

16. Jane L. Mendillo, *Annual Endowment Report, Harvard Management Company Inc.* (2014), at www.hmc.harvard.edu/docs/Final_Annual_Report_2014.pdf

17. Charlie Eaton, Charlie Dioun, Cyrus Godoy, Daniela García Santibáñez et al., *Borrowing Against the Future: The Hidden Costs of Financing U.S. Higher Education*, Berkeley: The Center for Culture, Organizations, and Politics (CCOP), 2014, pp. 3, 6.

18. Caroline Salas Gage and Janet Lorin, "Student Loans, the Next Big Threat to the U.S. Economy?," *Bloomberg Business Week*, January 16, 2014, www.bloomberg.com.

19. Henry Giroux, *America's Education Deficit and the War on Youth*, New York: Monthly Review Press, 2013, p. 189.

20. Andrew Rossi, "How American Universities Turned into Corporations," *Time*, May 22, 2014.

21. Andy Pinto, "Chancellor Names UC Berkeley's First Vice Chancellor for Real Estate," UC Berkeley NewsCenter, December 17, 2013, at http://NewsCenter. Berkeley.Edu.

22. The White House, "FACT SHEET on the President's Plan to Make College More Affordable: A Better Bargain for the Middle Class," August 22, 2013, at www.whitehouse.gov.

23. John Ingram Gilderbloom, *Promise and Betrayal: Universities and the Battle for Sustainable Urban Neighborhoods*, New York: State University of New York Press, 2005, p. 157.

24. Enrico Moretti, *The New Geography of Jobs*, New York: Houghton Mifflin Harcourt, 2013, pp. 194–7.

25. Clifford Tan Kuan Lu, "Do University Rankings Matter for Growth?," University of Nottingham-Malaysia Campus, MPRA Paper No. 52705, December 19, 2013, at ssrn.com/abstract=2377249

26. Andrew Ross, "Universities and the Urban Growth Machine," *Dissent: A Quarterly of Politics and Culture*, October 4, 2012.

27. Kevin Carey, "A Tale of 'Too Big to Fail' in Higher Education: City College of San Francisco Survives," *New York Times*, July 14, 2014.

28. C.S. Scott and J.J. Siegfried, "American Economic Association Universal Academic Questionnaire Summary Statistics," *American Economic Review: Papers & Proceedings*, Vol. 101, 2011, pp. 664–7.

29. Daniel Kleinman, Noah Feinstein, and Greg Downey, "Beyond Commercialization: Science Higher Education and the Culture of Neoliberalism," *Science & Education*, Vol. 22, No. 10, 2013, pp. 2385–401.

30. Steven Ward, *Neoliberalism and the Global Restructuring of Knowledge and Education*, New York: Routledge, 2012, pp. 3–8; Chris Lorenz and Joachim Urlauf, "If You're So Smart Why Are You Under Surveillance: Universities, Neoliberalism, and New Public Management," *Critical Inquiry*, Vol. 38, No. 3, 2012, pp. 599–629.

31. Rachelle L. Brooks, "Measuring University Quality," *Review of Higher Education*, Vol. 29, No. 1, 2005, pp. 1–21.

32. Frank Donoghue, *The Last Professors: The Corporate University and the Fate of the Humanities*, New York: Fordham University, 2008, p. xvi.

33. Alex Callinicos, *Universities in a Neoliberal World*, London: Bookmarks, 2006, p. 9.

34. Donoghue, *The Last Professors*, pp. 83–4, 121–4.

35. Newfield, *Ivy and Industry*.

36. Richard Munch, *Academic Capitalism: Universities in the Global Struggle for Excellence*, New York: Routledge, 2014.

37. Ibid., p. 1.

38. Ibid., pp. 10–11.

39. Ibid., pp. 22–41.

40. Kevin Carey, "Americans Think We Have the World's Best Colleges. We Don't," *New York Times*, June 28, 2014.

41. Donoghue, *The Last Professors*, p. 119.

42. Sheila Slaughter and Gary Rhoades, "The Academic Capitalist Knowledge/Learning Regime," in *The Exchange University: Corporatization of Academic Culture*, ed. Adrienne S. Chan and Donald Fisher, Vancouver, Toronto: UBC Press, 2008, p. 24.

43. Ibid., p. 25.

44. Michael Perelman, *Steal This Idea: Intellectual Property Rights and the Corporate Confiscation of Creativity*, New York: Palgrave, 2002, p. 3.

45. Ibid., p. 77.

46. Ibid., p. 93.

47. Ibid., pp. 99, 103.

48. Ibid., p. 104.

49. Ibid., p. 107.

50. Jonathan Haber, *MIT Press Essential Knowledge: MOOCs*, Cambridge: MIT Press, 2014, p. 39.

51. Ibid., pp. 1, 3.

52. Ryan Derousseau, "California's Multimillion-dollar Online Education Flop is Another Blow for MOOCs," *The Hechinger Report*, 2014, at http://hechinger-report.org.

53. Gary Rhoades, *Managed Professionals: Unionized Faculty and Restructuring Academic Labor*, Albany: State University of New York Press, 1998, p. 74.

54. Colleen Flaherty, "Time for a Union?," *Inside Higher Education*, February 21, 2014.

55. Robert A. Rhoads and Gary Rhoades, "Graduate Student Unionization as a Postindustrial Social Movement: Identity, Ideology, and the Contested U.S. Academy," in *The University, State and Market*, p. 278, 281, 289.

56. Tamar Lewin, "More College Adjuncts See Strength in Union Numbers," *New York Times*, December 3, 2013.

57. Justine Coyne, "Pitt Faculty Launch Campaign to Unionize," *Pittsburgh Business News*, October 26, 2015.

58. Joe Berry and Helena Worthen, "Wave of Contingent-Faculty Organizing Sweeps Onto Campuses," *Labor Notes*, October 8, 2014, www.labornotes.org.

59. Piya Chattererjee and Sunaina Maira, *The Imperial University: Academic Repression and Scholarly Dissent*, Minneapolis: University of Minnesota Press, 2014, pp. 3–5.

60. Alex Callinicos, *Deciphering Capital: Marx's Capital and Its Destiny*, London: Bookmarks, 2014, pp. 13–15.

61. Carlos Alberto Torres, "Public Universities and the Neoliberal Common Sense: Seven Iconoclastic Theses," *International Studies in Sociology of Education*, Vol. 21, No. 3, 2011, p. 197.

Bibliography

Aboul-Ela, Hosam, "Is There an Arab (Yet) in This Field? Postcolonialism, Comparative Literature, and the Middle Eastern Horizon of Said's Discourse Analysis," *Modern Fiction Studies*, Vol. 56, No. 4, 2010, pp. 729–50.

Adorno, T.W. et al., *The Authoritarian Personality*, New York: Harper & Row, 1950.

Albo, Greg, "Neoliberalism, the State and the Left: A Canadian Perspective," *Monthly Review*, Vol. 53, No. 12, 2002, pp. 46–55.

Anderson, Perry, "Components of the National Culture," *New Left Review*, No. 50, July–August, 1968, pp. 1–57.

— *In the Tracks of Historical Materialism*, London: Verso, 1981.

— *The Origins of Postmodernity*, London: Verso, 1998.

Ansart, Dorothy and Judith Grier, *Inventory to the Records of the Office of Public Information on the Vietnam War Teach-Ins, 1965–1966*, Special Collections and University Archives, Rutgers University Libraries, AnsartRG 07/A2/01, at http://www2.scc.rutgers.edu/ead/uarchives/teachinsb.html#series1

Armon, Adi, "Leo Strauss: Reading Karl Marx During the Cold War," in *Against the Grain: Jewish Intellectuals in Hard Times*, ed. Ezra Mendelson, Stafani Hoffman and Richard I. Cohen, New York: Berghahn Books, 2014, pp. 32–50.

Aronowitz, Stanley, *The Knowledge Factory: Dismantling the Corporate University and Creating True Higher Learning*, Boston: Beacon Press, 2000.

Assad, Talal, "Two European Images of Non-European Rule," in *Anthropology and the Colonial Encounter*, Ithaca, NY: Ithaca Press, 1975, pp. 103–18.

Bagchi, Amiya Kumar, "Contextual Political Economy, Not Whig Economics," *Cambridge Journal of Economics*, Vol. 38, No. 2, 2014, pp. 545–62.

Ball, Stephen J., *Global Education Inc.: New Policy Networks and the Neo-Liberal Imaginary*, London and New York: Routledge, 2012.

Baker, Keith Michael, *Condorcet: From Natural Philosophy to Social Mathematics*, Chicago: University of Chicago Press, 1975.

Baker, Keith Michael and Joseph Zizek, "The American Historiography of the French Revolution," in *Imagined Histories: American Historians Interpret the Past*, ed. Anthony Molho and Gordon S. Wood, Princeton: Princeton University Press, 1998, pp. 363–93.

Barber, David, *Hard Rain Fell: SDS and Why It Failed*, Jackson: University of Mississippi Press, 2008.

Barber, William J., "The Career of Alvin H. Hansen in the 1920s and 1930s: A Study of Intellectual Transformation," *History of Political Economy*, Vol. 19, No. 2, 1987, pp. 191–205.

— "Reconfiguring in Economics," in *American Academic Culture in Transition: Fifty Years, Four Disciplines*, ed. Thomas Bender and Carl E. Schorske, Princeton: Princeton University Press, 1997, pp. 105–21.

Barrat, James R., "Class Act: An Interview with David Montgomery," *Labor: Studies in Working-Class History of the Americas*, Vol. 1, No.1, 2004, pp. 23–54.

Barrow, Clyde W., *Universities and the Capitalist State: Corporate Liberalism and the Reconstruction of American Higher Education, 1894–1928*, Madison: University of Wisconsin Press, 1990.

Barseghyan, Levon, "Lucas, Robert," in *The New Palgrave Dictionary of Economics*, 2nd edn, ed. Steven N. Durlauf and Lawrence E. Blume, Basingstoke: Palgrave Macmillan, 2008.

Beasley, Chris, *What is Feminism? An Introduction to Feminist Theory*, Thousand Oaks and London: Sage, 1999.

Bell, David, *Cyberculture Theorists: Manuel Castells and Donna Haraway*, London and New York: Routledge, 2007.

Bellamy Foster, John, *The Ecological Revolution: Making Peace With the Planet*, New York: Monthly Review Press, 2009.

Bender, Thomas, "Politics, Intellect and the American University 1945–95," in *American Academic Culture in Transition: Fifty Years, Four Disciplines*, ed. Thomas Bender and Carl E. Schorske, Princeton: Princeton University Press, 1997, pp. 17–54.

Berlin, James A., *Rhetorics, Poetics, and Cultures: Refiguring College English Studies*, Urbana: National Council of Teachers of English, 1996.

Berry, Joe and Helena Worthen, "Wave of Contingent-Faculty Organizing Sweeps onto Campuses," *Labor Notes*, October 8, 2014, labornotes.org.

Bhabha, Homi K., *The Location of Culture*, London: Routledge, 1994.

Biondi, Martha, *The Black Revolution on Campus*, Berkeley: University of California Press, 2012.

Bu, Liping, *Making The World Like Us: Education, Cultural Expansion, and the American Century*, Westport: Praeger, 2003.

Buhle, Paul and Dan Georgakas, "Communist Party, USA," in *Encyclopedia of the American Left*, ed. Paul Buhle, Dan Georgkas, and Mari Jo Buhle, New York: Garland, 1990, pp. 147–57.

Burkett, Paul, *Marxism and Ecological Economics: Toward A Red and Green Political Economy*, Leiden: Brill, 2006.

Butler, Judith, *Gender Trouble: Feminism and the Subversion of Identity*, New York: Routledge, 1990.

Cain, Timothy Reese, *Establishing Academic Freedom: Politics, Principles, and the Development of Core Values*, Basingstoke: Palgrave Macmillan, 2012.

—— "Unionised Faculty and the Political Left: Communism and the American Federation of Teachers on the Eve of the Second World War," *History of Education: Journal of the History of Education Society*, Vol. 41, No. 4, 2012, pp. 515–35.

Callinicos, Alex, *Universities in a Neoliberal World*, London: Bookmarks, 2006.

—— *Deciphering Capital: Marx's Capital and Its Destiny*, London: Bookmarks, 2014.

Capps, John, "Sidney Hook and Anti-Communism," *Transactions of the Charles S. Peirce Society*, Vol. 40, No. 4, 2004, pp. 803–16.

Carey, Kevin, "Americans Think We Have the World's Best Colleges. We Don't," *New York Times*, June 28, 2014, at http://www.nytimes.com/2014/06/29

— "A Tale of 'Too Big to Fail' in Higher Education: City College of San Francisco Survives," *New York Times*, July 14, 2014, at http://www.nytimes.com/2014/07/14

Carroll, Joseph Cephas, *Slave Insurrections in the United States, 1800–65*, Newburyport: Dover, 2012.

Carruthers, Susan L., "'The Manchurian Candidate' (1962) and the Cold War Brainwashing Scare," *Historical Journal of Film, Radio and Television*, Vol. 18, No. 1, 1998, pp. 75–94.

Ceplair, Larry, *Anti-Communism in Twentieth-Century America*, Santa Barbara: Clio, 2011.

Chartier, Roger, *Cultural History: Between Practices and Representations*, Ithaca: Cornell University Press, 1988.

Chattererjee, Piya and Sunaina Maira, *The Imperial University: Academic Repression and Scholarly Dissent*, Minneapolis: University of Minnesota Press, 2014.

Chibber, Vivek, *Postcolonial Theory and the Specter of Capital*, London: Verso, 2013.

— "L'universalisme, une arme pour la gauche," *Le Monde diplomatique*, May 2014.

Chomsky, Noam, "The Responsibility of the Intellectuals," *New York Review of Books*, February 23, 1967, at http://www.chomsky.info/articles/19670223.htm

— *American Power and the New Mandarins*, New York: Pantheon, 1969.

Cobban, Alfred, *The Social Interpretation of the French Revolution*, Cambridge: Cambridge University Press, 1968.

Cohen, Robert, *When the Old Left Was Young: Student Radicals and America's First Mass Student Movement, 1929–1941*, New York: Oxford University Press, 1993.

— "The Many Meanings of the FSM," in *The Free Speech Movement: Reflections on Berkeley in the 1960s*, ed. Robert Cohen and Reginald E. Zelnick, Berkeley: University of California Press, 2002, pp. 1–53.

Cohen-Cole, Jamie, *The Open Mind: Cold War Politics and the Science of Human Nature*, Chicago: University of Chicago Press, 2014.

Colander, David and Harry Landreth, "Political Influence on the Textbook Keynesian Revolution: God, Man, and Laurie Tarshis at Yale," in O.F. Hamouda and B.B. Price, *Keynesianism and the Keynesian Revolution in America: A Memorial Volume in Honour of Lorie Tarshis*, Cheltenham: Edward Elgar, 1998, pp. 59–72.

Colby, Gerard, *Thy Will be Done: The Conquest of the Amazon. Nelson Rockefeller and Evangelism in the Age of Oil*, New York: HarperCollins, 1995.

Cole, Jonathan R., *The Great American University: Its Rise to Preeminence, Its Indispensable National Role, Why It Must Be Protected*, New York: Public Affairs, 2009.

Cole, Juan, "State Universities Versus State Prisons: And Marijuana Legalization as a Solution," *Informed Comment*, December 2008, at http://www.juancole.com/2008/12/state-universities-versus-state-prisons.html

Coyne, Justine, "Pitt Faculty Launch Campaign to Unionize," *Pittsburgh Business News*, October 2015, at http://www.bizjournals.com/pittsburgh/news/2015/10/26

Christofferson, Michael Scott, "François Furet: Between History and Journalism, 1958–65," *French History*, Vol. 15, No. 4, 2001, pp. 420–47.

— "Les 'passeurs,' du 'depasseur': les historiens américains de la Révolution française et François Furet," in *Passeurs de révolution*, ed. Jean-Numa Ducange and Michel Biard, Paris: Société des études robespierristes, 2013, pp. 57–68.

Churchill, David S. 2008, "Spectres of Anti-communism: Richard Rorty and Leftist Thought in Twentieth-Century America," *Canadian Review of American Studies*, Vol. 38, No. 2, 2008, pp. 275–91.

Cumings, Bruce, *The Origins of the Korean War*, 2 vols, Princeton: Princeton University Press, 1981, 1990.

Cusset, François, *French Theory: How Foucault, Derrida, Deleuze & Co. Transformed the Intellectual Life of the United States*, Minneapolis: University of Minnesota Press, 2008.

Cypher, James M., "From Military Keynesianism to Global-Neoliberal Militarism," *Monthly Review*, Vol. 59, No. 2, 2007, pp. 37–55.

Damousi, Joy and Mariano Ben Plotkin, *Psychoanalysis and Politics: Histories of Psychoanalysis Under Conditions of Restricted Political Freedom*, New York: Oxford University Press, 2012.

Darnton, Robert, *The Great Cat Massacre and Other Episodes in French Cultural History*, New York: Basic Books, 1984.

Deckard, Natalie Delia and Alison Heslin 2016, "After Postnational Citizenship: Constructing the Boundaries of Inclusion in Neoliberal Contexts," *Sociology Compass*, Vol. 10, No. 4, pp. 294–305.

Deeb, Lara and Jessica Winegar, *Anthropology's Politics: Disciplining the Middle East*, Stanford: Stanford University Press, 2016.

Denning, Michael, *The Cultural Front: The Laboring of American Culture in the Twentieth Century*, London and New York: Verso, 1998.

Derousseau, Ryan, "California's Multimillion-dollar Online Education Flop is Another Blow for MOOCs," *The Hechinger Report*, 2014, at http://hechingerreport.org/californias-multi-million-dollar-online-education-flop-is-another-blow-for-moocs

Diamond, Sigmund, *Compromised Campus: The Collaboration of Universities with the Intelligence Community, 1945–1955*, New York: Oxford University Press, 1992.

Dimick, Matthew, "Arma et Leges: A Critique of Michael Mann's Concept of the State," Paper presented at the annual meeting of the American Sociological Association, Montreal Convention Center, Montreal, Quebec, Canada, August 11, 2006, at http://citation.allacademic.com/meta/p105087_index.html

Domhoff, William G., *Who Rules America?*, Englewood Cliffs: Prentice-Hall, 1967.

Donoghue, Frank, *The Last Professors: The Corporate University and the Fate of the Humanities*, New York: Fordham University, 2008.

Draper, Hal, *The Mind of Clark Kerr* (October 1964), Marxist Internet Archive, at http://www.marxists.org/archive/draper/1964/10/kerr.htm

— *Berkeley: The New Student Revolt*, Introduction by Mario Savio, Alameda: Center for Socialist History, 1965.

— *Karl Marx's Theory of Revolution*, 2 vols, New York: Monthly Review Press, 1977.

Drury, Shadia B., *The Political Ideas of Leo Strauss*, New York: Palgrave Macmillan, 2005.

Duménil, Gerard and Dominique Lévy, *The Crisis of Neoliberalism*, Cambridge MA: Harvard University Press, 2011.

Eagleton, Terry, *Against the Grain: Essays, 1975–1985*, London: Verso, 1986.

— *Marxism and Literary Criticism*, Hoboken: Taylor and Francis, 2012.

Eaton, Charlie, Cyrus Dioun, Daniela García Santibáñez Godoy et al., *Borrowing Against the Future: The Hidden Costs of Financing U.S. Higher Education*, Berkeley: The Center for Culture, Organizations, and Politics (CCOP), 2014.

Edsall, Thomas E., "How the Other Fifth Lives," *New York Times*, April 27, 2016, at http://www.nytimes.com/2016/04/27/opinion/campaign-stops/how-the-other-fifth-lives.html

Elbaum, Max, *Revolution in the Air: Sixties Radicals Turn to Lenin, Mao and Che*, London and New York: Verso, 2002.

Eley, Geoff and Keith Nield, *The Future of Class in History: What's Left of the Social?*, Ann Arbor: University of Michigan Press, 2007.

Engels, Friedrich, *The Origin of the Family, Private Property and the State in the Light of the Researches of Lewis H. Morgan*, London: Lawrence & Wishart, 1972.

Ewen, Stuart, *PR! A Social History of Spin*, New York: Basic Books, 1996.

Fain, Paul, "'Nearing the Bottom': Inside Higher Education," *Inside Higher Education*, May 15, 2014, at https://www.insidehighered.com/news/2014/05/15/new-data-show-slowing-national-enrollment-decline

Fine, Ben, "The General Impossibility of Neo-Classical Economics," *Ensayos Revista de Economia*, Vol. 20, No. 1, 2011, pp. 1–22.

Fisher, Donald, *Fundamental Development of the Social Sciences: Rockefeller Philanthropy and the United States Social Science Research Council*, Ann Arbor: University of Michigan Press, 1993.

Flaherty, Colleen, "Time for a Union?," *Inside Higher Education*, February 21, 2014, at https://www.insidehighered.com

Foner, Eric, *Who Owns History? Rethinking the Past*, New York: Hill and Wang, 2002.

Fossum, Donna, Lawrence S. Painter, Elisa Eiseman et al., *Federal Investment in Research and Development at the Nation's Universities and Colleges*, Santa Monica: Rand Corporation, 2004.

Foster, John Bellamy, "Afterword," in *In Defense of History: Marxism and the Postmodern Agenda*, ed. John Bellamy Foster and Ellen Meiskins Wood, New York: Monthly Review Press, 1997, pp. 84–94.

Freedman, Estelle, *No Turning Back: The History of Feminism and the Future of Women*, New York: Ballantine, 2007.

Freeman, Jo, "From Freedom Now! To Free Speech: The FSM's Roots in the Bay Area Civil Rights Movement," in *The Free Speech Movement: Reflections on Berkeley in the 1960s*, ed. Robert Cohen and Reginald E. Zelnick, Berkeley: University of California Press, 2002, pp. 73–83.

Furet, François, *Penser la Revolution française*, Paris: Gallimard, 1978.

— and Denis Richet, *La Revolution française*, Paris: Fayard, 1973.

Gage, Caroline Salas and Janet Lorin, "Student Loans, the Next Big Threat to the U.S. Economy?," *Bloomberg Business Week*, January 16., 2014, at www.bloomberg.com/.../2014...16/student-loans-the-next-big-threat-to-the-u-dot-s-dot-economy

Gardner, Katy and David Lewis, *Anthropology, Development, and the Post-Modern Challenge*, London: Pluto Press, 1996.

Geertz, Clifford, *The Interpretation of Culture*, New York: Basic Books, 1973.

Gendzier, Irene L., *Managing Political Change: Social Scientists and the Third World*, Boulder: Westview, 1985.

Genovese, Eugene D., *The Political Economy of Slavery: Studies in the Economy and the Society of the Slave South*, New York: Pantheon, 1965.

— *Roll, Jordan, Roll: The World the Slaves Made*, New York: Vintage, 1976.

Gilderbloom, John Ingram, *Promise and Betrayal: Universities and the Battle for Sustainable Urban Neighborhoods*, New York: State University of New York Press, 2005.

Gilman, Nils, *Mandarins of the Future: Modernization Theory in Cold War America*, Baltimore: Johns Hopkins University Press, 2003.

Ginsberg, Benjamin, *The Fall of the Faculty: The Rise of the All-Administrative University and Why It Matters*, New York: Oxford University Press, 2011.

Giroux, Henry, *America's Education Deficit and the War on Youth*, New York: Monthly Review Press, 2013.

Glowa, Josef K., *Spielwelten: Performanz und Inszenierung in der Renaissance* by Klaus W. Hempfer, review by Helmut Pfeiffer, *Sixteenth Century Journal*, Vol. 35, No. 4, 2004, pp. 1226–8.

Godelier, Maurice, *Rationality and Irrationality in Economics*, London: New Left Books, 1972.

Goddard David, "Limits of British Anthropology," *New Left Review*, No. 58, 1969, pp. 69–79.

Goffman, Erving, *The Presentation of Self in Everyday Life*, Garden City: Doubleday, 1959.

Goody, Jack, *The Theft of History*, Cambridge: Cambridge University Press, 2007.

Gordon, Larry, "College Ratings System Proposed by Obama is Scrapped," *Los Angeles Times*, July 22, 2015, at http://www.latimes.com/local/california/la-me-higher-learning-ratings-20150722-story.html

Gough, Kathleen, "Anthropology: Child of Imperialism," *Monthly Review*, Vol. 19, No. 11, 1967.

Gouldner, Alvin Ward, *The Coming Crisis in Western Sociology*, New York: Basic Books, 1970.

Gramsci, Antonio, *The Open Marxism of Antonio Gramsci*, ed. Carl Marzani, New York: Cameron Associates, 1957.

Grebowicz, Margret, Donna Jeanne Haraway, and Helen Merrick, *Beyond the Cyborg: Adventures with Donna Haraway*, New York: Columbia University Press, 2013.

Gross, Neil, *Richard Rorty: The Making of an American Philosopher*, Chicago: University of Chicago Press, 2008.

Guignon, Charles and David R. Hiley, *Richard Rorty: Contemporary Philosophy in Focus*, Cambridge: Cambridge University Press, 2003.

Gunnell, John G., "The Historiography of American Political Science," in *The Development of Political Science: A Comparative Survey*, ed. John G. Gunnell, David Easton, and Luigi Graziano, London and New York: Routledge, 2002, pp. 13–33.

— "The Reconstitution of Political Theory: David Easton, Behavioralism and the Long Road to System," *Journal of the History of the Behavioral Sciences*, Vol. 49, No. 2, 2013, pp. 190–210.

Haber, Jonathan, *MIT Press Essential Knowledge: MOOCs*, Cambridge: MIT Press, 2014.

Haraway, Donna, "A Cyborg Manifesto: Science, Technology, and Socialist-Feminism in the Late Twentieth Century," in *Simians, Cyborgs and Women: The Reinvention of Nature*, New York: Routledge, 1991, pp. 149–81.

Harlow, Harry, I. E. Farber, and Louis Jolyon West, "Brainwashing, Conditioning, and DDD (Debility, Dependency, and Dread)," *Sociometry*, Vol. 20, No. 4, 1957, pp. 271–85.

Harman, Chris, "Theorising Neoliberalism," *International Socialism*, Vol. 117, 2007, at http://www.isj.org.uk/?id=399

Harris, Marvin, *Cultural Materialism: The Struggle for a Science of Culture*, New York: Random House, 1979.

Hartman, Andrew, *A War for the Soul of America: A History of the Culture Wars*, Chicago: University of Chicago Press, 2015.

Harvey, David, *Seventeen Contradictions and the End of Capitalism*, Oxford: Oxford University Press, 2014.

Havers, Grant, "The Right-Wing Postmodernism of Marshall McLuhan," *Media Culture Society*, Vol. 25, No. 4, 2003, pp. 511–27.

Heineman, Kenneth J., *Campus Wars: The Peace Movement at American State Universities in the Vietnam Era*, New York: New York University, 1993.

— *Put Your Bodies on the Wheels: Student Revolt in the 1960s*, Chicago: Ivan R. Dee, 2001.

Heller, Henry, *The Cold War and the New Imperialism: A Global History, 1945–2005*, New York: Monthly Review Press, 2005.

— *The Birth of Capitalism*, London: Pluto, 2011.

Hendry, Joy and Laara Fitznor, *Anthropologists, Indigenous Scholars and the Research Endeavour: Seeking Bridges Towards Mutual Respect*, London and New York: Routledge, 2012.

Herman, Ellen, *The Romance of American Psychology: Political Culture in the Age of Experts*, Berkeley: University of California Press, 1995.

Hexter, Jack, "The Historian and His Day," *Political Science Quarterly*, Vol. 69, No. 2, 1954, pp. 219–33.

— *Reappraisals in History*, New York: Longmans, 1961.

Higham, John, "The Collapse of Consensus History," *Journal of American History*, Vol. 76, No. 2, 1989, pp. 460–66.

Hilton, Rodney Howard et al., *The Transition from Feudalism to Capitalism*, London: New Left Books, 1976.

Hobsbawm, Eric, *The Age of Extremes*, New York: Vintage, 1996.

Hogan, Wesley C., *Many Minds, One Heart: SNCC's Dream for a New America*, Chapel Hill: University of North Carolina Press, 2007.

Homer, S.I., *A Short History of the Marxist Literary Group*, at http://mlg.eserver.org/about/a-short-history-of-the-mlg

Horst, Frank C.P. van der, Helen A. LeRoy, and René van der Veer, "'When Strangers Meet': John Bowlby and Harry Harlow on Attachment Behavior," *Integrative Psychological and Behavioral Science*, Vol. 42, No. 4, 2008, pp. 370–88.

Huddart, David, *Homi K. Bhabha*, London: Routledge, 2006.

Inderjeet, Parmat, *Foundations of the American Century: The Ford, Carnegie, and Rockefeller Foundations in the Rise of American Power*, New York: Columbia University Press, 2012.

Isaac, Joel, *Working Knowledge: Making the Human Sciences from Parsons to Kuhn*, Cambridge MA: Harvard University Press, 2012.

Isserman, Maurice and Michael Kazin, *America Divided: The Civil War of the 1960s*, New York: Oxford University Press, 2012.

Jacobsen, Michael, *The Contemporary Goffman*, London and New York: Routledge, 2010.

Jacoby, Russell, *Social Amnesia: A Critique of Conformist Psychology from Adler to Laing*, Boston: Beacon Press, 1975.

— *The Last Intellectuals: American Culture in the Age of Academe*, New York: Basic Books, 1987.

Jameson, Fredric, *Postmodernism, or, The Cultural Logic of Late Capitalism*, Durham: Duke University Press, 1991.

Jappe, Anselme, "Sohn-Rethal and the Origin of 'Real Abstraction': A Critique of Production or a Critique of Circulation," *Historical Materialism Journal*, Vol. 21, No. 1, 2013, pp. 3–14.

Jay, Martin, *The Dialectical Imagination: A History of the Frankfurt School and the Institute for Social Research*, London: Heinemann, 1973.

Kaufman, Eric P., *The Rise and Fall of Anglo-America*, Cambridge MA: Harvard University Press, 2004.

Kauppinen, Illka, "Academic Capitalism and the Informational Fraction of the Transnational Capitalist Class," *Globalisation, Societies and Education*, Vol. 11, No. 1, 2013, pp. 1–22.

Kaye, Harvey J., *The British Marxist Historians: An Introductory Analysis*, London: Polity Press, 1984.

Kerr, Clark, *The Uses of the University*, Cambridge MA: Harvard University Press, 1963.

Keucheyan, Razmig, *The Left Hemisphere: Mapping Critical Theory Today*, London and New York: Verso, 2013.

Kimmage, Michael, *The Conservative Turn: Lionel Trilling, Whittaker Chambers, and the Lessons of Anti-Communism*, Cambridge MA: Harvard University Press, 2009.

Kirby, Vicki, *Judith Butler: Live Theory*, New York: Continuum, 2006.

Kleinman, Daniel, Noah Feinstein, and Greg Downey, "Beyond Commercialization: Science, Higher Education, and the Culture of Neoliberalism," *Science & Education*, Vol. 22, No. 10, 2013, pp. 2385–401.

Kroker, Arthur, *Body Drift: Butler, Hayles, Haraway*, Minneapolis: University of Minnesota Press, 2012.

Kuhn, Thomas S., *The Structure of Scientific Revolutions*, Chicago: University of Chicago Press, 1962.

Kurzman, Charles, "The Stubborn Parochialism of American Social Sciences," *The Chronicle of Higher Education*, January 19, 2015, http://chronicle.com/article

Laidler, David, "Chicago Monetary Traditions," in *The Elgar Companion to the Chicago School of Economics*, ed. Ross B. Emmett, Cheltenham: Elgar, 2010, pp. 70–80.

Lamont, Michèle, "How Has Bourdieu Been Good to Think With? The Case of the United States," *Sociological Forum*, Vol. 27, No.1, 2012, pp. 228–37.

Larsen, Neil, "Marxism, Postcolonialism and the *Eighteenth Brumaire*," in *Marxism, Modernity and Post-Colonial Studies*, ed. Crystal Bartolovich, Cambridge: Cambridge University Press, 2002, pp. 204–20.

Lazarus, Neil, "The Fetish of 'the West,' in Postcolonial Theory," in *Marxism, Modernity and Post-Colonial Studies*, ed. Crystal Bartolovich, Cambridge: Cambridge University Press, 2002, pp. 43–64.

Leacock, Eleanor, "Anthropology," in *The Left Academy: Marxist Scholarship on American Campuses*, ed. Bertell Ollman and Edward Vernoff, New York: McGraw-Hill, 1982.

Lebovic, Sam, "From War Junk to Educational Exchange: The World War II Origins of the Fulbright Program and the Foundations of American Cultural Globalism, 1945–1950," *Diplomatic History*, Vol. 37, No. 2, 2013, pp. 280–312.

Levant, Alex and Vesa Oittinenen, *Dialectics of the Ideal: Evald Ilyenkov and Creative Soviet Marxism*, Leiden: Brill, 2013.

Lewin, Tamar, "More College Adjuncts See Strength in Union Numbers," *New York Times*, December 3, 2013.

Lewis, William S., *Louis Althusser and the Traditions of French Marxism*, New York: Lexington Books, 2005.

Lewontin, Richard C., "The Cold War and the Transformation of the Academy," in *The Cold War and the University: Toward an Intellectual History of the Post-War Years*, ed. Noam Chomsky et al., New York: New Press, 1997, pp. 1–34.

Lindsay, Tom, "More U.S. Colleges Poised to Go Bankrupt, According to Three Studies," November 18, 2015, *Forbes Magazine*, at www.forbes.com

Lingua Franca editors, *Sokal Hoax: The Sham That Shook the Academy*, Lincoln: University of Nebraska, 2000.

Link, Arthur S., "Annual Address of the President of the American Historical Association, Delivered on December 28, 1984," *American Historical Review*, Vol. 90, No. 1, 1985, pp. 1–17.

Loewen, Rebecca S., *Creating The Cold War University: The Transformation of Stanford*, Berkeley: University of California Press, 1997.

Lohmann, Susanne, "Rational Choice and Political Science," in *The New Palgrave Dictionary of Economics*, 2nd edn, ed. Steven N. Durlauf and Lawrence E. Blume, Basingstoke: Palgrave Macmillan, 2008.

López, Alfred J. and Robert P. Marzec, "Postcolonial Studies at the Twenty-Five Year Mark," *Modern Fiction Studies*, Vol. 56, No. 4, 2010, pp. 677–88.

Lorenz, Chris and Joachim Urlauf, "If You're So Smart Why Are You Under Surveillance: Universities, Neoliberalism, and New Public Management," *Critical Inquiry*, Vol. 38, No. 3, 2012, pp. 599–629.

Losurdo, Domenico, "Toward a Critique of the Concept of Totalitarianism," *Historical Materialism*, Vol. 12, No. 2, 2004, pp. 25–55.

Lu, Tan Kuan, "University Rankings Game and Its Relation to GDP Per Capita and GDP," Growth," *International Journal for Innovation Education and Research*, Vol. 2, No.4, 2014, pp. 1–33.

Lukács, Gyorgy, *History and Class Consciousness*, London: New Left Books, 1971.

McCoy, Alfred M., *A Question of Torture: CIA Interrogation, From the Cold War to the War on Terror*, Metropolitan Books: Henry Holt, 2006.

McLuhan, Marshall, "Mussolini is the Message," *Manitoban*, December 1, 1933, republished in *Canadian Dimension*, Vol. 32, Issue 3, May/June 1998.

Marcuse, Herbert, *One-Dimensional Man: Studies in Ideology of Advanced Industrial Society*, Boston: Beacon Press, 1964.

Marks, John, *The Search for the "Manchurian Candidate,"* New York: Times Books, 1979.

— and Vincent Marchetti, *The CIA and the Cult of Intelligence*, New York: Knopf, 1975.

Marlowe, Anne, "The Picture Awaits: The Birth of Modern Counterinsurgency," *World Affairs*, summer 2009, at http://www.worldaffairsjournal.org/article/picture-awaits-birth-modern-counterinsurgency

Marx, Karl, Letter to Arnold Ruge, Kreuznach, September 1843, *Letters from the Deutsch-Französische Jahrbücher*, at https://www.marxists.org/archive/marx/works/1843/letters/43_09.htm

Mathies, Charles and Sheila Slaughter, "University Trustees as Channels Between Academe and Industry: Toward An Understanding of the Executive Science Network," *Research Policy*, Vol. 29, No. 1, 2013, pp. 1–21.

Medema, Steven G., "Ronald Harry Coase," in *The Elgar Companion to the Chicago School of Economics*, ed. Ross B. Emmett, Cheltenham: Elgar, 2010, pp. 258–64.

Meiksins, Peter F., "A Critique of Wright's Theory of Contradictory Class Locations," in *The Debate on Classes*, ed. Erik Olin Wright, London and New York: Verso, 1989, pp. 173–83.

Melman, Seymour, *Pentagon Capitalism*, New York: McGraw-Hill, 1971.

Mendillo, Jane L., *Annual Endowment Report, Harvard Management Company Inc.* (2014), at www.hmc.harvard.edu/docs/Final_Annual_Report_2014.pdf

Messerly, Megan, "Dirks Names UC Berkeley Alumnus Robert Lalanne First-Ever Vice Chancellor for Real Estate," *Daily Californian*, December 17, 2013.

Mészáros, István, *Social Structures and Forms of Consciousness*, 2 vols, New York: Monthly Review Press, 2010–11.

Mills, C. Wright, *White Collar: The American Middle Classes*, New York and Oxford: Oxford University Press, 1951.

— *The Power Elite*, New York and Oxford: Oxford University Press, 1956.

— *The Sociological Imagination*, New York and Oxford: Oxford University Press, 1959.

— *Letters and Autobiographical Writings*, Berkeley: University of California Press, 2001.

Milne, David, *America's Rasputin: Walt Rostow and the Vietnam War*, New York: Hill and Wang, 2008.

Mirowski, Philip, and Dieter Plewhe, eds, *The Road from Mont Pèlerin: The Making of the Neoliberal Thought Collective*, Cambridge MA: Harvard University Press, 2009.

Mojab, Sharzad, *Marxism and Feminism*, London: Zed Books, 2015.

Montgomery, David, *The Fall of the House of Labor: The Workplace, the State and American Labor Activism, 1865–1925*, Cambridge: Cambridge University Press, 1987.

— "Introduction: Prosperity Under the Shadow of the Bomb," in *The Cold War and the University: Toward an Intellectual History of the Postwar Years*, ed. Noam Chomsky et al., New York: New Press, 1997, pp. xi–xxxvii.

Moore, Jr., Barrington, *Social Origins of Dictatorship and Democracy: Lord and Peasant in the Making of the Modern World*, Boston: Beacon Press, 1966.

Moretti, Enrico, *The New Geography of Jobs*, New York: Houghton Mifflin Harcourt, 2013.

Morris, Aldon, "Black Southern Student Sit-in Movement: An Analysis of Internal Organization," *American Sociological Review*, Vol. 4, No. 6, 1981, pp. 744–67.

Morrow, Raymond A., "Foreword—Critical Theory and Higher Education: Political Economy and the Cul-de-Sac of the Postmodernist Turn," in *The University, State and Market: The Political Economy of Globalization in the Americas*, ed. Robert A. Rhoads and Carlos Alberto Torres, Stanford: Stanford University Press, 2006, pp. xvii–xxxiii.

Munch, Richard, *Academic Capitalism: Universities in the Global Struggle for Excellence*, New York: Routledge, 2014.

Murrell, Gary, "On Herbert Aptheker and His Side of History: An Interview with Eric Foner," *Radical History Review*, Vol. 78, No. 3, 2000, pp. 6–26.

N.a., "Angels of the Right 2.0: Conservative Foundations," angelsoftheright.net

N.a., "Apollo Group," Wikipedia, https://en.wikipedia.org

N.a., "Koch Family Foundations 2016," *The Center for Media and Democracy*, http://www.sourcewatch.org/index.php/Koch_Family_Foundations#Koch_University_Funding_-_Koch_and_Academic_Freedom

N.a., "University of Phoenix," Wikipedia, https://en.wikipedia.org

National Association of College and University Business Officers, *NACUBO-Commonfund Study of Endowments 2015*, at www.nacubo.org/.../NACUBO-Commonfund_Study_of_Endowments.html

Needell, Allan, "Project Troy and the Cold War Annexation of the Social Sciences," in *Universities and Empire: Money and Politics in the Social Sciences During the Cold War*, ed. Christopher Simpson, New York: New Press, 1998, pp. 3–38.

Newfield, Christopher, *Ivy and Industry: Business and the Making of the American University, 1880–1980*, Durham NC: Duke University Press, 2003.

— "The Humanities as Service Departments: Facing the Budget Logic," December 16, 2015, at https://profession.commons.mla.org/2015/12/16/the-humanities-as-service-departments-facing-the-budget-logic

Nicolaus, Martin, "The Professional Organization of Sociology: A View from Below," in *Ideology in Social Science: Readings in Critical Social Theory*, London: Fontana, 1972, pp. 45–60.

NikKhah, Edward, "George J. Stigler," in *The Elgar Companion to the Chicago School of Economics*, ed. Ross B. Emmett, Cheltenham: Elgar, 2010, pp. 337–441.

Ninkovich, Frank A., *The Diplomacy of Ideas: US Foreign Policy and Cultural Relations, 1938–1950*, Cambridge: Cambridge University Press, 1981.

Novick, Peter, *That Noble Dream: The "Objectivity Question," and the American Historical Profession*, Cambridge: Cambridge University Press, 1988.

Nugent, David, "Knowledge and Empire: The Social Sciences and United States Imperial Expansion," *Identities*, Vol. 17, No. 1, 2010, pp. 2–44.

Ohmann, Richard, *English in America: A Radical View of the Profession*, New York: Oxford University Press, 1976.

Paget, Karen M., *Patriotic Betrayal: The Inside Story of the CIA's Secret Campaign to Enroll American Students in the Crusade Against Communism*, New Haven: Yale University Press, 2015.

Panitch, Leo and Martijn Konings, "Myths of Neoliberal Deregulation," *New Left Review*, Vol. 57, 2009, pp. 67–83.

Parker, David, *Ideology, Absolutism and the English Revolution: Debates of the British Communist Historians*, London: Lawrence & Wishart, 2008.

Patterson, Thomas C., *A Social History of Anthropology in the United States*, Oxford and New York: Berg, 2002.

Pawling, Christopher, "The American Lukács? Fredric Jameson and Dialectical Thought," in *Fredric Jameson: A Critical Reader*, ed. Sean Homer and Douglas Kellner, Basingstoke: Palgrave Macmillan, 2004, pp. 22–41.

Peace, William J., *Leslie A. White: Evolution and Revolution in Anthropology*, Lincoln: University of Nebraska Press, 2004.

Perelman, Michael, *Steal This Idea: Intellectual Property Rights and the Corporate Confiscation of Creativity*, New York: Palgrave, 2002.

Phelps, Christopher, "Why Wouldn't Sidney Hook Permit the Republication of His Best Book," *Historical Materialism*, Vol. 11, No. 4, 2003, pp. 305–15.

Pijl, Kees van der, "Historicising the International: Modes of Foreign Relations and Political Economy," *Historical Materialism*, Vol. 18, No. 2, 2010, pp. 3–34.

Pinkoski, Marc, "American Colonialism at the Dawn of the Cold War," in *Anthropology at the Dawn of the Cold War: The Influence of Foundations, McCarthyism and the Cold War*, ed. Dustin Wax, London: Pluto Press, 2008.

Pinto, Andy, "Chancellor Names UC Berkeley's First Vice Chancellor For Real Estate," UC Berkeley NewsCenter, December 17, 2013, at http://NewsCenter. Berkeley.Edu/2013/12/17/Vice-Chancellor-For-Real-Estate

Plewhe, Dieter, "Introduction," *The Road From Mont Pèlerin*, ed. Philip Mirowski and Dieter Plewhe, Cambridge MA: Harvard University Press, 2009, pp. 1–41.

Port Huron Statement 1962, at http://coursesa.matrix.msu.edu/~hst306/documents/huron.html

Poster, Mark, *Existential Marxism in Postwar France: From Sartre to Althusser*, Princeton: Princeton University Press, 1975.

Price, David H., "Cold War Anthropology: Collaborators and Victims of the National Security State," *Identities: Global Studies in Culture and Power*, Vol. 4, No. 3–4, 1998, pp. 389–430.

— *Threatening Anthropology: McCarthyism and the FBI's Surveillance of Activist Anthropologists*, Durham NC: Duke University Press, 2004.

— "Uninvited Guests: A Short History of the CIA on Campus," in *The CIA on Campus: Essays on Academic Freedom and the National Security State*, ed. Philip Zwerling, Jefferson, NC: McFarland, 2011, pp. 33–60.

Pye, Lucian W., *Guerilla Communism in Malaya, Its Social and Political Meaning*, Princeton: Princeton University Press, 1956.

Reardon, S.F. and Karen Bischoff, "The Continuing Increase in Income Segregation, 2007–2012," *American Journal of Sociology*, Vol. 116, No. 4, 2011, pp. 1092–153.

Reisch George A., *How the Cold War Transformed Philosophy of Science: To the Icy Slopes of Logic*, Cambridge: Cambridge University Press, 2005.

Reising, Russell J., "Lionel Trilling, the Liberal Imagination, and the Emergence of the Cultural Discourse of Anti-Stalinism," *Boundary 2*, Vol. 20, No. 1, 1993, pp. 94–124.

Rhoads, Robert A. and Gary Rhoades, "Graduate Student Unionization as a Postindustrial Social Movement: Identity, Ideology, and the Contested U.S. Academy," in *The University, State and Market: The Political Economy of Globalization in the Americas*, ed. Robert Rhoads and Carlos Alberto Torres, Stanford: Stanford University Press, 2006, pp. 275–98.

Rhoades, Gary, *Managed Professionals: Unionized Faculty and Restructuring Academic Labor*, Albany: State University of New York Press, 1998.

Robin, Ron T., *The Making of the Cold War Enemy: Culture and Politics in the Military-Intellectual Complex*, Princeton: Princeton University Press, 2001.

Rodgers, Ibram H., *The Black Campus Movement: Black Students and the Racial Reconstitution of Higher Education, 1965–1972*, New York: Palgrave Macmillan, 2012.

Rogin, Michael Paul, *The Intellectuals and McCarthy: The Radical Specter*, Cambridge MA: MIT Press, 1967.

Rooks, Noliwe M., *Black Power/White Money: The Surprising History of African American Studies and the Crisis of Race in Higher Education*, Boston: Beacon Press, 2006.

Rorabaugh, W.J., *Berkeley at War: The 1960s*, New York: Oxford University Press, 1990.

Rosenfeld, Seth, *Subversives: The FBI's War on Student Radicals and Reagan's Rise to Power*, New York: Farrar, Straus and Giroux, 2012.

Ross, Andrew, "Universities and the Urban Growth Machine," *Dissent: A Quarterly of Politics and Culture*, October 4, 2012, at http://www.dissentmagazine.org/online_articles/universities-and-the-urban-growth-machine

Rossi, Andrew, "How American Universities Turned into Corporations", *Time*, May 22, 2014.

Rostow, Walt Whitman, *The Stages of Economic Growth: A Non-Communist Manifesto*, Cambridge: Cambridge University Press, 1960.

Sahlins, Marshall, *Culture and Practical Reason*, Chicago: University of Chicago Press, 1976.

— *Stone Age Economics*, London: Routledge, 2003.

Said, Edward W., *Orientalism*, New York: Vintage, 1978.

Sallaz, J. and J. Zavisca, "Pierre Bourdieu in American Sociology, 1980–2005," *Annual Review of Sociology*, Vol. 33, 2007, pp. 21–41.

Salzberg, Steven, "Scott Walker Takes $250 Million from U. Wisconsin, Gives $250M to Billionaire Sports Team Owners," *Forbes*, August 14, 2015, at www.forbes.com

Sanderson, Stephen K., "The Neo-Weberian Revolution: A Theoretical Balance Sheet," *Sociological Forum*, Vol. 3, No. 2, 1988, pp. 307–14.

Sandler, Peter, *Return from the Natives: How Margaret Mead Won the Second World War and Lost the Cold War*, New Haven: Yale University Press, 2013.

San Juan Jr., E., "The Limits of Postcolonial Criticism: The Discourse of Edward Said," *Against the Current*, Vol. 77, 1998, at http://www.solidarity-us.org/site/node/1781

— "Post-colonialism and the Problematic of Uneven Development," in *Marxism, Modernity and Post-Colonial Studies*, ed. Crystal Bartolovich, Cambridge: Cambridge University Press, 2002, pp. 221–39.

Saunders, Francis Stonor, *Who Paid the Piper? The CIA and the Cultural Cold War*, London: Granta Books, 1999.

Savio, Mario, "Sit-In Address on the Steps of Sproul Hall," December 2, 1964, at http://www.americanrhetoric.com/speeches/mariosaviosproulhallsitin.htm

Schoenfeld, A. Clay, "The University-Environmental Marriage," *Journal of Higher Education*, Vol. 50, No. 3, 1979, pp. 289–309.

Schorske, Carl, "The New Rigorism in the Human Sciences," *Daedalus*, Vol. 126, No. 1, 1997, pp. 289–309.

Schrecker, Ellen, *No Ivory Tower: McCarthyism and the Universities*, New York: Oxford University Press, 1986.

— *Many are the Crimes: McCarthyism in America*, Boston: Little, Brown, 1998.

Sciolli, D., "Talcott Parsons," in *International Encyclopedia of the Social and Behavioural Sciences*, 26 vols, ed. Neil Smelser and Paul B. Balte, Amsterdam and Paris: Elsevier, 2001.

Scott, C.S. and J.J. Siegfried, "American Economic Association Universal Academic Questionnaire Summary Statistics," *American Economic Review: Papers & Proceedings*, Vol. 101, 2011, pp. 664–7.

Scott, Joan Wallach, *The Politics of the Veil*, Princeton: Princeton University Press, 2007.

— "Introduction: Feminism's Critical Edge," in *Women's Studies on the Edge*, ed. Joan Wallach Scott, Durham NC: Duke University Press, 2008, pp. 1–13.

Scott-Smith, Giles, *The Politics of Apolitical Culture: The Congress for Cultural Freedom and the Political Economy of American Hegemony, 1945–1955*, New York: Routledge, 2002.

Seale, Bobby, "Seale Speech," May 10, 1967, San Francisco Bay Area Television Archive, https://diva.sfsu.edu/collections/sfbatv/bundles/190420

Shapiro, Herbert, "The Impact of the Aptheker Thesis: A Retrospective View of 'American Negro Slave Revolts'," *Science & Society*, Vol. 48, No. 1, 1984, pp. 52–73.

Shumar, Wesley, *College for Sale: A Critique of the Commodification of Higher Education*, London: Falmer Press, 1997.

Sim Stuart, "Postmodernism and Philosophy," *The Routledge Companion to Postmodernism*, London: Taylor & Francis, 2005, pp. 3–11.

Simpson, Christopher, *Science of Coercion: Communication Research and Psychological Warfare, 1945–1960*, New York: Oxford University Press, 1994.

Skocpol, Theda, *States and Social Revolutions*, New York: Cambridge University Press, 1979.

Slaughter, Sheila, *The Higher Learning and High Technology: Dynamics of Higher Education Policy Formation*, Albany: State University of New York Press, 1990.

— and Gary Rhoades, "The Academic Capitalist Knowledge/Learning Regime," in *The Exchange University: Corporatization of Academic Culture*, ed. Adrienne S. Chan and Donald Fisher, Vancouver, Toronto: UBC Press, 2008, pp. 19–48.

Slonecker, Blake, "The Columbia Coalition: African Americans, New Leftist Counterculture at the Columbia University Protest of 1968," *Journal of Social History*, Vol. 41, No. 4, 2008, pp. 967–96.

Smith, Ashley A., "Obama Steps Up Push for Free Tuition," *Inside Higher Education*, September 9, 2015, at https://www.insidehighered.com

Smith, David N., *Who Rules the Universities? An Essay in Class Analysis*, New York: Monthly Review Press, 1974.

Smith, Neil, *American Empire: Roosevelt's Geographer and the Prelude to Globalization*, Berkeley: University of California Press, 2003.

Smooth, Wendy G., "Intersectionality from Theoretical Framework to Policy Intervention," in *Situating Intersectionality: Politics, Policy, and Power*, London: Palgrave Macmillan, 2013, pp. 11–41.

Solovey Mark, "Project Camelot and the 1960s Epistemological Revolution: Rethinking the Politics-Patronage-Social Science Nexus," *Social Studies of Science*, Vol. 31, No. 2, 2001, pp. 171–206.

Soo, M. and C. Carson, "Managing the Research University: Clark Kerr and the University of California," *Minerva*, Vol. 42, No. 3, 2004, pp. 215–36.

Spivak, Gayatri Chakravorty, "Can the Subaltern Speak?," in *Marxism and the Interpretation of Culture*, ed. Cary Nelson and Larry Grossberg, Chicago: University of Illinois Press, 1988, pp. 271–313.

Spofford, Tim, *Lynch Street: The May 1970 Slayings at Jackson State College*, Kent, Ohio: Kent State University Press, 1998.

Sproule, J. Michael, *Propaganda and Democracy: The American Experience of Media and Mass Persuasion*, Cambridge: Cambridge University Press, 1996.

Steck, Henry, "Corporatization of the University: Seeking Conceptual Clarity," *Annals of the American Academy of Political and Social Science*, Vol. 585, No. 1, 2003, pp. 66–83.

Stone, Bailey, *The Anatomy of Revolution Revisited: A Comparative Analysis of England, France and Russia*, Cambridge, New York: Cambridge University Press, 2013.

Stone, I.F., *The Killings at Kent State: How Murder Went Unpunished*, New York: Vintage Books, 1971.

Strathern, Marilyn, *Audit Cultures: Anthropological Studies in Accountability, Ethics, and the Academy*, New York: Routledge, 2000.

Tai, Li-Chaun, *L'anthropologie français entre sciences coloniales et decolonisation*, Paris: Publications de la société française d'histoire d'outre-mer, 2010.

Tally, Robert T., *Fredric Jameson: The Project of Dialectical Criticism*, London: Pluto, 2014.

Tan Kuan Lu, Clifford, "Do University Rankings Matter for Growth?," University of Nottingham–Malaysia Campus, MPRA Paper No. 52705, December 19, 2013, at ssrn.com/abstract=2377249

Tanenhouse, Sam, "Fear and Loathing: How Leslie Fiedler Turned American Criticism on its Head," *Slate*, February 4, 2003, at http://www.slate.com/articles/news_and_politics/obit/2003/02/fear_and_loathing.html

Teixera, Pedro Nuno, "Gary S. Becker," in *The Elgar Companion to the Chicago School of Economics*, ed. Ross B. Emmett, Cheltenham: Elgar, 2010, pp. 253–8.

Terray, Emmanuel, *Marxism and Primitive Societies: Two Studies*, New York: Monthly Review Press, 1972.

Thelin, John R., *A History of American Higher Education*, 2nd edn, Baltimore: Johns Hopkins University Press, 2011.

Thomas, Peter D., *The Gramscian Moment: Philosophy, Hegemony, Marxism*, Leiden, Boston: Brill, 2009.

Torres, Carlos Alberto, "Public Universities and the Neoliberal Common Sense: Seven Iconoclastic Theses," *International Studies in Sociology of Education*, Vol. 21, No. 3, 2011, pp. 177–97.

Townsend, Robert B., *History's Babel: Scholarship, Professionalization, and the Historical Enterprise in the United States, 1880–1940*, Chicago: University of Chicago Press, 2013.

Trillin, Calvin, "Letter From Berkeley," *The New Yorker*, March 13, 1965, at http://www.fsm-a.org/stacks/trillin.html

Turner, B.S., "Weber, Giddens and Modernity," *Theory, Culture and Society*, Vol. 9, No. 2, 1992, pp. 141–6.

Veblen, Thorstein, *The Higher Learning in America: A Memorandum on the Conduct of Universities by Business Men*, New York: A.M. Kelley, 1965.

Vercellone, Carlo, "From the Mass Worker to Cognitive Labour: Historical and Theoretical Considerations," in *Beyond Marx: Theorizing the Global Labour Relations of the Twenty-First Century*, ed. Marcel van der Linden and Karl Heinz Roth, Leiden and Boston: Brill, 2014, pp. 217–43.

Vries, Jan de, "Great Expectations: Early Modern History and the Social Sciences," *Review*, Vol. 22, No. 1, 1999, pp. 121–49.

Wald, Alan M., *The New York Intellectuals: The Rise and Decline of the Anti-Stalinist Left from the 1930s to the 1980s*, Chapel Hill: University of North Carolina Press, 1987.

Waldo, Martin, "Holding One Another: Mario Savio and the Freedom Struggle in Mississippi and Berkeley," in *The Free Speech Movement: Reflections on Berkeley in the 1960s*, ed. Robert Cohen and Reginald E. Zelnick, Berkeley: University of California Press, 2002, pp. 83–102.

Walhout, Mark, "New Criticism and the Crisis of American Liberalism," *College English*, Vol. 49, No. 8, 1987, pp. 861–71.

Wallerstein, Immanuel, *The Modern World System*, New York: Academic Press, 1974.

— "Unintended Consequences," in *The Cold War and the University: Toward an Intellectual History of the Post-War Years*, ed. Noam Chomsky et al., New York: New Press, 1997, pp. 195–231.

Wang, Jessica, *American Science in an Age of Anxiety: Scientists, Anticommunism, and the Cold War*, Chapel Hill: University of North Carolina Press, 1999.

Wang, Shuibo, "They Chose China" (2005), National Film Board of Canada, at www.nfb.ca/film/they_chose_china

Ward, Steven, *Neoliberalism and the Global Restructuring of Knowledge and Education*, New York: Routledge, 2012.

Watson, George, "The Empire of Lionel Trilling," *Sewanee Review*, Vol. 115, No. 3, 2007, pp. 484–90.

The White House, "FACT SHEET on the President's Plan to Make College More Affordable: A Better Bargain for the Middle Class," August 22, 2013, at https://www.whitehouse.gov/.../fact-sheet-president-s-plan-make-college-more-affordable-better-bargain- https://www.insidehighered.com

Wiegman, Robyn, "Feminism, Institutionalism and the Idiom of Failure," in *Women's Studies on the Edge*, ed. Joan Wallach Scott, Durham NC: Duke University Press, 2008, pp. 39–66.

Williams, Raymond, *Culture and Society, 1780–1950*, London: Chatto & Windus, 1958.

Williams, William Appleman, *The Tragedy of American Diplomacy*, New York: Dell, 1950.

Winks, Robin W., *Cloak & Gown: Scholars and the Secret War: 1939–61*, New York: Morrow, 1987.

Wolf, Eric R., *Europe and the People Without History*, Berkeley: University of California Press, 1982.

Woodworth, Jed, "Feminism, Third-wave," in *Culture Wars in America: An Encyclopedia of Issues, Viewpoints, and Voices*, ed. Roger Chapman and James Ciment, London: Routledge, 2013, at http://uml.idm.oclc.org/login?url=http://search.credoreference.com/content/entry/sharpecw/feminism_third_wave/o

Young, Robert, "Postcolonial Remains," *New Literary History*, Vol. 43, No. 1, 2012, pp. 19–43.

Index

Beard, Charles 50, 52
Becker, Gary 14
Behaviorism 77–8, 80–1, 83, 88
Bell, Daniel 35, 51
Benedict, Ruth 70, 71, 72
Bennett, William 137
Bentley University 197
Bergmann, Gustav 65
Berman, Marshall xiv
Bernstein, Barton 123
Birmingham Centre for Contemporary
    Cultural Studies 147
Birmingham protests 101, 102
Bissell, Richard 29–30
Black Christianity 123
Black colleges 9, 102
Black nationalism 114
Black Power movement 11, 92, 104, 107,
    110, 114, 115, 167, 171
Black slave revolts 52–3
Black slavery 83
Black Studies 11, 119
Blacks 11, 46, 52, 137, 172
Bloch, Ernst 89–90
Bloom, Alan 137
Boas, Franz 69, 153
Boasians 71, 72, 74, 75, 78, 137, 152
Bohm, David Joseph 37
Boorstin, Daniel 50
Bourdieu, Pierre 7, 13, 44, 150–1, 189
Bourgeois Democracy 127
Bowie, Robert 86
Bowlby, John 80
Bowman, Isaiah 85
Boycott, Divestment and Sanctions
    Movement 4, 198
Brainwashing 81–2
Braudel, Fernand 157
Brenner, Robert xiv, 125, 126, 127
Brinton, Crane 48–9
British Marxist historians xiv, 11, 89, 92,
    122, 125, 159
Brookings Institution 19
Browder, Earl 36

Brown versus the Board of Education
    Decision 102
Bundy, McGeorge 117
Bureau of Indian Affairs 71
Bush, George W. 12
Business Higher Education Forum 175
Butler, Judith 80
Butler, Nicholas Murray 59, 72

California 94, 115
Callinicoss, Alex 186
Cambodia, invasion of 114
Cambridge University 130
Canada x
Canguilheim, Georges 150
Cantril, Hadley 30
Capitalism viii, xi, xii, xiv, xv, 2, 5, 9, 10,
    11, 14, 28–9, 41, 43, 44, 50, 54, 64, 88,
    95, 108, 110, 118, 121, 127, 128, 134,
    138, 146, 160, crisis of xiii, 1, 4, 5, 6,
    28, 57–8, 135, 136, 156, 167, 169, 172,
    175, 188, 199, 202, finance capital
    136, 139, 144, 145, 159, 176, late
    capitalism 144–5
Capitalist accumulation 93
Capitalist class 10, 32, 161
Capitalist transition debate 125–7
Carleton College 17
Carmichael, Stokeley 114
Carnap Rudolf 65, 67–8, 166
Carnegie Foundation 19, 55, 87, 115
Carnegie Institution 86
Carnegie-Mellon University 173
Cason, Sandra "Casey" 104
Castro, Fidel 11, 92, 122
Catholicism 130–1, 146
Central America 12
Chakrabarty, Dipesh 156
Chayanov, Alexander 160
Che Guevera 122
Chicago State University 175
Chicano Studies 11, 92, 119
Chile 128
China 38, 39, 55, 107, 109, 127, 135, 186
Chinese Revolution 46